Politics in Rhodesia

Politics in Rhodesia

White Power in an African State

Larry W. Bowman

Harvard University Press

Cambridge, Massachusetts

1973

For Clifford A. Bowman

IN MEMORIAM

Preface

This book took shape during the 1960's as Rhodesia found itself increasingly in the limelight of world attention over its internal racial policies. I was in Rhodesia for two years during this period and much of my analysis pertains to relatively current issues. I have found, however, that Rhodesia's present dilemmas are impossible to abstract from the history of white-black contact and conflict within this unhappy land. Therefore I have tried, sometimes in far less depth than I would have liked, to express contemporary conflicts within the context of the complete history of Rhodesia's race and colonial relations.

In general, the writing of this book has been an immensely solitary experience. Nonetheless, many people have given me assistance during the years in which this book was in process. At the University of Chicago in 1963–1964, Aristide R. Zolberg and Colin Leys were instrumental in helping me to obtain an appointment at the University College of Rhodesia and Nyasaland. In Rhodesia I had a great deal of help from Eileen Haddon, then editor of the *Central African Examiner*. When the *Examiner* was forced to cease publication in late 1965, I had the extraordinary good fortune to have almost complete access to files the magazine had built up since 1957. I have used that material at different places throughout the book. While in Rhodesia I conducted extensive interviews with more than seventy persons. I am grateful to all of them for the hospitality they showed me and for their willingness to answer my questions, often at great length; few will agree with much of what I have written here, but I could not have done many sections without their help. I am particularly grateful to Sir Roy Welensky and Clifford Pocket for their time and assistance. In Salisbury, I worked for many months at the National Archives, the Legislative Assembly Library, and the *Rhodesia Herald* library. At each I was given much assistance, which I deeply appreciate.

Back in the United States, Beverly Gray and Doris Calvin at the African Studies Center Library of Boston University were unfailingly gracious in helping me keep up with Rhodesian events; they make the library a wonderful place in which to work. It gives me great pleasure and satisfaction to be able to thank Ruth Schachter Morgenthau, Kenneth N. Waltz, and James Duffy—my dissertation committee at Brandeis University—for the encouragement and help they gave me throughout. They were wise enough to know when to leave me alone, and concerned enough to give me a prod when I needed that. They have been good friends.

As the dissertation made the considerable transformation into a book, I was given much guidance by Dorothy Whitney, then of Harvard University Press; it was a pleasure to work with her. Vivian B. Wheeler edited the book for Harvard and suggested numerous improvements for which I am grateful. My good friend and colleague, J. Garry Clifford, read the complete manuscript and found ways to eliminate a sentence or so from every paragraph. The readers of the book will be as thankful to him as I am pleased to acknowledge his assistance. The University of Connecticut Research Foundation helped with preparation of the manuscript, and I much appreciate the prompt and professional typing done for me by Marjorie Bentley.

Three special friends—Shirley K. Fischer, Monica Williams, and Stephen Williams—have, in different ways, been part of my life for many years and I want to share this book with them. My late yellow labrador, Mwalimu, gave me countless hours of much-needed diversion in both Salisbury and Cambridge as this book was evolving. Finally, I want to thank my wife Ruth for her encouragement and support over many years. I wish to note, however, that she had nothing to do with the editing and typing of this manuscript. Instead she turned her considerable talents toward developing her own career, thus making for a far more meaningful relationship.

Contents

	Introduction	1
1	The Foundation of White Political Control	5
2	White Rhodesian Politics, 1954–1962	21
3	The African Nationalist Challenge	45
4	Rhodesia's Drive to Independence	62
5	The Rhodesian Front: Political Power in Contemporary Rhodesia	91
6	Isolation and Survival: White Rhodesia under International Sanctions	110
7	Internal Politics and Control since the Unilateral Declaration of Independence	133
	Conclusion: Past Policies and Future Politics	151
	Appendixes	159
	Notes	166
	Selected Bibliography	191
	Index	201

Tables

1	Rhodesian land apportionment, 1894–1969	12
2	Rhodesian population growth, 1901–1970	13
3	Federal gross domestic product (at factor cost) by territory, 1954–1963	23
4	Percentages of federal government revenue derived from and expended in each territory, 1954–1963	24
5	1958 Rhodesian election results	32
6	1962 Rhodesian election results	36
7	Africans employed in various industrial sectors of the Rhodesian economy, 1936–1968	47
8	Average annual wages of Rhodesian Africans in major employment sectors, 1954 and 1963	48
9	Disposition of African criminal cases in Rhodesia and total prison population by year, 1959–1965	61
10	1965 Rhodesian general election: summary of constituency results	82
11	Electoral district B-roll voting in the 1962 and 1965 Rhodesian elections	83
12	Rural-urban breakdown of Rhodesian Front party organization, 1967	98
13	Party branches per Rhodesian Front division and European voter, 1967	99
14	Rhodesian Front officers, 1962–1971	101
15	Occupational structure of Europeans in Rhodesia compared to Rhodesian Front candidates in 1962 and 1965	104
16	Residence in Rhodesia for immigrants born outside the federation and Rhodesian Front members of parliament	105
17	Rhodesian Front caucuses and cabinets by prior political affiliation	106
18	Selected economic indicators for Rhodesia, 1964–1970	114
19	Use of selected security legislation in Rhodesia, 1964–1969	145

Politics in Rhodesia

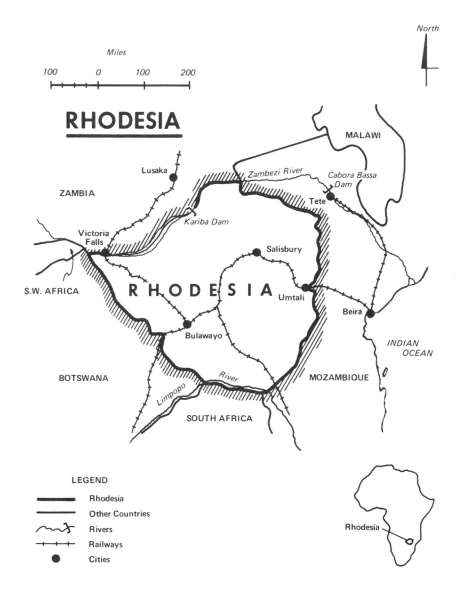

Miles

100   0   100   200

North

RHODESIA

MALAWI

Lusaka

Zambezi River

Cabora Bassa Dam

ZAMBIA

Tete

Kariba Dam

Victoria Falls

Salisbury

S.W. AFRICA

R H O D E S I A

Umtali

Beira

INDIAN OCEAN

Bulawayo

BOTSWANA

River

Limpopo

MOZAMBIQUE

SOUTH AFRICA

LEGEND

Rhodesia
Other Countries
Rivers
Railways
Cities

Rhodesia

Introduction

In November 1965 the white Rhodesian government headed by Prime Minister Ian D. Smith unilaterally declared itself independent. Ties with Britain which stretched back to the end of the nineteenth century were severed, and Rhodesia, because of the nature of its action and the style of its domestic racial policy, became the pariah of the international community.

Brigadier Andrew Skeen, Rhodesia's high commissioner to London in the months preceding the independence declaration, wrote in his memoir of this period:

Twice in the history of the world pressures from the East sought to overwhelm Western culture and civilisation . . . In both cases this Eastern tide was halted and ultimately turned back by a few determined and resolute people. The first time was when the Greek states halted the Persian hordes at Thermopylae . . . The second time was when the Turks were defeated in the sea battle of Lepanto in 1571 . . . In the twentieth century the forces of the East, which again seek to overwhelm the Western world, are fighting with subtler weapons, such as the ideology of Communism, the various methods of trans-

1

mitting information and by exploiting world organisations originally dedicated to the cause of peace . . . This process had gone a long way by the summer of 1965 when it received its first serious check . . . when Rhodesia assumed the role of champion of Western civilisation.[1]

Rhodesia's unilateral declaration of independence (UDI) provoked substantial international controversy. More than seven years after the declaration, no nation in the world had formally recognized the rebel Rhodesian government. Acting through the United Nations, the world community voted for the first time in its history to impose mandatory economic sanctions in an effort to force Rhodesia to renounce its action. And yet, white Rhodesia survives. Less than one-quarter million white Rhodesians ("a few determined and resolute people") continue to dominate five million Africans and to fend off all internal and international pressures.

White settlers entered Rhodesia to stay in 1890. By the end of the decade (following substantial African resistance), the settlers had succeeded in subduing the Africans. From that time until today, a small white minority (never more than 5 percent of the population) has dominated the life of the country and regimented the African majority to serve its economic needs and confirm its social prejudices. The major components of the social system constructed by the whites include the apportionment of the land between the two racial groups; the development of an industrial color bar that defines jobs, wages, and employment opportunities by race; and the implementation of almost total segregation. Through a variety of thinly disguised ruses, access to the political system is foreclosed to all but a handful of Africans.

The white settlers were able to construct this system for two reasons. They possessed the technological and organizational skills necessary to conquer and then directly administer the far larger African population, and their nominal political and constitutional mentor—the British government—allowed them internal autonomy and made no effort to inhibit the growth of a segregated society. This was true both under the British South African Company, which administered Rhodesia from 1890 to 1923, and under Rhodesia's unique responsible government constitution after 1923.

Few challenges were posed to this system until after World War II. Policies differed little from those practiced elsewhere in Africa—both to the north and to the south of Rhodesia—and the whites contemplated the future with equanimity and with little thought that the "Rhodesian Way of Life" would ever change. As possessors of advanced technology and bearers of racial and cultural attitudes prevalent in the West, the settlers had little reason to doubt either the moral premises of their society or their indefinite right to perpetuate that same society.

2

Belief in cultural superiority (identified with race) and national progress (identified with white class privilege) dovetailed nicely to reinforce the white community's determination to preserve the society it had organized.

For the past two decades Rhodesian political life has been dominated by the challenge posed to settler rule by the emergence of an indigenous African nationalist movement calling for independence on the basis of majority rule and by the settler demands for independence from Britain —independence under white minority government. These demands are obviously incompatible. One calls for a complete restructuring of Rhodesian politics; the other looks toward establishing conditions that will guarantee the permanence of the system constructed after 1890. This book is about the social, political, and economic developments that gave rise to these demands, their articulation both internally and externally, the conflicts that arose from these demands, and the nature of their resolution.

Three different political interactions will dominate our discussion. The first is between white and black in Rhodesia and concerns the distribution of power within the country. African nationalism (and now guerrilla warfare) pose a substantial threat to maintenance of the white system. The Europeans (so far successfully) have responded to these pressures by adding vast new security legislation to buttress the restrictive social and economic legislation from the pre-World War II period.

The second interaction is between the local white government and the British government over the limits of white authority within Rhodesia. A persistent issue of Rhodesian white politics has been the demand for ever-increasing white autonomy. The formation of the Central African Federation in the early 1950's and the new Rhodesian constitution in 1961 were important stages in the withdrawal of British control from Rhodesia. When Britain finally refused to give way fully to white Rhodesian demands in 1965, the government seized independence in defiance of Britain and the world. Although this action may fall somewhat short of Rhodesia's assuming "the role of champion of Western civilisation," it certainly reflects white Rhodesia's commitment to defend its privileged system. Britain has never been prepared to take the steps necessary to challenge this system in any meaningful way.

The third interaction is within the white community itself. In the course of white Rhodesian political history, there has been considerable conflict over the best strategies and tactics to ensure continued white political domination, and thus economic and social privilege. This conflict takes place within a "democratic" political process restricted to the white oligarchy united on the fundamental issue of maintaining the system. The heated white political controversy sometimes seen in Rhodesia should not prevent us from observing the fundamental reality, namely, that white conflict concerns what strategies or priorities to follow in the preservation of the white system. Political conflict in this setting is not synonymous with the offering of real choice.

The scope of this book embraces all these interactions from the arrival of the Europeans in Rhodesia until the present. The major focus, however, is from the beginning of the Central African Federation in 1953 to the May 1972 rejection (by the Pearce Commission) of the British and Rhodesian governments' attempt to resolve their differences over UDI. During this period the African challenge to the white system became manifest, the white Rhodesian demand for independence became persistent, the lack of British authority became evident, and Rhodesia's conflicts assumed an international character.

1

The Foundation of
White Political Control

Prior to the founding of Fort Salisbury, European penetration of the southern African interior was only scattered. A few intrepid Portuguese explorers had come before 1850. Dr. David Livingstone reached Victoria Falls in 1855; Carl Mauch explored the Zimbabwe ruins in 1871; and Dr. Robert Moffat founded the first permanent European settlement at the Inyati mission station in 1859.[1]

Toward the end of the 1880's Cecil Rhodes, Cape Colony politician and mining magnate, sent agents northward to seek mineral and commercial concessions from local chiefs. Although imperial designs played some part in his plans, Rhodes and his associates primarily hoped to repeat elsewhere the dazzling mineral discoveries made at Kimberley and on the Witswatersrand; Rhodesia was thought to be rich in gold.

Rhodes' agents received numerous concessions, but the Rudd Concession negotiated with Lobengula (chief of the Ndebele nation centered in southwestern Rhodesia) gave Rhodes mineral rights to an area which was ultimately interpreted to embrace all of the present boundaries of Rhodesia and Zambia (formerly Northern Rhodesia).[2] With this concession in hand, Rhodes was able to obtain a royal charter from the British government for the British South Africa Company (BSAC). The charter gave the BSAC rights to settle and administer an unspecified area to the north of South Africa and Bechuanaland; neither of these prerogatives had been included in the Rudd Concession.

Under the aegis of the BSAC, a small group of adventurers (the Pioneer Column) moved northward across the Limpopo River and on September 12, 1890, established a settlement near present-day Salisbury. During the first decade of European occupation there was substantial African resistance, including massive rebellions in 1896–1897; however, the Europeans' superior organization and technology overcame greater African numbers, and the indigenous population had little option but to concede defeat, succumb to white administration, and make the best of their conquered status.

The Absence of External Restraints

The BSAC administered Rhodesia from 1890 to 1923. The decision to turn local administration over to a chartered company quickly narrowed the possible forms of political evolution likely to occur in Rhodesia. In opting against direct administration, Britain effectively conceded local autonomy to the new settlers. Her decision was based on the desire not to become financially involved in administering Rhodesia and on the expectation that Rhodesia would eventually join a larger white-run South African federation or union.[3] During the company's rule, the only British official in Rhodesia was the resident commissioner. This situation, different from that in any other British colony, substantially affected the nature of British-Rhodesian relations and left the settlers free to shape their own political practices and institutions.

Britain intermittently professed concern with the trend of developments in Rhodesia (particularly those dealing with the African population), but it became apparent to the settlers and to company officials that Britain was rarely prepared to act. During the first six years of company administration, when the impact on the African societies was nothing short of devastating, the British representative was seldom in the country. British officials admitted their limited interest in, and ability to control, the shape of Rhodesia's African administration. The British high commissioner to South Africa wrote to the British prime minister as follows:

> Nothing is more certain than that if the Imperial Government were to be seen taking a strong line against the Company for the protection of the blacks, the whole of Dutch opinion in South Africa would swing round to the side of the Company and the bulk of—not the whole of—British Colonial opinion would go with it. You might indeed unite Dutch and English by protecting the black man, but you would unite them against yourself and your policy of protection.

6

[The "great thing" is] to secure the appointment of honourable and capable men as magistrates and native commissioners. If that can be done, I think the lot of the natives may be a very tolerable one and that even a system of compulsory labour indeed, under fair conditions and proper safeguards, may be turned to their advantage.[4]

This policy of not offending white opinion while remaining solicitous of Africans was contradictory in theory and unworkable in practice. Nevertheless, it was to be the hallmark of Britain's Rhodesia policy from 1890 on. The Southern Rhodesia Order in Council of 1898 called for a partially elected legislative council, thus granting a major feature of representative government to a European community only eight years old. Britain appointed a resident commissioner to supervise the BSAC, but because the British government, the BSAC, and the settlers shared many values about the purpose and goals of African administration, there was rarely any open disagreement.[5]

The major focus of white conflict before 1923 concerned disagreements over BSAC policies and the long-run political future of Rhodesia. Tensions between the company and the settlers arose initially when the settlers became angered over the company's inability to protect them during the African rebellions. More lasting disagreements emerged over development policy. The settlers resented the company's effective ownership of the land and felt that its policies were not directed toward long-term development of the country but only toward short-term profit. From 1907, when they achieved an effective majority in the Legislative Council, the settlers actively pursued the goal of responsible government, which would give them control over Rhodesia's internal affairs.

In 1918 the British Privy Council ruled that Rhodesian land belonged to the crown and not to the company. With this ruling the company lost interest in continuing to administer Rhodesia, for its hopes of recouping past losses through gains in land speculation, appreciation, and sales were now foreclosed.[6] From 1918 until 1922 negotiations between the company, the settlers, the Union of South Africa, and the British government took place with regard to two specific points—the financial settlement to be made with the company and the future context of Rhodesian political life. The choices were responsible government under the British crown or amalgamation with the Union of South Africa; whether Britain or South Africa would have to reach a financial settlement with the BSAC depended upon the choice made by the local settler electorate.

On October 27, 1922, the Rhodesian electorate (almost entirely white) chose responsible government over union with South Africa by 8,774 to 5,989.[7] This choice represented a defeat for South Africa, Britain, and the company—all of whom wanted Rhodesia to join South Africa.[8]

The Responsible Government Association carried the referendum by playing on fears among different sections of the white population. Rhodesian whites were predominantly English-speaking, and Rhodesian civil servants were particularly apprehensive that their careers would be jeopardized if Rhodesia joined the union. Some feared that unlimited white immigration from the south would lead to the growth of a poor Afrikaner community, while white workers opposed the harsh stand of the South African government during the famous 1922 Rand strike.[9]

Once the results of the referendum were known, Britain had little choice but to integrate Rhodesia into the British Empire; Rhodesia was annexed as a colony and on October 1, 1923, Rhodesia officially came under a system of responsible government. At the same time Northern Rhodesia made the transition from company to colonial office rule—a distinction that did not seem important at the time but was to loom large in the subsequent history of the two Rhodesias.

The system of responsible government allowed for internal self-government, subject to certain specific limitations. Thus the governor (who replaced the resident commissioner as Britain's sole representative in Rhodesia) was required to reserve certain legislation for British government surveillance and judgment.[10] In practice, supervision of legislation falling under the reserve clauses operated much like Britain's supervision of company rule. Britain retained control over African legislation in principle, but this control was seldom exercised. The governor and Rhodesian political leaders informally cleared potentially controversial legislation, thereby avoiding any open imbroglio. Sir Godfrey Huggins, Rhodesian prime minister for more than half the time the reserve clauses were operative, publicly described them as "a tremendous embarrassment to the Government that happens to be in power in the United Kingdom." [11] In 1937, when supervisory functions shifted to the more remote control of the secretary of state for the dominions, Huggins with characteristic bluntness acknowledged that "we do not want anybody messing about with our affairs who understands too much about them. We simply want someone who can satisfy a section of the House of Commons. The less he knows, I think, the better." [12] Typically, legislation was couched in nondiscriminatory language, even though in its practical application the effect was entirely discriminatory.

There was considerable continuity in Rhodesian politics both before and after World War II.[13] While seven elections were held between 1924 and 1948, except for a short period in 1933–1934 the Rhodesia Party (later called the United Party) formed the government. Huggins was prime minister from 1933 until 1953, when he became the first prime minister of the new Central African Federation. Africans played no part in political life; fewer than five hundred were ever enfranchised, and decisions concerning African policy regularly revealed the cohesion of white racial interests.

The Pattern of African Controls

From the first days of white occupation, the Europeans implemented laws and ordinances aimed at regulating the African population to serve white needs. Pass laws controlled entry into, and movement within, urban areas. Land was rapidly alienated to European farmers and mining syndicates. Taxes were imposed to force the Africans into wage employment, and the Europeans' monopoly on skills and education severely limited the jobs and wages to which Africans could aspire. In the political sphere, the Cape Colony's "nonracial" common-roll franchise was adopted, but qualifications were so high that Africans were effectively excluded.

These European institutions, policies, and practices were not immediately accepted by the Africans as the benefits of advanced civilization. Rebellions in 1896–1897 stand out in the history of all Africa as among the most successful attempts to resist European penetration. Yet once these rebellions were crushed, the Africans were forced to make accommodations to their new conquered status.

The African population that the Europeans found when they occupied Rhodesia had undergone considerable change in the preceding century—change which the advancing Europeans little understood or appreciated. The primary development had been that the Shona-speaking peoples (the most prominent group in the area for many centuries) had come under the partial domination of the Ndebele. The Ndebele (a Zulu offshoot) had established a small and highly centralized military raiding state in southwestern Rhodesia near modern-day Bulawayo.[14] Shona culture and religious traditions, as well as long-standing trade with Portuguese towns on the Zambezi River, had not been disturbed, but Ndebele raiding had led to the establishment of a general modus vivendi whereby many Shonas paid tribute in cattle to the Ndebele.[15]

The Shona initially ignored the Pioneer Column. They had no reason to believe that the intent of these men was different from that of previous hunters, traders, and concession seekers. Thus it was with surprise, bewilderment, then anger that the Shona reacted to the rapid implementation of tax, labor, and administrative measures by the BSAC.

In Matabeleland there had actually been more contact with whites because of the intense pressure placed upon Lobengula, the Ndebele king, by Rhodes' agents and other concession hunters. Until the late 1880's, however, the kingdom was so strong and self-sufficient that it could prevent significant white intrusion. When Frank Johnson, a would-be prospector, was denied entry into Mashonaland by Lobengula in 1887, he wrote, "Oh ye spirits of departed negrophilists and followers of 'Exeter Hall' if only you could feel what is felt by us today, at the knowledge that we white men and *Englishmen* too, are under the thumb and utterly in the power of a lot of black scoundrels . . . To feel oneself under the power of a nigger is worse than being in prison and quite enough to bring on fever." [16]

Missionaries had similar feelings. For nearly a generation Lobengula kept them completely isolated in Matabeleland and he exercised sufficient suzerainty over access routes to Mashonaland that no missionaries were even established there. As a result, missionaries were all too ready to help the company undermine the African position. When whites initially occupied Shona areas in 1890 (itself a tribute to Lobengula's ability to keep whites at bay in Matabeleland), missionaries from Matabeleland rejoiced that "the hateful Matabele rule is doomed. We as missionaries with our thirty years history behind us, have little to bind our sympathies to the Matabele people, neither can we pity the fall of their power, but we earnestly rejoice in the deliverance of the Mashona." [17]

Lobengula tried desperately to limit the extent of the white advance, but he was double-crossed by Rhodes. Verbal guarantees of limited white penetration (given to Lobengula in order to attain the Rudd Concession) were not honored.[18] In October 1893, under a manufactured pretext, the BSAC police invaded the Ndebele kingdom, destroyed its major towns, confiscated its land and cattle, and effectively ended the kingdom. Lobengula died in retreat.

The Shona and Ndebele had many grievances, but to organize a sustained resistance against the white settlers was an exceptional achievement. In his study of the rebellion, T. O. Ranger has argued that the remarkable thing about it was the Africans' ability to overcome the problem of scale—of expanding the commitment to the rebellion over a large area and among peoples of traditional rivalries.[19] Resistance expanded from that of the African soldiers alone to that of the entire society. This was achieved because a genuinely revolutionary leadership emerged which appealed to racial unity against the whites and promised success, invulnerability, and immortality to those who participated. At the core of this revolutionary leadership were the traditional Shona religious leaders—the spirit mediums and the priests of the Mwari cult, the latter being the critical link between the Shona and the Ndebele. These religious leaders were the most militant champions of the rebellion. Even after the Ndebele sued for peace with Rhodes in 1896, they urged continued resistance, and the Mashonaland struggle lasted well into 1897.

If the Africans had faced the Rhodesian whites as their only enemy, the rebellions might have succeeded. About 10 percent of the whites in Rhodesia in 1896 were killed, and all were vulnerable to attack. But the whites had allies in South Africa and Britain; with their assistance, the rebellions were inevitably crushed.

At best, the rebellions produced only minor improvements for the Africans. Whites retained the land and cattle, and taxes and labor impressment continued almost unaltered. In 1898 the Southern Rhodesia

Order in Council and Southern Rhodesia Native Regulations were promulgated. The former (designed in theory to introduce more explicit British supervision over company activities) in fact contained all the pass laws, labor control measures, urban controls, and land legislation the company had implemented since 1890. The latter established the structure for administering the African population that has remained virtually unchanged to the present day.

Under the 1898 regulations a policy of direct rule was implemented throughout African areas. This policy was administered by the Native Affairs Department, which had the authority to appoint all chiefs and headmen and to amalgamate and subdivide tribes. In theory the chain of command ran from the British government through the local European administration to the chiefs, headmen, kraalheads, and on to the African people, but in practice native commissioners had vast discretionary authority. They combined administrative, judicial, and legislative functions and no aspect of African life failed to come under their purview.[20] Native commissioners were in charge of land allocation, tax collection, and pass administration. The Native Affairs Act (NAA) of 1927 consolidated all previous rules and regulations and gave the native commissioners new jurisdiction in African civil cases and in criminal cases where the accused was an African. More importantly, the NAA gave native commissioners exclusive criminal jurisdiction over NAA-stipulated offenses. All Africans were bound to "obey and comply promptly" with any order given by a native commissioner, chief, or headman. Furthermore, any African who made a statement that was deemed to "undermine the authority" of these men could be given both a fine and prison sentence. The native commissioner became prosecutor, plantiff, witness, and judge over these broadly defined offenses.

The Native Affairs Department administered the pass laws. A 1902 act required every adult male to register with his native commissioner upon reaching age 14. He then received a registration certificate (*situpa*) which he was required to carry at all times. Other laws regulated movement of the Africans from their home districts and entry into urban areas. The Native Registration Act (NRA) of 1936 and the Native (Urban Areas) Accommodation and Registration Act (NUA) of 1946 consolidated previous regulations and augmented the methods of urban control. The NRA required that Africans in towns carry at least one pass in addition to the situpa. The NUA provided the statutory basis for wide-ranging new controls that were implemented as the African urban population expanded following World War II. These passes (required of all Africans, including nonindigenous workers) were always a major source of internal discord.

Another persistent source of tension has been land segregation. This complex feature of Rhodesian life permeates all questions of economic, social, and political life, and no aspect of Rhodesian politics can be understood without some knowledge of land policy.[21] Within a few years of white occupation, large areas of land were alienated to settlers, companies, and syndicates. Although small reserves were established for Africans in remote parts of Rhodesia, in reality little concern was paid to African land use. Both the settlers and the British government thought it proper for white Rhodesians to allocate the land, and any thought that Africans had a right to more than a fraction of it was dismissed as an absurdity.[22] By 1923, when Rhodesia moved to responsible government, reserves totaled about 21 million acres. This land, in theory, was for "the sole and exclusive use and occupation of natives"; in fact, Europeans retained all mineral rights on land assigned to Africans.[23] Under the reserve clauses, any subsequent alienation of reserve land was subject to British approval.

The division of Rhodesian land was formalized in 1930 by the passage of the Land Apportionment Act—an act that remained the cornerstone of Rhodesian segregation until the passage of the similar Land Tenure Act in 1969. The pattern of Rhodesian land apportionment since the end of the nineteenth century is summarized in Table 1. The crucial result of the Land Apportionment Act (LAA) was to divide the land into African and European areas.[24] Henceforth no African was to hold or occupy land in European areas except "under condition that he supply labour to such [European] owner or occupier."

Table 1. Rhodesian land apportionment, 1894–1969.
Figures are given in thousands of acres.

Year	Assigned to Africans	Assigned to whites	Undetermined or unassigned	National parks and forests
1894	2,200	—	—	—
1913	21,390	21,947	44,000	—
1925	21,595	31,588	42,149	894
1930	29,065	49,149	17,889	591
1941	29,500	49,700	17,900	600
1953	30,651	47,408	14,268	3,977
1959	41,950	48,062	57	7,190
1963	43,821	38,137	5,472	9,756
1969	45,000	45,000	—	6,500

SOURCE: *Second Report of the Select Committee on Resettlement of Natives* (Salisbury, Government Printing Office, 1960) and Land Tenure Act, 1969.

Land apportionment was based on the presumption that the land belonged to the Europeans and that it was theirs to allocate as they saw fit. In Rhodesia, however, many felt differently. Africans, hundreds of whom had presented evidence against the bill, saw it as continuing the pillage they had been subject to since 1890. African associations met in

1929 and voted unanimously to reject it. One Shona speaker said, "Let us tell the Government that this bill is wrong. Our people have been driven to lands where they cannot live. Our cattle die for want of water . . . Let us tell the Government that the bill is no good. It is all for the white man. Rhodesia is big. Let them cut the land in half and let us live on the one side and the white man on the other. If they cannot do this they should at least give us a place for reserves where there is water." [25]

African reserves were assigned in the most remote and least fertile areas of Rhodesia.[26] As Table 2 shows, the African population grew rapidly, and as early as the 1930's agricultural experts agreed that the reserve land was fully populated and could not support a larger African

Table 2. Rhodesian population growth, 1901–1970.

Year	Africans [a]	Europeans	Total [b]
1901	500,000	11,000	510,000
1907	670,000	14,000	690,000
1911	740,000	23,600	770,000
1921	860,000	33,600	900,000
1926	930,000	39,200	970,000
1931	1,080,000	49,900	1,130,000
1936	1,260,000	55,400	1,320,000
1941	1,400,000	69,000	1,480,000
1946	1,770,000	82,400	1,860,000
1951	2,170,000	135,600	2,320,000
1956	2,990,000	177,100	3,180,000
1961	3,550,000	221,500	3,790,000
1965	4,070,000	224,000	4,320,000
1970	5,130,000	249,000	5,405,000

SOURCE: *1961 Census of the European, Asian and Coloured Population* (Salisbury, Central Statistical Office, 1965?) and *Economic Survey for Rhodesia for 1970* (Salisbury, Government Printing Office, 1971).

[a] All figures for the African population prior to 1956 are estimates and are now considered to be undervalued. Moreover, because of changes in methods in estimation, the figures above and below the two lines (1941 and 1946) are not comparable. The figures from 1961 on are much more reliable.
[b] The total includes the small Asian and Coloured populations. Early totals are estimates, subject to the qualifications mentioned on the accuracy of African population figures.

population. Land deterioration became a permanent feature of reserve life, leading to urban migration and extensive African squatting on white land. Until well into the 1950's little was done to change this basic picture. Europeans steadily consolidated their hold on the best land, even though much of it remained unused. Africans were left with the choice of remaining on deteriorating land or working on European land in exchange for a place to live. Either choice brought the Africans under further administrative domination.

Four years after the occupation, a hut tax of ten shillings per year was promulgated by the BSAC. This tax quickly came to be enforced as an annual fee assigned to each adult male African in the country, both indigenous and nonindigenous.[27] The tax was increased to one pound in 1904, where it remained until 1956 when it doubled again. This tax compelled Africans living far from European settlement to migrate for at least part of the year to work on European farms and mines and forced those already resident on land alienated to Europeans into a tenancy relationship whereby their right to live on the land would be dependent upon their working part of the year for the white owner. These direct labor taxes were not opposed by the British government. The British high commissioner in South Africa declared that he personally favored "a well-regulated system of state compulsion under proper securities for good treatment and for adequate remuneration." [28] Forced labor was undoubtedly used in many areas, and L. H. Gann has computed that with the possible exception of the Transvaal, the Rhodesian African tax was the highest anywhere in Southern Africa.[29]

Wages offered were generally so low and conditions so deplorable that Rhodesian Africans only reluctantly joined the wage economy. The common pattern was for an African male to migrate to a job for a few months and then return to his rural home. Because this pattern did not satisfy white demands for a stable labor force, a system of labor migration to Rhodesia from outside was soon established. Whites favored workers from Mozambique and Nyasaland because they stayed longer and accepted lower wages than indigenous Africans. Foreign labor has seldom totaled less than half the number of Africans in wage employment in Rhodesia, and their constant presence in the country has had a profound effect on the evolution of African politics.[30]

African workers are subject to numerous regulations that channel them into certain jobs and delimit their rights and opportunities. The Master and Servants Act (MSA) of 1891 is still the basic legislation controlling Africans in domestic service and on European farms—two job categories which together comprise over 50 percent of the total African work force. Under the MSA it is an offense not to obey the "lawful" order of an employer, and an employee can be charged for "insulting his master, neglecting his master's property and deserting from his master's service."

The Industrial Conciliation Act (ICA) stands with the Land Apportionment Act as a major cornerstone of Rhodesia's white supremacist society. The ICA was passed in 1934 at the behest of white workers whose overriding purposes were to protect the white wage structure and to control access to employment opportunities. The term "employee" was defined to include only white workers. Africans thus were neatly excluded from the wage bargaining structure and from the skilled trades because only "employees" had the right to bargain collectively or to become apprentices. Not only did the ICA guarantee white control over scarce skills by preventing Africans from learning, it also instituted the practice of paying "the rate for the job" (also identified by the slogan "equal pay for equal work"). Since it was highly unlikely that any European employer would wish to pay an African the same wage as a European, the African was guaranteed unskilled, poorly paid work.

The government rarely felt the need to justify its African policies. The differences in capability and achievement between the primitive African population and the technologically advanced Europeans were so pronounced in white eyes that their domination was seen as beneficial, mandatory, and timeless. Little thought was given to the effect these rules and regulations had upon African life or upon the character of European society.

During the 1930's the government occasionally articulated the theory that Africans could rise to any heights within their own area. This was called the two-pyramid or parallel development policy. Huggins explained:

> The Europeans in this country can be likened to an island of white in a sea of black, with the artisan and the tradesman forming the shores and the professional classes the highlands in the centre. Is the native to be allowed to erode away the shores and gradually attack the highlands? To permit this would mean that the leaven of civilisation would be removed from the country, and the black man would inevitably revert to a barbarism worse than ever before . . .
>
> While there is yet time and space, the country should be divided into separate areas for black and white. In the Native area the black man must be allowed to rise to any position to which he is capable of climbing. Every step in the industrial and social pyramid must be open to him, excepting only—and always—the very top . . . The Native may be his own lawyer, doctor, builder, journalist or priest, and he must be protected from white competition in his own area. In the European area the black man will be welcomed, when, tempted by wages, he offers his services as a labourer, but it will be on the understanding that he shall merely assist, and not compete with, the white man, . . . the interest of each race will be paramount in its own sphere.[31]

The two-pyramid policy thus promised to protect all white jobs from African competition and retain political control in white hands. The notion that Africans could rise to any position was flagrant deception. Regulations dealing with training, wages, and education excluded Africans from attaining the skills necessary to be a "lawyer, doctor, builder, journalist or priest." Further, the concentration of economic development in European areas made it unrealistic in the extreme to think that any important opportunities for employment existed where Africans would not have to "merely assist, and not compete with, the white man." The point was driven home by the Public Services Act of 1931, which shut off government administrative jobs—even those in the African reserves—to nonwhites. The whole system worked smoothly to protect whites from competition and restrict Africans to menial roles.

Africans tended toward resigned acceptance of white rule. Early organizations such as the Rhodesian Bantu Voters Association and the African National Congress, formed in the 1920's and 1930's, were tiny elite organizations formed by a few educated Africans.[32] Their petitioning and lobbying efforts focused on improving conditions for themselves; because they were so far removed from the masses, the Rhodesian authorities and the British government paid them little attention. This state of affairs was not lost on Abraham Twala, a black South African resident of Rhodesia, who wrote in 1922 that "experience has taught us that our salvation does not lie in Downing Street. I strongly advise our fledglings in Southern Rhodesia, indulging in politics, to find out and make their friends in Southern Rhodesia. When this has been done, we shall see what the harvest shall be." [33] The tragedy of Rhodesian African politics before World War II, and far more explicitly and obviously afterward, lay in the fact that this well-put advice was never adhered to by leaders of the African people.

Discontent occasionally was manifested, but it rarely took a sustained form. Independent church movements, of which the Watchtower movement and Matthew Zwimba's Church of the White Bird were the most important, intermittently swept through Shona areas.[34] The Industrial and Commercial Union held regular meetings in Salisbury and Bulawayo in the late 1920's until its leaders were suppressed or deported. For the most part, however, "the mass of the population in Southern Rhodesia were politically inert, passive and virtually powerless . . . The rule of the white man was apparently accepted almost as inevitable, open resentment was rarely manifested; European privileges and prestige seemed inviolable, white supremacy appeared to be permanently established." [35]

The Drive to Federation

It is an irony of African politics that copper was discovered in Northern Rhodesia in 1924—only one year after the two Rhodesias took separate constitutional paths and only two years after both might have joined South Africa. The copper boom brought many new whites to Northern Rhodesia who soon looked enviously southward at Rhodesia's superior constitutional position. White Rhodesians, for their part, wished to use Northern Rhodesia's wealth to finance their own economic development.

From the middle of the 1920's on, whites in the two Rhodesias periodically advocated amalgamation of their territories. In 1929 and in 1938 Britain sent major commissions to Africa to consider this question, but both rejected the settlers' demands—mainly on the grounds that Rhodesia's racial policies were unacceptable; nevertheless, the Bledisloe Commission in 1938 accepted the idea of amalgamation "in principle" and recommended an interterritorial council to coordinate planning and services.[36] Despite disappointments, white leaders in the Rhodesias continued to press for closer association. Their supreme achievement after World War II was to overcome British inhibitions without in any meaningful way altering their internal racial policies. The key move on the settlers' part was to shift their goal from complete amalgamation to federation.[37]

The decision to form the Central African Federation emerged from a series of five conferences held between 1951 and 1953.[38] Negotiations were initiated by the British Labour government and completed by the Conservatives who came to power in November 1951. Africans from the three territories that were eventually federated (Rhodesia, Northern Rhodesia, and Nyasaland) were almost entirely excluded from the pre-federal negotiations. The one conference at which a few Africans were allowed to voice their discontent was derisively referred to by Huggins as "a Native Benefit meeting led by the . . . Secretary of State for the Colonies." [39] Africans in Northern Rhodesia and Nyasaland rightfully perceived the federal scheme as an effort to extend white Rhodesian influence into the two northern territories; their vigorous objections, however, were only occasionally heard and never taken seriously by the British government.

The federal White Paper was a formal constitutional document, but in reality it represented a British-Rhodesian bargain. Indeed, the agreement enshrined settler aims. For little more than agreeing to disavow amalgamation, a federation was proposed with a strong central government having considerable autonomy. Except for control over the political advance of Africans in the two northern territories, nearly all political, social, and economic responsibilities were to be granted to a locally based white minority government. Rhodesia retained complete control over its internal affairs (including African administration) while gaining effective economic control in the north. Twenty-nine of the thirty-five members of the proposed federal legislative assembly were *required* to be white; despite this, Huggins commented that "by the time you have got [six Africans in Parliament] you may have exceeded the total number of Africans in the three territories who are really fitted to be in any of these positions." [40] Many other guarantees made it certain that the settlers would completely dominate federal political life; short of complete amalgamation, the settlers could not have struck a political bargain with fewer risks for themselves.

What made the settler demand for closer association become a reality in 1953 when it had been denied for so many years? Answers range over a wide field of economic, imperial, strategic, moral, and humanitarian considerations. The key, however, is that the settlers were united, determined, and in a strong position vis-à-vis Britain, and that Britain in the early 1950's lacked a coherent African policy and was thus susceptible to settler pressure.

Britain and Rhodesia were drawn together because both wished to stabilize the situation in Northern Rhodesia, continue a British presence in the region, and promote economic development. Britain had no viable alternative to the unceasing demands of Northern Rhodesian settlers for greater autonomy—primarily because the big mining houses supported the settlers and Britain's own financial needs required stability on the Copperbelt.[41] Rhodesian whites saw federation as an effective way to shore up Northern Rhodesian whites as a potential buffer against African nationalism; they also were aware of the economic potential for Rhodesia in having access to the riches of the Copperbelt.

Britain believed its interests in Central Africa were threatened by the Nationalist Party which had come to power in South Africa in 1948. Huggins and Roy Welensky, the Northern Rhodesian leader, skillfully exploited ties of kith-and-kin by endlessly implying that the only alternative to federation on their terms was increased South African influence. Britain liked to think that her mere presence in Rhodesia was a guarantee against apartheid, and this theme became a primary British rationalization for federation.[42]

Both Britain and Rhodesia took it for granted, moreover, that federation would promote development by widening the local market, by diversifying the regional economy, by facilitating more efficient use of regional resources, and by making the area more attractive to foreign investors. These motivations have been brilliantly reviewed by Arthur Hazlewood, who demonstrated that the economic case for federation was always assumed and was never subjected to more than perfunctory analysis.[43] Nonetheless, economic development became another convenient rationale for federation; in the abstract it appealed to everyone, and the social and political implications were never worked out.

The package of Stability + British Way of Life + Economic Development was finally given the name Partnership. This was a fitting slogan because in its undefined state it provided a sophisticated cover for what was in fact a hard political bargain. British officials tended to prefer imagery capturing the notion of a great British multiracial state in Central Africa, while Huggins spoke far more candidly of a partnership of "junior and senior partners, and as a junior in this case the native gradually works himself up in the business."[44] Federation was approved by the British House of Commons on March 24, 1953. This left only a referendum vote in Rhodesia to be taken before the federal scheme could be implemented.

Despite the favorable terms, there was considerable white Rhodesian opposition to federation. The root of the conflict lay in disagreement over the best strategy to follow to protect white interests. The United Party Huggins led had long supported some form of closer association with Northern Rhodesia. The opposition Liberal Party (holding but five of thirty seats in the Rhodesian Legislative Assembly) was committed to a policy of "Southern Rhodesia First"—meaning that Rhodesia should obtain dominion status (that is, independence from the potential British use of the reserve clauses) before embarking on any constitutional ventures outside her borders. The Liberals feared that either amalgamation or federation would delay Rhodesia's own constitutional advance.[45] Their differences turned on degrees of skepticism with respect to Britain. Huggins was disdainful of the reserve clauses and never really feared that Britain would interfere with white control in Rhodesia; the Liberals were less certain.

The referendum was set for April 9, 1953, and the campaign engaged all white political leaders. The opposition to federation included three of Huggins' former finance ministers (Sir Ernest Guest, J. H. Smit, and Max Danziger), Charles Olley from the White Rhodesia Council, R. O. Stockil, leader of the parliamentary opposition, and several figures who would later become prominent in the Rhodesian Front government of the 1960's.[46] These men focused on puncturing Huggins' optimism about federation by developing three themes: loss of status, concern about Britain's African policy, and rejection of partnership.[47]

The opposition argued that Rhodesia would be unable to advance constitutionally while joined to two territories of less advanced status. They feared continued British control of the pace of African advance in Northern Rhodesia and Nyasaland and believed that the seating of six Africans in the federal legislative assembly would inevitably lead to similar pressure in the territorial sphere and thus threaten the well-established segregated industrial, political, and social system of Rhodesia.[48] Partnership as a slogan was viewed as undermining everything white Rhodesians had advocated since 1890. The opposition stood for white Rhodesia alone and not for providing assistance to northern territory Europeans or the British government.

Huggins, Welensky, and other supporters of federation played down opposition criticism. They implied that the full federation would attain dominion status at the Federal Review Conference, already set for seven to nine years hence.[49] Huggins handled the criticism of African advance by bluntly reminding the House that "in the face of world opinion, the United Kingdom Government are trusting the Europeans of Central Africa sufficiently to hand over 6,000,000 primitive people to a

Parliament dominated by local Europeans." [50] As far as partnership was concerned, proponents of federation preferred to leave the impression that it would evolve out of experience, custom, and circumstance, implying that it would be far in the future before any marked deviation from current norms occurred.

Federal advocates struck their strongest arguments in proclaiming the great potentialities of the proposed system. "Pray God our greatness may not fail through craven fears of being great"—this was the slogan under which they fought the referendum campaign. Federation was seen as an opportunity for Rhodesia to extend its influence across the Zambezi in a permanent way. One profederation placard claimed that by voting for federation, Rhodesians "will be taking part in one of the greatest movements and in one of the greatest missions that any civilised part of the world has ever taken part in." [51]

When the ballots were counted, federation was approved by 25,570 (63.5 percent) to 14,729 (36.5 percent). The portion of the electorate going to the polls was 82.1 percent—even today the highest for any referendum or general election in Rhodesia's history. Of the African population of about 2.3 million, a total of 429 individuals were eligible to vote. The federal victory can be attributed to the Rhodesian economic boom of the postwar years and to the continued confidence white Rhodesians had in their political leaders. Between 1938 and 1952 the value of construction and manufacturing production increased tenfold. The value of Rhodesian exports, 10.6 million pounds in 1938, reached 54 million pounds in 1953; national income in the same period increased from 25.2 to 125.1 million pounds.[52] The growing European population (summarized in Table 2) reaped considerable personal benefits from this growth; Yudelman has estimated that in the eighteen years from 1938 to 1956 (and taking inflation into account), for Europeans "the average annual increase in real incomes amounted to 30 percent." [53]

This rapid rise in their standard of living induced white Rhodesians to support Huggins. He offered them the opportunity to play a heroic role: "The scheme in front of us now is for the emancipation of Northern Rhodesia and Nyasaland and for the preservation of Southern Rhodesia." [54] And he sweetened the pot with promises of continued prosperity and no racial risks. Linked to the sixty-year tradition of complete white domination in which Britain had concurred, there was little reason to believe federation was anything but another victory for white Rhodesians.

2

White Rhodesian Politics, 1954–1962

Federation complicated Rhodesian political life. A new government and civil service was established, but the territorial government and civil service remained. The federal government generally assumed functions that pertained to the entire area (defense, external affairs, economic growth and development, commerce, and nearly all revenue responsibilities); the territorial government was left with the more limited, but ultimately crucial, responsibility for handling African affairs.

White interests were carried forward on two levels. The federal government (wholly dominated by white Rhodesians) pressed unceasingly for federation-wide independence, skewing economic development and other financial matters to Rhodesia's advantage. At the same time, Rhodesia retained its internal self-government constitution as a fall-back position for white interests if federation failed.

The federation has been called "the world's most overgoverned country." [1] With three territorial governments, the federal government, and Britain all involved in the administration of little over six million people (in 1954), this description may be true. More important, however, is the fact that from 1954 to 1963, white Rhodesians had two en-

21

trenched governments actively promoting and defending their narrow racial interests. Although there was considerable white political competition, particularly in the territorial sphere, it all occurred within the general framework of united resistance to African nationalism and centered on the selection of political strategies that would best sustain white rule. A prime concern was how to entice new constitutional concessions from Britain. The federal leadership and those who governed Rhodesia through 1962 believed that the small concesssion encased in liberal-sounding rhetoric was the best ploy for handling Britain; the Rhodesian Front (which came to power in 1962) was less willing to make the verbal gesture. Before the Rhodesian Front came to power, however, Britain consented to the 1961 Rhodesian constitution that granted new autonomy to Rhodesia without jeopardizing white rule. This constitution again reflected Britain's limited ability and interest in effecting political change in Rhodesia.

Economic Development, Partnership, and the Federal Experience

The referendum victory left Huggins with the responsibility for forming the first federal government. White leaders from all three territories (Rhodesia, Northern Rhodesia, and Nyasaland) quickly joined his new Federal Party—a party that was little more than a federation-wide extension of Rhodesia's United Party.

Huggins and Roy Welensky completely dominated federal political life. Huggins was prime minister until 1956; Welensky served as prime minister until the federation dissolved at the end of 1963. Their leadership was never challenged within the political system. The Federal Party held 26 of 35 seats after the 1954 election, 46 of 59 seats after the 1958 election, and 54 of 59 seats after the 1962 election.[2] Federal Party domination led to complete political rigidity. The men who conceived federation saw it through, and there was never any circulation of new leadership, new ideas, or new policies. Nothing about the federation is more remarkable than its unchanging vision during ten years of dramatic political development elsewhere in Africa.

Although political change was negligible during these years, economic development did occur. The federal area experienced steady but unspectacular growth from 1954 to 1963. Copper, tobacco, and tea were the major exports both before and after federation; overall the gross domestic product rose 54 percent in real terms. Table 3 summarizes federal economic growth by territory.

Two questions must be answered about this growth: was it attributable to federation, and who benefited? Literature on the federal economy provides conclusive answers. Aside from perhaps the Kariba Dam project, economic growth in the region can in no way be attributed to

22

Table 3. Federal gross domestic product (at factor cost)
by territory, 1954–1963.
Figures are given in millions of pounds.

Year	Southern Rhodesia	Northern Rhodesia	Nyasaland	Total
1954	161.5	138.8	29.5	329.8
1955	180.7	169.5	31.8	382.0
1956	206.8	188.1	34.1	429.0
1957	231.2	155.2	35.9	422.3
1958	241.4	141.0	38.2	420.6
1959	256.9	188.1	39.9	484.9
1960	274.7	207.4	42.1	524.2
1961	290.4	200.6	43.5	534.5
1962	295.0	198.2	45.5	538.7
1963	306.3	207.5	46.7	560.5

SOURCE: *National Accounts and Balance of Payments of Northern Rhodesia, Nyasaland, and Southern Rhodesia 1954–1963* (Salisbury, Central Statistical Office, 1964), Tables 1, 51, and 140.

federation. The economic benefits accrued largely to Rhodesia and occasionally to Nyasaland; Northern Rhodesia financed their growth.[3] In his review of federal economic life, Hazlewood showed that during the first five years of federation, only in Rhodesia did the net domestic product grow faster than in the five years preceding federation. Moreover, growth throughout the federal area was faster between 1949 and 1953 than in either the 1954–1958 or 1959–1963 periods.[4] At the very least, federation did not induce the dramatic growth that often was predicted.

Rhodesia, however, did very well. The allocation of responsibilities between the federal and territorial governments was extremely advantageous to Rhodesia. Federation assumed functions such as the education of Europeans and white agriculture. Since the great preponderance of whites lived in the territory of Rhodesia, the effect was that federal revenues paid for white Rhodesian services. Analogous advantages arose out of federal fiscal arrangements. At the start of federation, the federal government assumed the public debt of the three territories. Since a high percentage of this debt was Rhodesia's, the servicing of the debt represented a federal subsidy to Rhodesia.

The collection and expenditure of federal revenues was an even more blatant source of Rhodesian exploitation of Northern Rhodesia. Federal revenue was distributed in the following percentages: federal government, 62 percent; Northern Rhodesia, 18 percent; Southern Rhodesia, 14 percent; and Nyasaland, 6 percent. These allocations derived from prefederal patterns of expenditure and thus perpetuated the territorial differences in development that existed in 1953 and maintained at 1953 levels the differences in expenditure between Africans and Europeans. In both ways this fiscal division worked to the advantage of white Rhodesians and to the disadvantage of everyone else. In every year but 1959, federal expenditure within Rhodesia exceeded revenues collected there. This never occurred in Northern Rhodesia.[5] Table 4 summarizes federal revenue and expenditure by territory.

Since political power remained in white Rhodesian hands, other advantages almost automatically fell to Rhodesia. The federal capital was sited in Rhodesia's capital, Salisbury; this assured that most federal government departments and jobs would be located in Rhodesia. The

Table 4. Percentages of federal government revenue derived from and expended in each territory, 1954–1963.

Year	Southern Rhodesia		Northern Rhodesia		Nyasaland	
	Revenue	Expenditure	Revenue	Expenditure	Revenue	Expenditure
1954	51	69	53	24	− 4	7
1955	45	66	56	28	− 1	6
1956	41	63	58	27	1	10
1957	47	63	55	29	− 2	8
1958	62	64	39	28	− 1	8
1959	70	64	29	28	1	8
1960	59	62	41	28	0	10
1961	55	61	45	30	0	9
1962	58	62	43	28	− 1	10
1963	56	64	44	27	0	9

SOURCE: *National Accounts and Balance of Payments of Northern Rhodesia, Nyasaland, and Southern Rhodesia 1954–1963* (Salisbury, Central Statistical Office, 1964), pp. 36, 58, 95, and Table 6(g). Computations to percentages done by the author.

federal decision to forego the previously agreed upon Kafue hydroelectric scheme in Northern Rhodesia in favor of the Kariba dam project on the Zambezi River between the two Rhodesias was an early indication that federation would serve white Rhodesian interests first.

Trends in manufacturing followed this same pattern. Considerable political pressure induced manufacturers to locate in Rhodesia, and it has been computed that "the value of manufacturing output increased during the federal period by nearly 30 million pounds in Southern Rhodesia compared with an increase of only 9 million pounds in the other two territories together."[6] This pattern cannot really be explained in terms of markets or raw materials, for the Northern Rhodesian Copperbelt (where the lack of development was striking) was perhaps the most concentrated federal area for sales. During federation, Rhodesian exports to Northern Rhodesia and Nyasaland grew from 15 to 30 percent of its exports; Northern Rhodesia could only increase its Rhodesia-Nyasaland exports from 2 to 4 percent.

Redistribution of wealth from the relatively undeveloped territory of Northern Rhodesia to Rhodesia amounted to some 70 million pounds over the ten-year span.[7] In terms of governmental expenditure, capital outlay, and general patterns of growth, Rhodesia and particularly the Salisbury area benefited greatly from federation. Rhodesia's economy was far more diversified in 1963. Its gross domestic product had nearly doubled, and these gains strengthened the growing white community. The prediction of some early opponents of federation that Rhodesia would milk the economic wealth of Northern Rhodesia was emphatically realized. These same prognosticators had also suggested that partnership would come to naught.

During federation, partnership was implemented in much the same fashion as economic development—progress was equated with Rhodesian growth, and partnership with indefinite white rule.[8] Defenders of federation commonly argued that the division of functions prevented the federal government from having access to the African population. Implicit was the notion that the federal government should not be blamed for shortcomings on racial questions. This argument is misleading. The federal government did little where it had a direct impact on African affairs, and federal politicians played a considerable role in Rhodesian territorial politics, where they invariably resisted any promotion of African interests. The federal government directly contacted Africans in transport, postal services, higher education, defense, and the federal public service. In any of these areas the federal government could have made a positive contribution to the idea of partnership. It never did.

During the mid-1950's the federal government recruited white immigrants throughout Europe for railway positions rather than challenge traditional patterns of social segregation and labor-wage regulations. Post offices were opened for integrated use only after years of African (and later British) protest.

The federal government employed about thirty thousand individuals. Here the government had an opportunity to influence profoundly employment practices throughout the area. By 1959 in public service Grade I (the top administrative grade) there were 12,428 Europeans and 53 non-Europeans. In Grades II to IV there were no Europeans and 17,065 non-Europeans. In the federal army, units were rigidly segregated. African privates earned 44 pounds per year; European reserves or trainees received 552 pounds annually.[9]

Federal resistance to change was equally noticeable whenever political advancement for Africans was broached. Huggins' and Welensky's statements against equality, integration, and partnership are legion. A remark commonly attributed to Huggins was that "partnership between black and white is the partnership between the horse and its rider." Another time he commented that "all the Federal Party wanted to integrate was the territories of British Central Africa." [10] Welensky was no less blunt: "We believe that the African should be given more say in the running of the country, as and when he shows his ability to contribute more to the general good, but we must make it clear that even when that day comes, *in a hundred or two hundred years' time,* he can never hope to dominate the partnership. He can achieve equal standing but not go beyond it." [11] Federal politicians cannot be criticized for failing to implement partnership. Their irrevocable commitment to white domination was never a secret; they always viewed partnership as a meaningless slogan to assuage British opinion.[12] Would Britain indefinitely accept the slogan without any substance? British-federal relations turned on the answer to this question.

Africans and Europeans engaged in a constant struggle for the ear of the British government. The whites desired full federal independence under white leadership and hoped to achieve this at the 1960 Federal Review Conference. Africans in the northern territories fought federation as an extension of white Rhodesian power. The key focus of conflict became the question as to whether Britain would make territorial changes objectionable to the federal government.

Britain's relations with the federal government were excellent until the late 1950's. In 1957–1958 Britain agreed to several constitutional changes that shattered all lingering hopes that partnership might come to mean something and strongly suggested Britain's willingness to consider federal independence under white rule. On April 27, 1957, Britain announced broad new concessions. Henceforth the federal government could receive diplomatic, trade, and consular representatives and acquire membership in international organizations. Moreover, Britain publicly acknowledged a convention "whereby the United Kingdom in practice does not initiate any legislation to amend or to repeal any Federal Act or to deal with any matter included within the competence of the Federal Legislature, except at the request of the Federal Government." Britain also agreed that the 1960 review conference "will consider a programme for the attainment of such status as would enable the Federation to become eligible for full membership in the Commonwealth." [13]

A Constitution Amendment Act approved by Britain later in 1957 gave further evidence of Britain's continued commitment to a white federation. This act increased the federal assembly from 35 to 59 members and substantially increased the ability of white voters to select African representatives and to control African political advance.

These settler gains in international prestige and constitutional prerogatives pointed toward early white independence and reconfirmed to Africans that they were to be systematically and indefinitely excluded from any meaningful access to the federal political system. Thus opponents of federation turned their attention to the federal government's one weak link—its limited control over territorial constitutional advance. The African nationalists in Northern Rhodesia and Nyasaland heightened their efforts in a last-ditch attempt to arouse concern and undermine political stability. They rightly believed that African political advance would doom federation, for white politicians would not be interested in a federation they did not fully dominate.

British support for federation dissipated after 1957, and by 1960 it was evident that the chance for a white independent federation had evaporated. This fundamental change occurred because trends elsewhere in Africa finally began to have an impact in Central Africa. Ghana achieved independence in 1957, and other British colonies were following Ghana's lead. In East Africa the Mau Mau emergency pointed up the high cost of supporting small white minorities. Moreover, the pressures that originally led Britain to support federation no longer seemed so important. Britain was now much more comfortable in dealing with black Africans. Far from believing that whites alone could guarantee stability, it became possible to argue that they were the major cause of instability. Britain's economic position was sounder by the end of the decade, and the copper companies (especially Roan Selection Trust) were prepared to come to an agreement with the African nationalists. Finally, Britain had dealt with the Afrikaners in Pretoria for more than ten years and rather than being a threat to British interests, South Africa had become a bigger and more important commercial partner than ever.

Two British Commissions of Inquiry pointed toward the end of federation. Patrick Devlin's report on the February-March 1959 state of emergency in Nyasaland had much the same effect as the Gold Coast's Watson Commission report of 1948. Devlin reported persuasively on the profound gulf between the British government in Nyasaland and the indigenous Africans, who invariably found federation to be the "cause of all the trouble." [14] Implicitly the Devlin report constituted a stinging attack on British policy throughout the federal area.

The Monckton Commission was established by Britain to prepare materials for the 1960 Federal Review Conference. Because its terms of reference were vague and its purpose unclear, the commission was received with skepticism or hostility by everyone. The Labour and Liberal parties in Britain and the African nationalists in Central Africa refused to participate at all. The federal government was only slightly less reluctant and bitterly fought any expansion of the Monckton Commission's terms of reference beyond the single question of federal political advance. [15]

Federal government fears were heightened in January-February 1960, during British Prime Minister Harold Macmillan's long trip through Africa. In Salisbury he remarked that "we will not remove the protection of the British government to either . . . Northern Rhodesia or Nyasaland until it is clear that the expressed wish of these peoples is to enter into a full and independent federation." [16] Two weeks later in a famous Cape Town address, Macmillan noted, "The wind of change is blowing through the continent. Whether we like it or not, this growth of national consciousness is a political fact. We must accept it as a fact. Our national policies must take account of it." [17]

The federal government was not cheered by these speeches, and the Monckton Commission report in October 1960 delivered the coup de grace. The commission concluded that racial hostility was so great that federation could not be maintained except by force or by introducing massive changes such as rapidly dismantling the discriminatory apparatus in Rhodesia, broadening the franchise, establishing racial parity in the federal house, granting self-government to Nyasaland and Northern Rhodesia, and barring constitutional advance without local acceptance.[18]

The federal government's position never changed. It defended white rule and endlessly castigated Britain and the African nationalists. In a typical broadside, Welensky lashed out:

> The British Government have ratted on us. They have gone back on the most solemn understandings and intentions. They have wrecked the foundation upon which they themselves built the Federation and on which they were determined at that time to construct a lasting edifice. They have been guilty of an act of treachery . . . I say that Britain has lost the will to govern in Africa and that Britain is utterly reckless of the fate of the inhabitants of the present Federation, including those of our own kith and kin. By contrast we in the Federation have neither lost faith in ourselves nor in our will to be governed decently and fairly.[19]

Welensky's outbursts embarrassed the British government, but it was a performance without hope or charity. Colonial Office administration gave way to African governments led by Dr. Banda in Nyasaland in 1961 and by Kenneth Kaunda in Northern Rhodesia in 1962. In Rhodesia, Welensky's white allies turned to protect their own, more limited, interests. No one—not Britain, not the federal government, not any of the territorial governments—really considered maintaining federation under governments headed by different races. Such was the achievement of partnership. Federation might have been saved by an African government in Rhodesia, but here the whites remained determined to resist and Britain possessed far less local power with which to induce change.

White Feuds and the Decline of the
United Federal Party

Rhodesia had two prime ministers between 1954 and 1962. Garfield Todd, a missionary and cattle rancher and a United Party back-bencher, became prime minister when Huggins assumed command of federation. In 1958 Todd was ousted in an internal party dispute and Sir Edgar Whitehead became the new leader. He remained in office until the Rhodesian Front defeated the United Federal Party (UFP) in Rhodesia's December 1962 election. Both the Todd and Whitehead governments supported federation, though not always without reservation. The Rhodesian Front, on the other hand, based its drive to power on a commitment to white Rhodesia alone. The erosion of support for federation and for UFP rule was the most dramatic change in white politics during this period.

From the outset of federation, there were tensions between the federal and Rhodesian governments. Even though both were located in Salisbury and the leading personalities were all acquaintances, disagreements arose. One constant source of tension was the Rhodesian government's limited ability to raise money. Fiscal functions were almost entirely federal, and territorial governments were limited to a surcharge of no more than 20 percent of the federal income tax. This meant that the Rhodesian government had little access to revenues which did not accord with federal spending priorities.

Another source of tension was the lack of intergovernmental consultation. Many territorial responsibilities (such as African agriculture, housing, irrigation and water development, lands, mining, and town planning) could not be intelligently handled without knowledge of federal priorities, yet these were seldom discussed with the territorial governments. Bad feeling was further engendered by status differences within the white society which favored the federal government.

These problems first came to a head in 1956 when Todd made several speeches criticizing the federal government.[20] Todd's attack led to increased consultation at both party and governmental levels, but it also alienated Welensky and set in motion events that would lead to his ouster as prime minister.

Three by-election defeats sustained by the Federal Party from 1955 to 1957 provided the immediate background. The most important of these came in June 1957 when Winston Field, president of the newly formed Dominion Party, defeated Evan Campbell, a prominent member of the Federal Party, for a federal seat.[21] These defeats did not remotely jeopardize Federal Party rule, but the leadership was concerned. Federal leaders still saw white Rhodesian opposition to federation as a greater threat than African opposition. They therefore moved to tighten their control over Rhodesian politics.

The first step was to arrange a merger between the two governing parties. This met with little opposition, for their membership was nearly identical. Todd favored fusion in the interest of closer governmental consultation; federal leaders favored it in the interest of greater political control. It is important to realize how important fusion was to the federal government, for this overt move could only heighten concern in Britain and the northern territories about the interchangeability of the Rhodesian and federal governments. The new party was called the United Federal Party (UFP). Within weeks of the merger, the Todd affair began—an event that shook the UFP to its roots and benefited only the Dominion Party—precisely the opponent that fusion had been designed to stop.

It is all but impossible to gather together the threads leading to Todd's ouster.[22] The public and private opinions of those involved often differ widely, and Todd's subsequent support of African nationalism has warped memories of this earlier event. The impetus, however, lay in personality conflicts, poor federal-territorial relations, and federal concern about Dominion Party strength in Rhodesia. On January 9, 1958, Todd's cabinet (at the instigation of senior federal ministers) resigned. They expected Todd to accept the inevitable and resign also. Instead, Todd accepted their resignations, formed a new cabinet, and thereby deepened the conflict to a degree far in excess of what the conspirators had anticipated. Todd could not muster a parliamentary majority, however, and a party congress was called to resolve the dispute.

The weeks preceding the UFP congress—set for February 8, 1958 —were marked by frenetic political moves to form branches that could be accredited at the upcoming congress. Nothing is more revealing about the state of white Rhodesian political parties at this time than the admission by all those who participated in the congress that most branches materialized out of thin air. Until the emergence of the Rhodesian Front in 1962, this was to be one of the rare moments in white political history in Rhodesia when the party played a role aside from the few weeks before elections. In this competition Todd was at a definite disadvantage, for the federal people controlled the money and the power in Rhodesia.

The congress was attended by about three hundred twenty people, but it was dominated by Julian Greenfield, federal Minister of Law, the congress chairman. The dissident ministers spoke first—attacking Todd for being a dictator, for taking all of the credit and absorbing none of the blame for territorial developments, and for doing Rhodesia a disservice by attacking the federal government. Todd, a brilliant orator, then skillfully rebutted their charges in an emotional address. Then nominations for the new prime minister were taken: first Todd, then Patrick

Fletcher (one of the dissident ministers), and finally a surprise candidate, Sir Edgar Whitehead, who at this time was *federal* minister in Washington, D.C. The nomination of Whitehead revealed the desire of federal leaders to find a candidate who could both unite the fractured party and faithfully support federation. Whitehead was perfect. He had been out of the country so was not implicated in the Todd ouster; as a former minister of finance in Huggins' Rhodesian government, he was part of the old guard who initiated federation. He was elected on the second ballot.

The drama still had not completely unfolded. Whitehead was not in parliament, so a UFP member from Bulawayo resigned and a by-election was set for April 16, 1958. Once again the Dominion Party defeated the UFP; Whitehead lost by 691 to 604 in a "safe" UFP constituency. Whitehead had no alternative but to call a general election, which was set for June 5. The election was contested under the terms of the 1957 Electoral Act, which had slightly broadened the franchise and established a system of preferential voting whereby voters could rank candidates. Three groups competed: the UFP led by Whitehead, the Dominion Party, and a small group led by Todd, who called themselves the United Rhodesia Party (URP). Todd's election slogan was "Forward without Fear," but its program differed little from the UFP.[23] It looked toward greater white autonomy and said little about African matters.

The UFP claimed to be the moderate party. It firmly associated itself with federal prosperity, and its election brochure was self-congratulatory about the 1957 Electoral Act, which it said would "ensure that political power [was] retained by civilised and responsible people." The UFP further promised "the removal of the remaining reservations in the Constitution."[24] The DP issued a party document, *What's the Difference?,* which was responded to by a UFP pamphlet, *This Is the Difference.* Both were exercises in nit-picking and hair-splitting and fully demonstrated that there was no difference between the parties on any matter of substance. Both favored continued white rule, dominion status, economic expansion, and the social and industrial legislation that protected white privileges.

The vote was so close that in ten of the thirty constituencies none of the candidates received a first-preference majority. In these cases the lowest candidate was eliminated and his ballots were checked for second preferences. In four cases the second-preference choices of those initially voting for URP (Todd) candidates was enough to push UFP nominees ahead of the DP—thus giving Whitehead a narrow victory (see Table 5).[25]

The 11.7 percent first-preference votes polled by the United Rhodesia Party represents the high-water mark in Rhodesian-style liberal politics. Although it had not yet looked so far ahead, this group might have con-

Table 5. 1958 Rhodesian election results.

Party	First preference			Final count		
	Votes	Percent	Seats leading	Votes	Percent	Seats won
Dominion Party	18,142	45.7	17	18,314	47.2	13
United Federal Party	16,840	42.4	13	17,416	44.9	17
United Rhodesia Party	4,652	11.7	0	2,981	7.7	0
Independent	67	0.2	0	67	0.2	0

SOURCE: F. M. G. Willson, ed., *Source Book of Parliamentary Elections and Referenda in Southern Rhodesia 1898–1962* (Salisbury, University College of Rhodesia and Nyasaland, 1963), p. 180.

sidered the possibility of a gradual transition to majority rule. Even this vague a possibility has not been offered since to the Rhodesian electorate.

The Todd affair and its lengthy aftermath has sometimes been seen as a turning point in white politics, at which it became apparent that there was no possibility of white and black working together. This is really more legend than fact and derives almost wholly from Todd's activities *after* he was prime minister rather than from anything he did while in office. As prime minister, his actions against African protest were rigid and forceful. His attitude toward Africans was, at the very least, exceedingly paternalistic—as this 1956 speech reveals:

> There are some people of course who talk as if we regretted that the African was in Africa, but surely one of the pleasant things in Africa is the people themselves. I do not know how many of us would have come to Africa if there had been no African people here. It may be that more would have come, I do not know, but I think that most people find that the African has helped to make life even more pleasant for him; and with their singing and their patience and good humour, they are a pleasant people.[26]

The racist stereotypes are too plentiful to need elaboration.

Todd firmly believed in federation and in one of his more noted remarks expressed the belief that he "should work himself out of a job"—meaning that he expected that territorial functions would be steadily given over to an ever more comprehensive federal government. Interpreting Todd most favorably, we could say that he tried to take some rough edges off the Rhodesian system. But it is crucial to note that the attacks against him by his dissident ministers seldom touched on racial questions. He was removed because he offended the *amour propre* of some federal politicians, not because he in any way was prepared to challenge the operation or correctness of the system itself.

Whitehead and the United Federal Party narrowly escaped defeat in 1958; they would not be so fortunate in 1962. In the intervening years the Dominion Party (later the Rhodesian Front) skillfully organized white voters and decided to forego support for federation. In taking this stand the DP-RF jettisoned federal dreams (about which it had always been skeptical) in order to better defend the security of white Rhodesia. Welensky and Whitehead, tied together in the same party and bound by the memories of the Todd affair, were unable and unwilling to admit white Rhodesia's disenchantment with federation until it was too late for both their governments.

The Dominion Party's appeal to white Rhodesians was summed up in its party slogan, "Rhodesia first, last, and always." This idea—the basis of earlier opposition to federation—had been adopted by many small white organizations that sprang up between 1958 and 1962.[27] Individually none of these organizations mattered very much, but they all articulated the same line: that white Rhodesians should unite and be careful. The objects of their distrust were Britain, federation, and ultimately the UFP. They were deeply hostile to British support for African nationalism elsewhere and feared that eventually British policy toward Rhodesia might change. Federation was seen as white Rhodesia's Achilles heel because the federal government had no control over African advance in the northern territories. The first manifesto of the Southern Rhodesia Association stated "the only way for Southern Rhodesia to avoid being passed over to African rule will be by seceding from the Federation, by achieving dominion status for itself, and taking whatever steps are necessary to ensure European rule shall continue." [28]

During this period many politicians believed that the emergence of so many different groups marked the fragmentation of the opposition to the UFP. Actually, it reflected the increasing politicization of white Rhodesians, who heretofore had been content to let Huggins or Welensky handle their political affairs. It was the particular genius of the early organizers of the Rhodesian Front that they were able to mobilize these many discontented whites into a *single* strong and effective political organization.

The Rhodesian Front was formed in March 1962 as an amalgam of the Dominion Party, the Southern Rhodesia Association, and the United Group.[29] The merger had two key elements. The Rhodesia First strategy of the DP and the SRA was accepted by the United Group and the DP members of the federal parliament (both of whom previously had supported Welensky's bid for federation-wide independence). In turn, leaders of the DP and the SRA in Rhodesia (most notably William Harper and Desmond Lardner-Burke) stood aside and let Winston Field and Clifford Dupont (both federal members of parliament) and Ian Smith (founder of the United Group) assume major leadership roles. Field became the RF's first president, Dupont the party chairman, and Smith the deputy chairman.

Once decisions were taken on leadership and federation, these groups easily meshed. Their commitment to Rhodesia First was quickly demonstrated by their boycott of the April 1962 federal elections. From March to December 1962 they built their strength in Rhodesia and at the election they were rewarded.

The 1962 election was conducted under the complex system established by the new 1961 constitution, which will be discussed more fully later on in this chapter. There were two types of seats (50 constituencies and 15 districts) and two classes of voters (A-roll and B-roll). Essentially the constituencies were European seats elected by A-roll voters and the districts were African seats determined by the B-roll. The A-roll had 90,785 registered voters; the B-roll had 10,632. A new provision allowed voters on each roll to vote for a candidate in both a district and a constituency. This was called cross-voting, and in theory it intended to give A-roll voters up to 25 percent influence in district voting and B-roll voters the same influence in constituencies. Where cross-voting exceeded 25 percent of the predominant roll's vote, the results would be devalued proportionately. Because so few Africans ever registered or voted, cross-voting had no effect in the two elections (1962 and 1965) held under the 1961 constitution.

Conditions in 1962 were more turbulent than those in 1958. Federation was under severe challenge in the two northern territories. Economic growth had slowed, white immigration had fallen off, and there was even a bit of white unemployment for the first time since the 1930's. Three African nationalist parties had been successively banned between 1959 and 1962, but there was no clear indication that this was a solution to internal unrest. The Congo troubles also made whites uneasy. Finally the 1961 constitution had just come into effect. This had been sold to the white voters as an independence constitution, but by 1962 the UFP's deceptive salesmanship was becoming evident.

The United Federal Party's primary objective was to win the election in such a way that Britain would grant Rhodesia white minority independence. The Rhodesian-British bargain incorporated in the 1961 constitution had made this a likely possibility. Whitehead believed that all he had to do for independence was show Britain that the UFP had political support from the "civilised and responsible" Africans registered on the B-roll. Thus his campaign was dominated by the gestures he deemed necessary to cultivate British and "civilised" African support. During the campaign the UFP promised to repeal the Land Apportionment Act (white land would be secured by new legislation), to continue to work toward "the repeal of existing racially discriminatory laws which are either unnecessary or are unfair," and to build a new Rhodesian nationalism where race would not matter.[30] Whitehead and Welensky also hammered hard on federal themes. They argued that an RF victory would doom federation and be an economic disaster for white Rhodesians. Welensky threatened that "this election will do much more than decide whether your property value will go up or down by a few percent; it will decide whether your property and the national investment have any value at all. It is not a case of some other person competing for your job; it is a case of whether or not there will be a job to compete for." [31]

The UFP had the considerable advantage of being the long-time defender of white interests and the major beneficiary of postwar white prosperity. The leadership believed that its relentless actions to destroy Rhodesia's African nationalist movement unreservedly demonstrated its commitment to white domination. And it further believed that its substantial victory for white interests in negotiating the 1961 constitution would carry over to the election. Overconfidence was rampant.

Whitehead's desire to show African support led him to make statements for British consumption that were misunderstood locally. When he traveled to the United Nations in October 1962 to speak to the Trusteeship Committee, he remarked, "There is no doubt that the African will have a majority within 15 years." [32] Two nights before the election he said that he might have an African in his new cabinet and he anticipated more in the future. It is essential to realize that Whitehead did not mean an African "majority" in the sense used elsewhere in Africa. African cabinet members would be those who supported UFP rule. An African majority *did not* mean majority rule, but a majority on the electoral rolls. Under the A-roll/B-roll division a "majority" meant nothing, since the tiny European electorate would always control 50 seats; even if all Africans were enfranchised, they would still elect only 15 members. Without understanding the deception in Whitehead's statements, it is easy to misinterpret his meaning.

The Rhodesian Front responded to the UFP campaign with a vigorous, well-financed effort. Their best issue was Rhodesia First. The RF argued that the UFP would be unable to halt the emergence of African governments in the two northern territories and that federation therefore was jeopardizing white security. The RF seized upon UFP plans for phasing out the Land Apportionment Act as an indicator of the UFP's diminishing commitment to European interests. In one famous campaign advertisement the RF used a photograph of white and black legs together (with a school in the background) and captioned it, RHODESIA IS NOT READY FOR THIS. The RF explicitly guaranteed that it would "ensure the permanent establishment of the European in Southern Rhodesia." [33] The RF's efforts were rewarded. It won a convincing victory with white voters by taking 35 of 50 seats. The UFP made the results close, however, by taking 14 of 15 electoral district seats.[34] The results are summarized in Table 6.

Table 6. 1962 Rhodesian election results.

Party	Constituencies (final count)[a]			Districts (final count)[b]			Seats won
	Votes	Percent	Seats	Votes	Percent	Seats	
Rhodesian Front	38,284	55.1	35	659	20.7	0	35
United Federal Party	30,470	43.8	15	2,117	66.4	14	29
Central Africa Party	104	0.1	0	361	11.3	0	0
Independent	671	1.0	0	50	1.6	1	1

SOURCE: F. M. G. Willson, ed., *Source Book of Parliamentary Elections and Referenda in Southern Rhodesia 1898–1962* (Salisbury, University College of Rhodesia and Nyasaland, 1963), p. 180.

[a] A-roll plus B-roll votes, no devaluation necessary in any constituency.

[b] A-roll plus B-roll *after* devaluation. In no instance did cross-voting and devaluation change the victor from the leader on the basis of B-roll or A-roll votes alone.

One interesting possibility must be considered. If the UFP had won but four more seats on the A-roll, it could have controlled a parliamentary majority with 33 members (19 white and 14 African). The question then is, in what sense would this have presented Rhodesia with a viable multiracial solution to its constitutional and racial problems. There can be little doubt that the UFP would have called for quick independence on the basis of this type of electoral victory. It probably would have been granted. Unfortunately, encouraging as this prospect may look on paper, it really had little to do with the shape of political conflict within Rhodesia. The 14 UFP African victors on the B-roll represented literally no one; *together* they had amassed a total of 1,870 votes in a country of over three million Africans. They were European-owned Africans and were treated as such by both the UFP and the African population of Rhodesia.

If the UFP Africans had attempted to strike out on an independent course, there can be no doubt that a new election would have been called to allow the Europeans to coalesce into a single party, as occurred in 1965 when the RF took all 50 seats. Because of the strong constitutional position held by the whites, there would have been little that either Britain or the Africans could have done, short of military intervention or revolution. With the whites in full control of the political system, a nonracial solution to Rhodesian problems was a dim likelihood at best. Whitehead was a master tactician for a certain type of white strategy. Despite his 1962 defeat, he was not trying to ease the Europeans out of political power by subterfuge. His schemes were designed to ease the British government out of Rhodesia; and in negotiating the 1961 constitution he very nearly succeeded.

Internal "Reforms" and the 1961 Constitution

Rhodesia's 1923 constitution provided for internal self-government, subject only to the rarely used reserve clauses. Whitehead took the position that since British policy elsewhere in Africa was changing, there was no reason to believe that its Rhodesian policy would be permanently immune from change. Therefore he sought discussions with Britain about removing the reserve clauses. His goal was complete white internal autonomy—a step that would move Rhodesia much closer to independence, regardless of what happened with federation.

Whitehead's efforts required considerable political skill. One problem was his commitment to federation. He did not want to undercut Welensky's larger plans by moving prematurely in Rhodesia. Other pressures, however, forced him toward action. Rhodesia's African nationalists were actively lobbying in London in favor of the reserve clauses and indeed were demanding that Britain use them against the white government.[35] This African support for the reserve clauses intensified Whitehead's desire to eliminate them. Another pressure arose from the Dominion Party's commitment to Rhodesia First, which required Whitehead to make clear his own commitment to protect white Rhodesia. The factor that most complicated Whitehead's position, however, was the realization that Britain would probably demand some concessions to Rhodesia's Africans in exchange for any constitutional advance. What these concessions might be, and whether they would be acceptable to white or black Rhodesians, was unknown.

Throughout 1959 and 1960 Whitehead evolved a subtle strategy that was designed to entice Britain without frightening Rhodesia's white electorate or jeopardizing white control. In no uncertain terms, Whitehead spelled out the limits of Rhodesia's commitment to federation. She would not remain in federation if African governments came to power in the north, for the "safety and integrity of Southern Rhodesia must be preserved at all costs . . . We are not going to give away our birthright . . . and I am not going to run away and sell Rhodesia down the river." [36] While making these assurances, Whitehead gave them substance by vigorous repression of Rhodesia's nationalist movement.

On the other hand, Whitehead lured Britain (far more than Rhodesia's Africans) with so-called liberal reforms which he hoped would prompt African support for his government. Two approaches to African political involvement were sponsored. One was a middle-class strategy associated with a highly restricted franchise and the idea that "civilised and responsible" Africans should have political rights. The second focused on the chiefs as the true African spokesmen. The Whitehead government utilized both approaches, but emphasized the former. Since 1962 the Rhodesian Front has stressed the latter. Both approaches fulfilled the key requirement of Rhodesian black-white relations—that the whites select the African "leaders." Under the middle-class strategy, the government controlled access routes to political participation through franchise manipulation; the chiefs, on the other hand, had long been beholden to the government for their appointment, salary, and safety. Furthermore, both strategies gave the appearance of African involvement without jeopardizing white domination. As political ploys used to get British concessions, they were quite successful; as steps toward better race relations, they were sheer fantasy. Both approaches share the dubious distinction of drawing almost all their support from their white sponsors. The reality of white-black relations lay in the government's repression of African nationalism.

Of the steps taken by the UFP in pursuit of the elusive "civilised" African, four should be briefly mentioned: land apportionment alterations, amendment of the Industrial Conciliation Act, opening of the public service, and repeal of the pass laws. A review of these reforms demonstrates that they combined minor modification of long-standing patterns of racial control with public relations efforts to convince Britain of the government's concern for Africans. They gave the appearance of progress toward a less rigidly segregated society, but in fact were either so trivial as to be unimportant or well-disguised additions to the European armory of African controls.

Land apportionment changes were suggested by a 1960 parliamentary select committee chaired by H. J. Quinton, Parliamentary Secretary to the Minister of Native Affairs in Whitehead's cabinet. The Quinton committee did not dispute the right of 234,000 Europeans to hold 48 million acres while 3.5 million Africans held 42 million acres, but it urged two changes: a halt to the constant shifting of Africans from one subsistence plot to another just to comply with the LAA, and the opening of all Rhodesian land to purchase by anyone.[37] The Quinton recommendations were designed to reduce wasteful expenditures on African resettlement and to open the reserves to European purchase. Neither change would undermine white control of the good Rhodesian land; indeed, the opening of land to purchase could only have the effect of driving up prices to levels few Africans could afford. All the same, nothing was done about the Quinton recommendations, because Welensky intervened and told Whitehead to shelve any changes until after the 1962 elections.

The 1959 amendment to the Industrial Conciliation Act was a "reform" that was passed. This amendment forced all Rhodesian unions to organize vertically by industry. This was done to foreclose the possibility that unskilled workers (in other words, Africans) would combine into a single national organization. Whitehead could now claim that Rhodesian unions were multiracial, but branches were segregated and voting rights were allocated on the basis of skill. S. M. Grant, the Chief Industrial Officer for Rhodesia, was quoted to the effect that the amendments were designed to keep industrial power in the hands of white workers and to contain African trade unions before they became powerful.[38] Unions were also firmly prohibited from undertaking political activity—a prohibition affecting only Africans. There was no new era here.

In 1960 the Whitehead government opened up the public service, from which Africans had been excluded since 1931. In doing so, the Minister of Justice and Internal Affairs promised that "each person who is seeking employment in our Public Service will be watched very carefully, not only from the point of view of academic qualifications, but from the point of view of other nebulous factors as character, judgment, sense of responsibility, sense of loyalty, sense of devotion, . . ." [39] Simultaneously, Whitehead announced new public service regulations that terminated automatic progression from the bottom to the top of the service. Whitehead admitted that this change was aimed at Africans and noted that "if anybody really gets to an important position in under thirty years he is doing extremely well." [40]

Pass law changes were even more dubious. The Native (Registration and Identification) Act of 1957 established a provision whereby Africans certified as "advanced" would not have to carry several passes in urban areas—only one; this was to be an identification card (pass?) which would tell any police official or urban location officer of his advanced status. The 1960 Pass Laws (Repeal) Bill dealt with regulations extant since 1895: the requirement that Africans have a registration certificate plus at least one additional pass to enter towns. The 1960 bill abolished the latter requirement because, as the Minister of Native Affairs explained, "after very careful and considered examination it has been decided that adequate control of the urban African population can be obtained by the registration certificate or identity card, and the rent cards issued by the township authorities." [41] The need to carry two documents instead of three was the type of liberal gesture that could only be appreciated by the Rhodesian and British governments. Few Africans could ever be found to take advantage of these "reforms."

Throughout 1959 and 1960, Britain put off Whitehead's overtures.[42] The federal issue took priority, and it was only after the Monckton Commission had reported that Britain agreed to consider Rhodesian matters separately. Whitehead had hoped to remove the reserve clauses by private governmental negotiations, but Britain insisted on calling a full constitutional conference with all Rhodesian political parties participating. The crucial discussions were held in Salisbury from January 30 to February 7, 1961.

At the conference the Rhodesian government attained its major objective when Britain agreed to remove the reserve clauses. Britain further gave up its authority to revoke or amend sections of the constitution conferring legislative power and publicly acknowledged the convention that it would not legislate on matters within the competence of the Rhodesian government.[43] In exchange for these concessions, the conference agreed to several political changes. A declaration of rights was introduced into the Rhodesian constitution, a constitutional council was established to review legislation, the Rhodesian parliament was expanded from 30 to 65 members, and the A-roll/B-roll mechanism was introduced.[44] The constitution in theory opened the way to African majority rule as the number of Africans on the A-roll grew. There were, however, so many variables—the future structure of African education, African employment, African wages, and African opportunities to own property—not to mention European willingness to let such a transition occur, that the constitution really guaranteed nothing but indefinite white rule.

The constitution was rigged with loopholes that negated any possibility that it would serve to curb the authoritarian propensities of the white government. The declaration of rights was a travesty. Each "right" was subject to many exceptions. The "right to personal liberty," for instance, had five major and thirteen minor clauses spelling out limitations. Moreover, the declaration *did not* pertain to extant legislation. Since the bulk of Rhodesia's restrictive and discriminatory legislation was already on the books, the declaration was assured of having no meaningful effect. The constitutional council was equally ineffectual. It could review legislation, but it had no enforcement power and could be overruled immediately by a two-thirds majority in parliament or by a simple majority after six months. Its purview did not apply to money bills, and it had no authority to initiate action against existing legislation. Further, if the prime minister asked for a certificate of urgency for any bill, the council was bypassed entirely.

The introduction of 15 B-roll seats was the major change agreed upon at the conference. Britain insisted on some African representation before withdrawing the reserve clauses. The Rhodesian government made this concession because the ratio of A-roll to B-roll seats could be amended by a two-thirds parliamentary vote. Since the whites were guaranteed control of the 50 A-roll seats indefinitely, only 44 white votes would be necessary to raise the number of A-roll seats or lower the number of B-roll seats. Thus the B-roll seats posed no threat to white rule so long as the whites remained united against the Africans. The *Bulletin of the International Commission of Jurists* noted that the constitution "provides a striking example of the futility of laying down human rights in the Constitution and thereafter subjecting those same human rights to the sway of a legislature which does not adequately represent the people of the country." [45]

Whitehead and the United Federal Party eagerly endorsed the new constitution. They realized that the withdrawal of the reserve clauses and Britain's public endorsement of the convention of noninterference marked a substantial white victory. In this spirit they attempted to sell the constitution to the Rhodesian electorate in a July 26, 1961, referendum.

The UFP's campaign resembled the 1953 federation campaign. They accepted the nominal liberalization required by Britain (in 1953 to support partnership, in 1961 to agree to 15 B-roll seats), at the same time demonstrating that the concessions were trivial in light of the gains won. White security was constantly stressed. Not only was it explicitly acknowledged that the 50 Europeans could always coalesce against the 15 Africans, but it was also noted that without the reserve clauses, the Africans would have a more difficult time enticing British help. Whitehead remarked that "The country has the opportunity now of getting these restrictions removed, and if this opportunity is lost I would be very surprised if equally favorable conditions ever presented themselves again." [46]

The UFP claimed that the new constitution meant independence for Rhodesia. Whitehead stated, "There is no doubt that the House of Commons do believe that they are giving us independence" and "The choice lies between the old constitution and acceptance of the new one which will give the colony independence." In a major parliamentary address, Whitehead said seven times that the new constitution gave Rhodesia independence.[47] Welensky backed Whitehead and made many speeches in favor of the constitution.

The Dominion Party had difficulty competing with this barrage of confident predictions. Its dilemma was clear. It had long stood for permanent white control and an independent Rhodesia: exactly what the UFP said the new constitution would bring. The central opposition argument was that the UFP was lying—that the new constitution would not bring independence and that too many concessions had been given for little real political advantage. The DP urged defeat of the proposals, retention of the current all-white parliament, and new constitutional talks leading to Rhodesian independence outside the federation.[48] The DP also warned that in light of British policy elsewhere in Africa, Britain's support for the new constitution was sufficient reason for white Rhodesia to oppose it.

Other groups urged a No vote. Ian Smith's United Group and the Southern Rhodesia Association were opposed because of the 15 B-roll seats. A group called the Rhodesian Vigilance Association emerged and ran ads asking, "Are you a coward, White Man? Vote No, make a stand and INSIST ON COMPLETE INDEPENDENCE FOR SOUTHERN RHODESIA out of the present Federation." [49] Finally, white liberals such as Sir Robert Tredgold (former Chief Justice of both the federation and Rhodesia) and Garfield Todd opposed the constitution because they felt its broad concessions to local settlers would permanently foreclose the possibility of white and black Rhodesians reaching a meaningful racial accord.[50]

When the vote was taken, the UFP won a substantial victory— 42,004 or 65.8 percent in favor versus 21,846 or 34.2 percent opposed. The turnout of eligible voters was 76.5 percent.

There is no way to prove explicitly that the UFP would have been granted independence on the basis of this constitution. When it was defeated in 1962, any private agreement that existed between the UFP and Britain vanished. But such an agreement had almost certainly existed. Further minor changes such as repeal of the Land Apportionment Act, an expanded B-roll franchise, and perhaps an increase in African representation to one-third of parliament would have led to white minority independence before the end of the British Conservative government's term of office (October 1964).[51] As it turned out, similar terms were offered the Rhodesian Front.

The constitution did not come into effect until November 1962. In the interim period Whitehead renewed his efforts at building African support for the United Federal Party. Between 50,000 and 100,000 pounds were raised for the Build-a-Nation Campaign (BANC), which intended to register African voters "who had education and had made a success of life." [52] Whitehead and Steve Kock, BANC organizer, predicted that 50,000 to 60,000 Africans would register in order to participate in this middle-class experiment.

The BANC was a shambles from beginning to end. All meetings were held unannounced for fear nationalist organizers would get to the site before BANC speakers. On January 16, 1962, Whitehead repeated the prediction that 50,000 Africans would register, but admitted that only 813 had so far come forward. In April 1962, Kock admitted that "we are not meeting with . . . marked enthusiasm." In August a scandal broke when the African schoolteachers' association charged that its members were being forced to register under threats of losing their jobs. In exasperation, Kock finally admitted that the UFP's middle-class strategy was a total failure and that the nationalists were strong throughout the country.[53] Other UFP sources all but admitted the same thing. *Federal Outlook* reported that "our African supporters today feel desperately lonely in their townships. They are a small minority of the population . . . the majority have gone with the swing of the tide." [54] By the end of 1962 there were 10,632 registered B-roll voters. Only 2,577 voted in the 1962 election. These figures hardly suggest African support for the political system. The idea that race was an incidental matter in Rhodesia and that Africans would find an acceptable political outlet in European parties was a transparent fraud.

The most important thing about the 1961 constitution and the UFP's African strategy was not that African support was negligible or that the constitution perpetuated white rule, but that the agreement was acceptable to Britain and to white Rhodesia. It provided a sophisticated cover for British withdrawal under the guise of opening opportunities for "civilised" Africans. It did not provide full independence; however, it gave white Rhodesians firm reasons to believe there would be no further British interference in their constitutional affairs or in their domestic dealings with the African population. This was almost equivalent to independence.

The new constitution reconfirmed Rhodesia's unique constitutional arrangement with Britain. Unlike other colonies where Britain withdrew her authority only after majority rule was established, the constitution considerably augmented local power without endangering white rule. The agreement was consonant with the entire history of British-Rhodesian relations. Rhodesia was different, because Britain had no local administration with which to implement her own policy. Furthermore (and this would become fully apparent only after the unilateral declaration of independence), Britain was unprepared to challenge white rule in Rhodesia because of South Africa's influence. Britain's own trade and investment ties with South Africa were far too important to jeopardize over the Rhodesian question. In dropping the reserve clauses and avowing the convention of noninterference, Britain deliberately shed the two constitutional means by which she might have tried to induce political change in Rhodesia. Whitehead gladly provided Britain with the illusion of liberalization while eagerly grasping the reality of local domination.

There are essentially two ways of viewing Rhodesian politics from 1954 to 1962. One sees a steady succession of shifts to the right—from the liberal paternalist Todd, to the vacillating Sir Edgar Whitehead, and then on to the stern leaders of the Rhodesian Front. An alternative interpretation would focus on the most stable feature of Rhodesian political life: the enduring demand that political control remain in white hands. In this case leadership or policy changes need not be seen as shifts to the right, but as part of a continual process of white reassessment (in the context of the times) of what was needed to protect white rule.

The immediate difficulty with the first interpretation comes in defining the meaning of right and left in Rhodesia. In probing social and economic policy pertaining to Europeans, the terms have no relevance. The Rhodesian white population is homogenous and white poverty has been all but nonexistent since the 1930's. On issues of *European* social and economic concern, each Rhodesian government probably has stood to the left of its predecessor. The paradox should be noted that the more stringent (that is, so-called right) a government is in impeding African political and economic advance, the more left it is in preserving a high and basically uniform standard of living for whites. It is also hard to use these terms with regard to African political advance. All white governments concurred in their fundamental right to select appropriate African leaders, to repress unacceptable ones, and to control the pace of African advance. Within this framework, minor differences of style or nuance did not matter. Finally, the notion of a left position in white politics is misleading insofar as it obscures the resolute defense of white privilege by all white parties.[55] Thus, although the Rhodesian Front attacked the United Federal Party for its persistent support of federation and for its concessions to obtain the 1961 constitution, no realistic appraisal of UFP actions could suggest that the UFP was less resolute in defense of white privileges. It simply favored a different strategy.

The second interpretation is more useful. It focuses on the delicate process by which Rhodesian governments attempted to thread their way between the concessions necessary for constitutional advance and the limited flexibility provided them by the white electorate. Those in power from 1954 to 1962 believed that small concessions would allow Rhodesia (or the federation) to become independent under a white government. The white political opposition was less trustful of Britain and feared that limited concessions would only whet the appetite of Britain and the African nationalists, thus permitting the situation to get out of hand.

European factions argued endlessly about these points, but the intensity of white debate was a symptom of white strength, not real disunity. They were able openly and bitterly to debate their differences about federation and Britain because there was overriding agreement within the white system that African nationalism should be crushed. To the uninitiated the clash of party competition understandably conveys the notion of choice. Extreme care must be taken, however, to distinguish between rhetorical and actual differences. White political rhetoric obscures reality and suggests difference on racial questions where none existed. White conflict was invariably over tactical variations on the same theme—how to structure relations internally with Africans so as to entice from Britain constitutional concessions leading to independence. On the question of permanent white control and the destruction of the nationalist movement, there was only one choice.

3

The African
Nationalist Challenge

African nationalism came very late to Rhodesia. The first mass-based, nationwide party—the African Nationalist Congress—was formed in 1957. By this time Ghana had become independent, Mau Mau was nearly over, and nationalist movements were already well established in neighboring Northern Rhodesia, Nyasaland, and South Africa. The nationalist movement in Rhodesia itself emerged from an indigenous African political tradition that had wavered between resistance and accommodation to the European settlers. Its goals were to redress social and economic grievances; to achieve this, the movement increasingly demanded independence under a majority-rule government.

Rhodesian African nationalists faced organizational problems which were common elsewhere in Africa, including those of ethnic conflict, of linking rural and urban discontent, and of overcoming the political indifference of nonindigenous migrant workers. These difficulties, however, paled beside the overriding factor of European resistance and repression. Like nationalist movements throughout the continent, Rhodesian Africans engaged in rural and urban protest via meetings, rallies, and strikes. They also engaged in international lobbying. In these activities they made one critical error. They presumed their struggle to be similar to that waged in other British colonies. In Rhodesia, however, the settlers controlled the political system, *and* this control was accepted by Britain. The British government was unwilling to intervene as the Rhodesian government passed the laws and took the steps necessary to destroy the nationalist movement. All that the settlers would concede to the African people was the right to participate nominally within political structures they utterly dominated. By 1964 the settlers had largely succeeded in curbing nationalist activity inside Rhodesia.

Urban Poverty and Land Hunger

From the end of the rebellions until World War II, African political activity was largely limited to a tiny elite who made intermittent efforts to achieve modest improvements in African living conditions. Following the war, Africans gradually turned to political protest to draw attention to their grievances. There was much uncertainty about how to proceed, however, and the African pattern continued to swing back and forth between active protest and hope for racial compromise.

In 1945 and 1948 Africans participated in two strikes which turned into the biggest mass actions since the rebellions. The strikes were prompted by worker unrest over low wages and the capricious implementation of various control measures. In each case the strike was short-lived, as the Africans were poorly organized, largely leaderless, and exceedingly vulnerable to government and employer pressures. Only minor changes in living and working conditions were achieved by the strikes. For Africans "a reaction of profound disullusionment" [1] set in. African organizations lapsed. From 1951 to 1953, when African nationalists in Northern Rhodesia and Nyasaland were vigorously working against federation, scarcely any activity was taking place in Rhodesia. The Southern Rhodesia All-African Convention briefly appeared in protest, but for the most part Rhodesian Africans were indifferent about federation because it did not affect their internal status. It would take other issues to raise mass consciousness in Rhodesia.

For a brief time in the 1950's a few Africans looked to multiracial organizations for solutions to their problems. The Interracial Association, the Capricorn Africa Society, and the Central Africa Party, among others, attempted to build social and political interaction across racial lines.[2] The problem with these organizations was not that they lacked either motivation or high purpose, but that they were powerless. They attracted a tiny group of generally wealthy, urban liberals. They were able to make contact only with those few Africans who were well educated. Each group tended to accept positively the idea of partnership, but none was in a position to give it substance except on an extremely narrow and personal level. Eventually the groups collapsed; the Africans joined nationalist parties and began their migration toward prison, those Europeans who retained their liberalism began their migration into exile. Multiracial parties never had a chance in Rhodesia so long as the whites firmly retained political power and did not believe they would have to give it up or share it. Each new repressive action drove this point home. Eventually Africans drew the obvious conclusion that they had no choice but to organize their own people first. Conditions both in towns and rural areas helped give rise to new African political organization and activity.

Africans moved to the towns for several reasons. Tax pressure forced males to earn some income each year. Overcrowded reserves were unable to provide sufficient land and food for the African population, and industrial expansion in Rhodesia provided new job opportunities. Table 7 reveals the rapid growth in African employment in the manufacturing sector following the Second World War.

Urban life for Africans was harsh. Studies made in the 1940's and

Table 7. Africans employed in various industrial sectors
of the Rhodesian economy, 1936–1968.

Year[a]	Mining		Agriculture		Manufac- turing[b]		Other[c]		Total[d]
	Num- ber	Per- cent	Num- ber	Per- cent	Num- ber	Per- cent	Num- ber	Per- cent	
1936	84,000	33	83,000	33	34,000	13	52,000	21	254,000
1941	85,000	28	103,000	34	47,000	15	69,000	23	303,000
1946	70,000	18	150,000	40	67,000	18	90,000	24	377,000
1951	64,000	12	226,000	43	149,000	28	91,000	17	530,000
1956	61,000	10	248,000	40	182,000	30	119,000	20	610,000
1961	49,000	8	249,000	40	184,000	29	143,000	23	624,000
1968	41,000	7	239,000	38	121,000	20	220,000	35	622,000

SOURCE: *Report of the Advisory Committee: The Development of the Economic Resources of Southern Rhodesia with Particular Reference to the Role of African Agriculture* (the Phillips Report) (Salisbury, Government Printing Office, 1962), p. 382, and *Economic Survey for Rhodesia for 1968* (Salisbury, Government Printing Office, 1969).

[a] Figures for 1936 to 1946 are not strictly comparable to the 1951 to 1968 figures because of changes in classification of occupation.
[b] Manufacturing figures include Africans employed in electrical and water services, construction, and transport and communication. Between 1951 and 1961 only, the manufacturing figure includes Africans working in commerce. The removal of this category largely accounts for the drop in the 1968 manufacturing figure.
[c] For the 1951 to 1968 period this category is almost wholly services; previously it had included some jobs now covered in manufacturing.
[d] Because of rounding, the totals do not always match.

1950's uniformly reveal conditions of extreme deprivation.[3] The 1943 investigations of Percy Ibbotson revealed that only 8.8 percent of married urban Africans earned a bare subsistence of four pounds, fifteen shillings a month.[4] Howman's committee agreed that many families were living perilously close to starvation. The 1958 report of the Plewman Commission (the most comprehensive study ever made of housing, tenure, wages, rents, and administrative controls in urban Rhodesia) reiterated the earlier themes. It revealed that 26.8 percent of single males in Salisbury had wages (and rations) which left them below the poverty datum line, while fully 47.2 percent of Salisbury families were "extremely impoverished" and only 34.5 percent of the African families had incomes within or above the poverty-datum-line limits.[5]

Wages for Africans did rise slowly in the postwar period. Overall the average annual wage for an employed African rose from 64 pounds per year in 1954 to 114 pounds in 1963. In terms of constant prices, however, this growth amounted to just over one pound per year.[6] Table 8 summarizes African wages by key industrial sectors.

Table 8. Average annual wages of Rhodesian
Africans in major employment sectors,
1954 and 1963.

	1954		1963	
	Number employed	Wages (pounds)	Number employed	Wages (pounds)
Agriculture	218,000	48	257,300	67
Mining	62,400	83	40,500	115
Manufacturing	62,500	65	66,500	184
Construction	51,000	65	30,800	150
Domestic service	76,100	71	95,000	105
Other	84,000	—	112,900	—
Total	554,000	64	603,000	114

SOURCE: *National Accounts and Balance of Payments of Northern Rhodesia, Nyasaland, and Southern Rhodesia 1954–1963* (Salisbury, Central Statistical Office, 1964), Table 161.

Other factors must also be taken into account. As can be seen in Table 7, the number of Africans employed has been static since the mid-1950's. Coupling this fact with the rapid growth of the African population, a steady decline in the proportion of employed Africans is apparent. Moreover, economists have shown persuasively that African income gains have been wiped out by rising costs and (more importantly) by the need to transfer money into the declining rural economy. The per capita income of the African population has probably been falling steadily since the mid-fifties.[7]

Bad as urban conditions were, rural conditions were probably even worse. Steady African population growth increased pressure on the already overcrowded reserves and led Africans to migrate to the towns or to squat illegally on white land. In the post-1945 period whites demanded stricter enforcement of the Land Apportionment Act, and in the decade following the war nearly 85,000 African families (perhaps 10 percent of the entire population) were resettled by government order.[8] This engendered considerable rural unrest. In 1951 the government passed the Native Land Husbandry Act (LHA) in an attempt to deal with the land problem. Presented as a conservation measure, the LHA established standards for controlling land fragmentation and for destocking African cattle. Its most important provision called for shifting land tenure relations on the reserves from communally held tenure to individually held tenure in order to assign responsibility more accurately for land care and usage.

The LHA had valid conservation purposes, but it met with tremendous African resistance. George Nyandoro, an important nationalist leader, called it "the best recruiter Congress ever had." [9] The principal reason for the adverse African reaction lay in the uncertainties the LHA introduced into African life. Destocking was unpopular because most Africans measured wealth and status by the number of cattle they owned. Land tenure issues were even more unsettling. Under Rhodesia's system of direct rule, one of the few important functions that the chiefs had retained was the right to allocate reserve land. Under the LHA, this right was withdrawn and the native commissioner became the local land registrar. Moreover, under the communal system operating on the reserves, all Africans had a right to claim a share of the land. It was theirs by birthright, their social security. The LHA jeopardized this cornerstone of African life, since it did not intend to provide land for all Africans. Those who did not receive land were expected to find "livelihood in the expanding industries of the Colony." [10]

The LHA did not work for a number of reasons.[11] From a conservation standpoint, assigning deteriorated land to individual tenure was often the worst thing possible. The land needed rest, not perpetual usage. The act failed because the underlying reason for its implementation—the white desire to save the Land Apportionment Act—set the conditions for its failure. There was, in fact, no land shortage in Rhodesia; in the 1950's ten million acres of European assigned land were still unallocated.[12] There were, however, political realities which prevented a rational or just land-use policy. While LHA land allocations averaged 6 acres per African farmer, European farmers held a minimum plot of 750 acres; 895 European farms were over 10,000 acres in size.[13] The Europeans told one another that Africans were incapable of caring for land, all the while ignoring the crucial cause of land deterioration—their own insistence on land segregation. Rubbing

salt into the wound, the government introduced a levy on African agricultural produce in order to finance the cost of LHA implementation.[14]
Furthermore, the act did not work because the Rhodesian economy did
not provide jobs for Africans who became landless; thus rural land
fragmentation and deterioration remained unchecked.

The LHA was a public admission by the government that African
rural conditions were bad. Unfortunately it did not deal with the more
basic problem of land segregation. Instead, the act had the unforeseen
consequence of heightening rural unrest by undermining the chiefs and
creating a class of landless Africans. The nationalists quickly capital-
ized on African resentment against the LHA and used it to link rural
and urban discontent.[15] In 1961 the government quietly abandoned the
LHA in tacit admission that it had played into the hands of the nationalists and because the government was moving toward a new African
strategy of supporting the chiefs. Returning their land-allocation functions was a first step in this process.

Nationalist Parties and Strategies

The nationalist movement has operated under different names because of recurring government suppression. The African National Congress (ANC) lasted from September 1957 to February 1959. It was
followed by the National Democratic Party (January 1960 to December
1961) and the Zimbabwe African Peoples Union, or ZAPU (December
1961 to September 1962). Following the ZAPU ban, the nationalist
movement split. The ZAPU was reconstituted as the People's Caretaker
Council and a new party, the Zimbabwe African National Union, was
formed. Both operated from August 1963 to August 1964, when they
too were banned. After that nationalist activity carried on either underground or in exile until the African National Council emerged in late
1971 to oppose the British and Rhodesian settlement over independence.[16]

The ANC grew out of the Youth League (YL) which had been active
in Salisbury from 1955 to 1957.[17] The thrust of Youth League activity
was toward discouraging multiracial activity and promoting African
self-confidence. *Mukayi Africa* (Wake-Up Africa), a YL political journal published in 1955–1956, argued that "the salvation of the African
race is entirely in the African." A second paper, *Chapupu* (Witness),
published in 1957 took the same position.[18]

The African National Congress announced its formation on September 12, 1957—the settlers' national holiday, Occupation Day. The first
president was Joshua Nkomo; James Chikerema and George Nyandoro,
the Youth League leaders, became vice-president and secretary general.
J. Z. Moyo, Paul Mushonga, and J. Msika were the other three officers.
The leadership was ethnically balanced. Nkomo and Moyo were Nde-

beles; Chikerema, Nyandoro, and Mushonga were Shonas; and Msika was a Shangani.[19]

The ANC deliberately projected a moderate image. Nkomo was selected as president because he did not have YL connections and because of his record of multiracial activities; he had even joined Huggins' delegation to one of the prefederal London conferences. African leaders agreed on the ANC's reformist and nonracialist stance because they did not wish to alarm the whites. The ANC's statement of principles, policy, and program was almost deferential in tone. Except for occasional suggestions that land was misallocated and the franchise unfair, an ANC program could easily stand as a Welensky or Huggins statement on the beauty of partnership. There was much talk of nonracialism and economic progress, little mention of overt discrimination or political power:

> The African National Congress of Southern Rhodesia is a people's movement, dedicated to a political programme, economic and educational advancement, social service and personal standards. Its aim is the NATIONAL UNITY of all inhabitants of the country in true partnership regardless of race, colour, and creed . . .
>
> Congress affirms complete loyalty to the Crown as the symbol of national unity. It is not a racial movement. It is equally opposed to tribalism and racialism . . .
>
> Congress believes that individual initiative and free enterprise are necessary to the life of a young country and must be fully encouraged, but that a considerable measure of Government control is necessary in a modern state . . .
>
> This country greatly needs capital from overseas . . . [and] Government must therefore establish conditions under which capital may be invested and industry established with sufficient security to encourage investors.[20]

Behind this low-key approach, however, the ANC quietly organized Africans throughout Rhodesia.[21] African resistance to the Land Husbandry Act provided a useful entry to the countryside, and ANC leaders garnered much support by bringing court cases against the government to halt LHA implementation. The ANC spoke directly to rural needs and succeeded in shattering the complacency with which the Native Affairs Department had long administered the rural areas. The result was the nationwide state of emergency and banning of the ANC in early 1959.

The suppression of the ANC dealt a stunning blow to the fledgling nationalist movement—a blow from which it never really recovered. Nearly five hundred ANC activists were detained for varying periods; Chikerema and Nyandoro, among others, were not released until 1963. The parties succeeding the ANC faced many new obstacles. The government introduced security legislation that prohibited many political activities used successfully by the ANC. Urban harassment and surveillance increased sharply, and stringent controls were placed on all nationalist activities in rural areas. In response, the National Democratic Party and then the Zimbabwe African Peoples Union evolved new strategic perspectives. They concentrated their attention on urban organization and on lobbying in Britain for constitutional political advance. These changes had important ramifications.

The nationalist movement regrouped as the National Democratic Party (NDP) on January 1, 1960. New leaders such as Matthew Mawema (a Shona teacher), George Silundika (a Kalanga teacher), and Enos Nkala (a Ndebele laborer) came forward to replace the imprisoned Nyandoro, Chikerema, and Mushonga. Though still president, Nkomo had been outside the country in February 1959 and would not return to Rhodesia until October 1960.

The urban orientation of the NDP and ZAPU led to activities (strikes, boycotts, occasionally even riots) that were difficult to sustain. In times of unrest the government could always seal off centers of activity. Africans were vulnerable to the plethora of urban regulations such as entry permits and housing allocations, not to mention more direct political controls. Further, an urban-oriented movement was handicapped by the fact that approximately half the employed males in Rhodesian towns were nonindigenous.[22] Their migrant status made them susceptible to official pressure to supply intelligence information for the security forces. In turning to an urban orientation, the NDP and ZAPU let lapse the intense pressure that the ANC had brought against white authority in rural areas.

The year of greatest political optimism for the nationalists was probably 1960. Mass rallies and urban marches captivated many Africans into believing that success was at hand. Francis Nehwati, a Ndebele trade-union activist, has noted the "high degree of unity of purpose" achieved by Africans in Bulawayo during 1960 protests.[23] Africans flowed from the multiracial groups into the NDP, uniting the Africans as never before. Among the Africans who made their commitment to the nationalist movement in 1960 were Herbert Chitepo and Enoch Dumbutshena, Rhodesia's two African attorneys; the Reverend Ndabaningi Sithole, teacher and minister and author of *African Nationalism,* published in 1959;[24] and Leopold Takawira, a Shona teacher who had long been a Central Africa Party organizer.[25] Sithole and Takawira quickly became national officers of the National Democratic Party.

Outside developments also seemed conducive to optimistic appraisals. The Monckton Report made clear that federation was in trouble. Both in Nyasaland and in Northern Rhodesia the nationalists seemed close to power. Could Rhodesia be far behind? Many clambered aboard the NDP bandwagon and began to worry about how cabinet positions would be allocated; the Africans made the critical error of mistaking foreign developments, tough talk, and urban unrest for solid organizing and a coherent political strategy. These grave errors were to become obvious all too soon.

The 1961 constitutional conference, held in Salisbury during January and February, was the critical moment for Rhodesian nationalists. Their admission as full participants was a dramatic victory for the NDP, which had regularly called for constitutional change. It seemed that Nkomo's endless travels to the United Nations, to London, and to numerous African and Third World conferences demanding "one man one vote" were about to pay off.[26] The fact that Britain had called a constitutional conference convinced Nkomo that the NDP could attain political advance through constitutional channels, just as in other British colonies.

Nkomo led the African delegation to the conference; he was joined by Sithole, Chitepo, and Silundika. Their performance at the conference was woefully inept. They jettisoned the NDP's strong previous position in favor of retaining the reserve clauses and agreed to their removal in exchange for the constitutional council, the declaration of rights, and the 15 seats—none of which began to threaten white control of the parliament or the repressive machinery of the state.[27] The withdrawal of the reserve clauses and the implicit sanctioning of extant discriminatory legislation all but guaranteed the nationalists a permanently ineffective role in Rhodesian politics. They apparently accepted these proposals because they anticipated having white allies in the new parliament, because they came to trust Duncan Sandys, the British chairman, in the course of the conference, and because they feared that NDP supporters would accuse them of failure if they rejected every proposal.[28] In the pressure of the conference situation, they made the error of assuming that any agreement would assist their cause and lead toward African rule. This was the pattern of other African countries. But Rhodesia was different, and the nationalists were not cautious enough to understand fully the implications of the pact so eagerly sought by Whitehead and the British government. They also were sadly out of touch with African opinion.

Almost immediately, other party members attacked the NDP leaders for their sellout at the conference. Takawira wired from London, where he handled the NDP's external relations: "We totally reject Southern Rhodesian constitutional conference agreement as treacherous to the future of the three million Africans. Agreement diabolical and disastrous. Outside world shocked by N.D.P.'s docile agreement." [29] This was a fairly accurate analysis of the agreement's effect, but the damage had been done. Nkomo quickly disavowed the agreement, but the nationalist movement had squandered its sole opportunity to achieve meaningful constitutional change.

The optimism of 1960 vanished. Whereas before the conference the NDP's journal, *Democratic Voice,* had seen "the tragic figure of jittery Sir Edgar Whitehead heading toward political damnation," despair and disorganization quickly followed.[30] The nationalists refused to participate in anything related to the 1961 constitution. At the time of the white referendum, the NDP held its own referendum and announced that 467,189 Africans voted against the constitution and 584 approved.[31] Subsequently the nationalists refused to participate in elections and worked successfully to keep Africans from registering to vote. This activity lacked direction, however, and it was augmented by increasingly aimless and undirected urban violence. In December 1961 the NDP was banned. The Zimbabwe African Peoples Union was quickly formed, but its goals, organization, and activities were indistinguishable from the NDP's. Nine months later it too was banned.

Following the ZAPU ban, the party leadership decided not to form a new party, since each successive banning led to governmental confiscation of party funds and equipment. It was expected that the movement would go underground and plan for more militant resistance against the Europeans. Before many months had passed, however, controversial decisions were taken which led nearly all ZAPU's leaders out of the country and into exile. This action prompted the split in the nationalist movement which continues to today.

Nkomo was out of Rhodesia when ZAPU was banned, but he soon returned and was immediately restricted for three months. In restriction he apparently became convinced that the government would soon seize independence. He thought the nationalists could best take advantage of this event if they were *outside* Rhodesia when it occurred, prepared to establish a government-in-exile that could compete with the whites for international recognition. There was considerable resistance to this suggestion within the former ZAPU executive (Nkomo's predilection for being outside Rhodesia had long been a source of discontent), but Nkomo persuaded the leaders that this strategy was approved by Julius Nyerere, President of Tanganyika, and other high-ranking Africans.

The departure of the executive to Dar es Salaam in early 1963 stirred widespread African resentment in Rhodesia. In Dar many ZAPU leaders were shocked when Nyerere strongly rebuked them for leaving Rhodesia. Talks at the May 1963 inaugural conference in Addis Ababa of the Organization of African Unity revealed to Sithole and others the grave reservations many African leaders had about Nkomo. Until this point, Nkomo's foreign experience had generally been deemed an asset and had given him an aura of expertise and experience that was hard to challenge. Now the doubters in the ZAPU executive had hard evidence to support their opposition to Nkomo's external strategies.

Immediately following the Addis Ababa conference, the executive returned to Dar where a power struggle ensued. Most of the officials now committed themselves to go back to Rhodesia. Before returning, however, they wanted to decide about leadership, whether or not to start a new party, and the nature of future action within Rhodesia. At this point Nkomo made a shrewd move that ever after made the dissidents' position very difficult. Rather than face them in Dar, he returned to Salisbury, where he precipitated the split by denouncing key nationalists as enemies to the movement.[32] This blunt and direct attack threw those opposing Nkomo (both inside and outside the country) off balance. Most of the executive in Dar faced immediate imprisonment in Rhodesia because they had jumped bail to leave; Nkomo, being in the country, was able to make use of the argument that had been most effectively used against him—that those outside the country really were not interested in struggling for the people.

A sad, wasteful, and useless struggle began. The executive returned from Dar and established the Zimbabwe African National Union (ZANU) under the Reverend Sithole's leadership. Nkomo reconstituted ZAPU as the People's Caretaker Council (PCC). The formation of open parties in itself was an admission of failure, for many leaders, particularly in ZANU, favored a militant underground campaign directed against the government.

The Zimbabwe African National Union was well financed by Nkrumah's Ghana, Malawi, Algeria, Tanzania, and (to Nkomo's outrage) by the Organization of African Unity Liberation Committee. Nigeria and Nasser's United Arab Republic supported the PCC. There is no way to gauge accurately which party had the greatest support, although the PCC probably was stronger. Neither party followed the single course that was most likely to lead to popular approval and internal ascendancy—that is, relentless struggle against the white regime.

The split was not based on tribal lines, although most Ndebeles stood by Nkomo. Of the fifteen (of seventeen) past members of the ANC, NDP, and ZAPU executive that can be accounted for, eight stayed with Nkomo and seven went with Sithole. The crux of the split was not even political, except as they differed over *past* actions (or the lack thereof). Both parties espoused similar goals: independent majority rule, relentless opposition to colonialism and imperialism, and commitment to African socialism and Pan-Africanism.[33]

The split was caused by Nkomo's leadership and this issue continues to divide Rhodesia's nationalists. In the year before both parties were banned, they engaged in dismal, internecine warfare. Little attention was paid to the putative enemy—the local settlers—who were free to pick off the nationalists as they pleased. Nkomo was restricted in April 1964; Sithole went to prison in May 1964. Neither has been free since, and the same can be said for many other nationalists. For the PCC,

"ZANU does not exist"; for ZANU, "no nationalist movement is possible if led by Nkomo." Behind these intractable positions, the Africans have stood divided against the white government since 1963.

Between 1959 and 1964 five major nationalist organizations were banned in Rhodesia. Could this have been avoided, or was it inevitable or even necessary? Davis M'Gabe, a Rhodesian African nationalist now in exile, has argued that the Rhodesian nationalist movement failed as "an effective revolutionary force because it moved from one European model to another, without ever sinking its roots deep into the African soil." [34] The *Zimbabwe Review,* the ZAPU party paper now published in exile, reviewed the African nationalist experience in the 1960's and concluded that it was "an unfortunate experiment in trying to defeat the enemy through the rules of his own game." [35] These African criticisms are the difficult lessons learned from negotiating experiences with Britain and from organizing experiences within Rhodesia.

In stressing primarily urban organization and constitutional political advance, the Africans implicitly accepted the possibility of internal suppression but expected that, in turn, Britain would eventually come to their rescue. As a result they never formulated a revolutionary perspective with which to confront the settler government. They expected external agents, not internal pressures, to alter the balance of power in Rhodesia.[36] They interpreted their struggle as analogous to that waged in Nyasaland, Northern Rhodesia, and other British colonies. The nationalists were wrong. The settler government was determined to resist nationalist pressure, and open nationalist organization played right into white hands. The nationalists also fundamentally misunderstood the nature of British-white Rhodesian relations and grossly overestimated Britain's commitment to Rhodesian Africans.

Should the nationalists have participated in the elections under terms of the 1961 constitution? Arguments in favor focus on the idea that if the nationalists had been in political office they would have been less vulnerable to government suppression and more effective in gaining British support.[37] This reasoning rests on many questionable assumptions. It was not obvious that 15 seats in parliament would have strengthened the nationalist cause. United white action could have passed any measure and pointed up African weakness, not strength. At the NDP congresses following the constitutional conference, one of the main reasons for rejecting the constitution was rank-and-file fear that those taking the 15 seats would again engage in multiracial politics.[38] The expectation that the white government would have been reluctant to suppress African members of parliament is entirely conjectural, but in view of government actions before and after 1961, it is hard to take this view seriously. Finally, this argument rests on the belief that 15 African seats would be but a stage in Rhodesia's constitutional evolution. The nationalists believed that both Britain and the whites viewed this not as a stage, but as the *culmination* of African advance—a culmination that would doom them to the certainty of minority impotence. All subsequent British and white Rhodesian action bears out this analysis. Thus, although their alternatives obviously were unsatisfactory, the nationalists stood outside the political process and hoped to build new pressure for more substantial political change.

One cannot conclude this analysis of nationalist strategy without noting the double standard that is in operation here. Britain assumed that the four nationalist leaders at the 1961 constitutional conference could make any decision without interaction with their constituency. But what if the Europeans had rejected the constitution? Would Britain then have sulked? Would no new conference have been called? The decision to implement the constitution arose out of British eagerness to disengage from Rhodesia, to accept the reality of local white power, and not from any effort to do equal justice to white and black.

The European Response to African Nationalism

The emergence of African protest in the postwar period elicited a relentless European response designed to exclude from political activity anyone unprepared to accept indefinite white rule. Increasingly harsh measures have been utilized to achieve this end, but the goal has always been broadly accepted within the white community.

From the outset of African protest, the government moved quickly to curb dissent. The 1948 African strike led to the Subversive Activities Act of 1950. This act gave the government power to ban meetings, to establish a secret police, and to ban "the propaganda or dissemination or inculcation or advocacy of all or any of the following ideas . . . [including] . . . undermining or destroying constitutional democratic government; . . . maintaining control over the people through fear, terrorism or brutality; or . . . passive resistance to any law." [39] In a society where whites dominated everything, it was not hard to judge in whose interest it was to call Rhodesia a "democratic government" or who would find it most useful to prohibit the "passive resistance to any law." Early Youth League activities led to the Public Order Act of 1955. This act provided the government with authority to detain and restrict people without charge or trial. During the 1956 Youth League bus boycott campaign, the Todd government detained over two hundred Africans and banned all open meetings and processions. [40]

The government also responded quickly to the attempts at rural organization by the African National Congress. The 1958 report of the chief native commissioner indicated extreme official displeasure:

Chiefs and Headmen encountered a new and strange influence bearing on them in the shape of the African National Congress. Blandishments, threats, disdain, ridicule and intimidation were meted out to them . . . This African National Congress . . . began to reach out tentacles into the rural areas during 1958, probing about for grievances and local talent on which to fasten, and then cleverly evoking an emotional response out of which local branches were created.[41]

In July 1958 all open meetings in the reserves were banned.

The 1959 emergency involved massive police and army actions, revealed the already advanced state of intelligence surveillance, and confirmed the intense white commitment to curbing nationalist protest. Prime Minister Whitehead was acclaimed in parliament by both government and opposition members when he promised new legislation to remove this "canker in our body politic" (as he called the ANC).[42]

In the aftermath of the emergency, new security legislation passed which broadened the government's control over every political activity within Rhodesia. The key measures were the Native Affairs Amendment Act, the Unlawful Organizations Act, and the Preventive Detention (Temporary Provisions) Act (all in 1959), and the Law and Order (Maintenance) Act and the Emergency Powers Act (both in 1960). Taken together, these acts all but eliminated the notion of the rule of law within Rhodesia.[43] They gave the government broad powers to curb freedom of speech, movement, privacy, expression, assembly, and association.

The Native Affairs Amendment Act was designed to stop nationalist organization in rural areas. Native commissioner approval was henceforth required for any meeting of 12 or more Africans. The penalty for holding an illegal meeting was up to a year in jail. As much as six months imprisonment (or a fine of up to 50 pounds) was provided for "any African who makes any statement or does any act or thing whatsoever which is likely to undermine the authority of any officer of the Government of Southern Rhodesia or of the Federation or of any chief or headman." [44]

The Unlawful Organizations Act gave the government authority to ban any organization "likely to raise disaffection among the inhabitants of Southern Rhodesia or to promote feelings of ill will or hostility between or within different races." Imprisonment of up to five years or a fine of 1,000 pounds was provided for anyone who belonged to a banned organization, or shouted any of their slogans, or made or carried any of their signs, or refused to provide police full information about members. Finally, any person who attended a meeting of an unlawful organization or who had in their possession any books, accounts, writings, papers, banners, or insignias were considered members of that organization "until and unless the contrary is proved." [45] This act has been used to ban all Rhodesia's nationalist parties.

The Preventive Detention (Temporary Provisions) Act (PDA) allowed for up to five years detention for anyone "concerned in any activities which in the opinion of Governor are potentially dangerous to public safety or public order." The only protection for those detained was the right to a hearing before a tribunal appointed by the minister of justice. The tribunal was a facade behind which the government operated at its pleasure, for the PDA provided that "a detention order and a restriction order shall not be subject to any appeal, review or other proceeding in any court of law nor shall any action, suit or other legal proceeding or remedy be available to any detained person in respect of his detention or restriction." [46]

The comprehensive Law and Order (Maintenance) Act (LOMA) added many new offenses to the Rhodesian statute book. In its printed form the LOMA runs to 34 pages—34 pages descriptive of what Africans cannot do and what will happen to them if they do. The act has been amended several times and includes provisions for, *inter alia:* the prohibition of meetings and of the right to attend meetings; police power to arrest and search without warrant; the banning of any publication; restriction without trial to any designated spot for up to five years; three-year prison sentences for intimidation; twenty-year sentences for possession of any "offensive weapon or material" (including a stone, acid, wire cutters, or inflammable substance); and sentences of up to five years for making "subversive statements." [47] In sum, the LOMA gave the government legal authority to prevent any party or person from challenging its notion of the political system.

The Emergency Powers Act gave sweeping new authority to the government during a state of emergency. The government could make regulations having absolute power of summary arrest and detention without trial, control businesses and employees, and generally make regulations to prevent interference with any essential service (such as transport, electricity, water, food, fuel, communications, and the like). States of emergency have been employed regularly in Rhodesia; in fact, since November 5, 1965, Rhodesia has been under a constant state of emergency. The Emergency Powers Act simply added the ultimate weapon of government by decree when all other legal weapons proved insufficient.

The introduction of this legislation met with broad white approval. The Dominion Party had no trouble in supporting the United Federal Party's actions against their real enemy, the African nationalist movement. Nor did Britain invoke the reserve clauses to inhibit the passage of this legislation. The UFP that brought this legislation forward was, ironically, the same party that Britain deemed a moderate organization seeking a nonracial solution to Rhodesia's problems.

The government did not hesitate to use its new laws. Parties were banned regularly. The reserves were all but closed to the nationalists from 1959 on. Meetings were banned throughout the country at several different junctures. After October 1962, political rallies were forbidden on Sundays and holidays. Since this was the only free time that most urban Africans had, it was a severe blow to any political organizing. This steady harassment prevented the nationalists from developing the momentum necessary to challenge the settlers seriously.

Party and organizational repression was matched by personal oppression. The LOMA was rapidly put to use, and from 1961 to 1965 the total number of arrests for LOMA violations was as follows: 1961—1,028; 1962—1,084; 1963—1,019; 1964—4,435; and 1965—2,143. From 1960 to May 1965, 6,301 Africans were formally prosecuted under this act and 3,448 were convicted. During the same period, 1,610 Africans were prosecuted under the Unlawful Organizations Act and 1,002 convicted.[48]

Detention and restriction were other weapons valued by the government. Detention (often for years) was primarily utilized during the 1959 emergency and in 1964 when states of emergency were declared in the two largest Salisbury African townships. The government detained 495 persons in 1959 and 1,791 from the beginning of 1964 to June 1965. Restriction has generally meant being sent to one of three restriction camps: Gonakudzingwa, Wha Wha, or Sikombela. Under the original LOMA, restriction orders were for three months, but they now can be for terms up to five years—and they are always renewable. The government restricted 296 persons in 1962, none in 1963, 690 in 1964, and 315 between January and July of 1965.[49] Except for those in exile, all the important nationalist leaders have been either restricted or detained since 1964.[50]

In addition to LOMA, other acts such as the Vagrancy Act, the Master and Servants Act, and the African (Registration and Identification) Act regularly applied administrative harassment to Africans. Whether by withdrawing rural land rights or an urban housing permit, or by having a man fired from his job, white authorities had many ways to make a political point without using overt security legislation. One indication of European willingness to act tough is the steady rise in the length of jail sentences and the size of the prison population. This is set forth in Table 9.

The government occasionally tried to justify its actions by arguing that the nationalists were an adjunct of the world Communist movement. One official analysis called nationalist activities "a classic example of the use of Communist methods of subversion from within." It added that nationalist activities "are aimed at producing fear in the minds of the vast majority of peace-loving Africans and to produce the desired effect overseas that there is an 'explosive situation' in Rhodesia, which is being exacerbated by the reactionary 'settler' Government, and therefore outside intervention is justified and necessary. As is well known the ultimate aim is the overthrow of Constitutional Govern-

Table 9. Disposition of African criminal cases in Rhodesia
and total prison population by year, 1959–1965.

Year	Separate counts	Fines under 25 pounds	Jail sentences under one month	Jail sentences one month to one year	Jail sentences over one year	Prison population[a]
1959	60,893	32,337	1,700	11,446	607	5,042
1960	54,606	25,747	1,668	10,732	668	5,417
1961	57,875	25,244	2,761	12,201	869	6,465
1962	51,312	20,836	1,782	10,017	788	6,901
1963	61,797	25,598	2,327	11,651	1,057	6,454
1964	70,033	29,674	1,349	10,164	3,264	8,837
1965	65,480	31,005	688	9,943	2,566	10,115

SOURCE: *Annual Reports of the Secretary for Justice.*

[a] Until 1964 the prison population figures (which are averages for the year) were computed from July 1 to June 30. Thus the figure 5,042 is the average for 1958–1959.

ment." [51] For the most part, however, both sides accepted the conflict as a simple power struggle. The Europeans used every weapon at their command to break the nationalist movement, and the nationalists did what they could in the face of this onslaught. Both sides looked to Britain. The Africans desired intervention; for white Rhodesia, however, British indifference was quite acceptable.

The nationalist movement posed the Rhodesian government with its most critical challenge. Earlier dealings with Britain had shown the whites that they had nothing to fear from that quarter. Thus they were free to take whatever steps they deemed necessary to crush the nationalist movement. From this base of internal dominance the whites prepared their final push for independence.

4

Rhodesia's Drive
to Independence

Nearly all white Rhodesians desired independence. The move to federation in 1953, Welensky's demand for dominion status in 1960, and Whitehead's negotiation of the 1961 constitution were all designed to promote this end. Where the Rhodesian Front (RF) came to differ from the previously governing United Federal Party was in its willingness to contemplate and then undertake a unilateral declaration of independence (UDI).[1]

The revolution that the Rhodesian Front capped with UDI was not an internal revolution, but only a revolution with respect to Rhodesian relations with Britain. Ties to Britain, once looked on as a secure lifeline to the rest of the world, came to be viewed as an unbearable threat to white survival. UDI was made possible by the linkage of two European fears: one that they would lose what they had if the African nationalists came to power, and the other that British policy toward Rhodesia was designed to achieve this very end. Taken together and fostered by propaganda and three years of fruitless independence negotiations, the traditionally close relations between Rhodesia and Britain broke down. In view of the fact that these relations had always been characterized by the ability of white Rhodesians to get their way, the breakdown over independence was perhaps inevitable.

Both RF prime ministers, Winston Field and Ian Smith, attempted to negotiate independence for Rhodesia. Field's efforts were inextricably linked with the complex problems associated with the dismantling of federation. Because of his failure to achieve independence for Rhodesia at the end of federation, Field's days were numbered and in April 1964 he was forced to resign. This change marked the shift from a traditional, autocratic type of Rhodesian prime minister (like Welensky and Huggins) to a new type of collegial authoritarianism based upon the well-oiled machine of the Rhodesian Front. From April 1964 on, this machine, with Smith as its spokesman, hardened its attitude toward Britain. Drawing upon a distorted picture of events in the rest of Africa and construing the demise of federation as the most recent example of British perfidy toward whites in Africa, the independence drive gathered momentum. The RF's success was in convincing the European electorate in Rhodesia that independence by any means was preferable to continued colonial status, however meaningless the reality of British control.

Winston Field's Approach to Independence

The RF's position on independence if federation were dissolved was "to seek under a suitable constitution sovereign independence within or outside the commonwealth." [2] This independence was to be consonant with party principles, which guaranteed the permanent establishment of Europeans in Rhodesia.

The early RF strategy, and one which had strong possibilities of success, was to tie the Rhodesian demand for independence to the British desire to extricate themselves from federation as amicably as possible. Just after assuming office, Field had a round of talks with R. A. Butler, British secretary of state for Central Africa, and it was apparent that he believed independence could be negotiated.[3] Further talks were held in March 1963. The Rhodesian position was that it would "not attend a Conference [on the dissolution of federation] unless we have received in writing from you an acceptable undertaking that Southern Rhodesia will receive its independence . . . on the first date when either [Northern Rhodesia or Nyasaland] is allowed to secede or obtain its independence." [4]

Rhodesia seemed in a strong position, for Welensky was vigorously backing Field's moves. In a May 11, 1963, speech Welensky noted that Field's "aim is exactly what mine was four years ago and what was Sir Edgar's aim during his period of office as Prime Minister—to achieve independence for Southern Rhodesia." [5] If both prime ministers insisted on Rhodesian independence as a prior condition for participation in the breakup of federation, it would pose complicated problems for Britain;

63

breaking up federation without their active assistance would be nearly impossible.

Britain's answer to Field drew the lines of conflict clearly. Though Britain would "accept in principle" that Rhodesia would proceed to independence, it was the desire of the British government to consider the "transitional arrangements" for dissolving federation and the "broad lines of a future relationship between the territories" *before* moving on to the specific question of Rhodesia's independence. At any rate, Britain added, Rhodesia could not possibly become independent while the federation still existed and Britain "would expect to convene a Conference to discuss financial, defense, constitutional and other matters," before granting Rhodesia full and sovereign independence.[6]

Rhodesia remained adamant and in a long letter dated April 20, 1963, Field rebutted each of the British contentions and reiterated Rhodesia's refusal to attend any conference without a written promise of independence.[7] Britain's answer was to try to split the problem of federal dissolution from that of Rhodesia's future constitutional position. Britain again asked the Rhodesian government to attend a conference to deal with the ending of federation and at the same time promised that if Rhodesian cooperation were forthcoming, "the British government will undertake to enter into negotiations on her independence with Southern Rhodesia not later than the date on which negotiations for the independence of either of the other Territories are initiated by us." [8]

The Rhodesian government was quick to see that this apparent concession offered her nothing and in another determined letter on May 9, the Field government again set out its position. In a form only slightly modified from earlier demands, Rhodesia now agreed to accept independence not later than the dissolution date of federation, but only if "the discussion, which you regard as a necessary prelude to independence, should take place *before* the conference on dissolution and future economic links, and that *agreement* should be reached between our two governments on all the requirements for independence before any other conference begins." [9] No concession was made to the British plea to deal with federal disssolution as a separate problem, distinct from Rhodesian independence.

Britain, increasingly worried about delay, agreed to Field's demands and scheduled a conference for the end of May in London. Butler added that "if it has not been found possible to complete our discussion on the terms on which Southern Rhodesia should proceed to independence before the conference [that is, the projected dissolution conference] I would undertake that discussion would be resumed at the earliest convenient date." [10] Rhodesia thus proceeded to the London conference without having made any promise about future attendance at a federal dissolution conference.

To this point, Rhodesia's independence strategy had been completely successful. Britain was in a dilemma over how to dismantle federation, and Rhodesia, by holding firm to the threat of nonparticipation, had forced London to convene a special Rhodesian independence conference. The London talks, however, proved unsuccessful and Field returned to Rhodesia on June 5 with no agreement on terms or on a time limit for independence. Britain's terms for Rhodesian independence, although not publicly announced, were thought to entail (1) a blocking one-third of the parliamentary seats to go to Africans; (2) a gradual repeal of the Land Apportionment Act; (3) the end of legalized racial discrimination; (4) the widening of the B-roll franchise; and (5) the retention of cross-voting.[11]

Two significant facts emerge from these and all subsequent Rhodesian independence talks. One is that the 1961 constitution was accepted as the basic working document in all negotiations despite the fact that most RF leaders had originally opposed it. Once in office, however, they quickly realized how easily they could live with it and how useless were its guarantees of orderly advancement to majority rule.[12] With both the RF and the opposition UFP supporting the constitution, Britain found herself in a very awkward position in asking for new constitutional changes, inasmuch as she had so recently oversold the "liberal" features of the constitution. The second point is that neither Britain nor Rhodesia expected that majority rule would precede the granting of independence. The context of British-Rhodesian negotiations, both before and after UDI, always was limited to the terms under which a white minority government would be granted independence.

At the beginning of June three sets of pressures were building up on Winston Field: an anxious party insisting on independence but unwilling to make any concession for it; the British government pushing hard for the federal dissolution conference and trying to show goodwill by convening the Rhodesian independence conference; and many Rhodesian citizens (especially the large civil service) facing employment uncertainty and desiring an agreeable, ordered end to federation. At this point Field began to reconsider the hard Rhodesian stand. In a letter to Butler on June 13, Field said that Rhodesia would be willing to reconsider its position "to avoid continuing the uncertainty for both the Federal government and its employees as well as for the people of Southern Rhodesia and, therefore we are inclined to reconsider the matter of our attendance at the Conference." [13] In turn, Rhodesia merely asked for an agreed agenda and a promise not to discuss the internal politics of any territory at the conference. It was, in fact, a complete capitulation to the British position and Butler was quick to accept. He eased the pressure on Field by agreeing to continue the Rhodesian independence talks during the two days prior to the opening of the federal dissolution conference. This conference was set for Victoria Falls beginning June 28, 1963— the independence talks to be held on the 26th and 27th.

Field defended the shift in the Rhodesian position in an address to parliament on June 18, 1963.[14] His major argument was that Britain (by agreeing to hold the earlier conference) had moved considerably and that Rhodesia should not provoke unnecessary bitterness by boycotting the federal dissolution conference. He claimed that Rhodesia was holding firm to her independence demands and would not bow to British pressure for the lowering of the A-roll franchise or for commonwealth participation in the independence negotiations. Unknown, of course, was the continued validity of a firm negotiating stance, once a key point of political leverage had been foresworn.

The shift in the Rhodesian position resulted from a personal decision on Field's part. He feared that the United Kingdom might break up federation without Rhodesia and that he must go to protect Rhodesia's interests. There were many financial matters to be discussed and Field, holding the defense portfolio, was eager to have the air force returned to Rhodesia. Even more decisive, however, was Field's essential goodwill. He got on well with Butler and he genuinely believed that with Butler, Rhodesia would be able to negotiate independence. He clearly saw the British dilemma if he refused to attend the breakup conference and he believed that goodwill on his part would engender the same on the part of the British government.[15] In taking this decision, Field indirectly sealed his own doom; most important RF figures were incensed at his apparent capitulation. Unfortunately for Field, his basis for optimism was cut away a few months later when Butler became the British foreign secretary and Duncan Sandys became the new commonwealth secretary. After his first round of talks with Sandys in January 1964, Field's optimism vanished and shortly thereafter he was forced out of office.

In accordance with the agreements made, Rhodesian and British leaders met on June 26–27 to further discuss Rhodesia's independence terms, but once again negotiations proved fruitless. Rhodesia then attended the dissolution conference from June 28 to July 3, 1963. Here all the machinery for the breakup of federation was established; committees composed of both ministers and civil servants from the five governments were set up to divide federal assets and liabilities, the federal civil service, the federal defense establishment, and to work out citizenship problems.[16]

In the months following the Victoria Falls conferences, the independence issue faded under the weight of the complicated administrative problems of breaking up the federation. This was a vast task, since more than thirty-five thousand civil servants were involved, many of whom wished to return to the Rhodesian civil service. The problems of reintegrating large numbers of people and preparing to assume all federal functions was a big bureaucratic task, especially since none of the Rhodesian ministers had ever held a government portfolio prior to December 1962. Despite the fact that the capitals of federation and Rhodesia were both in Salisbury and that many federal ministries could be transferred almost en masse to Rhodesian jurisdiction, enough difficulties remained so as to push independence into the background for a few months. Indeed, between the Victoria Falls Conference and November 1963, no published messages on independence passed between the two governments.

In November 1963 Ian Smith, Rhodesia's treasury minister, traveled to London primarily to deal with financial and investment matters, but his visit prompted a reopening of moves relating to independence. These renewed contracts led to a trip by Field to London in January 1964. Duncan Sandys was now the man in charge of Central African affairs and Sir Alec Douglas-Home had become the new prime minister. Rhodesia too had made changes, and Evan Campbell, a prominent Rhodesia tobacco farmer, ex-UFP politician, and close friend of Winston Field, had become Rhodesian high commissioner to London.

Home and Field managed to evolve a cordial working relationship, but Sandys and the Rhodesian officials could not see eye to eye. The result of these talks was again total failure, and Field once more returned to Salisbury empty-handed. The stalemate at this point was probably not caused solely by Rhodesian intransigence, for the Conservatives were anxious not to get involved in a troublesome colonial situation during an election year. But the Tories' problems were of little concern within Rhodesia, where it soon became clear that Field was in serious political difficulty for failing in a primary objective of the Rhodesian Front government.

Field was clearly dispirited about independence and uncertain about how to proceed. He attempted to deflect criticism in February 1964 by saying, "Let no one think we have accepted defeat on the independence question—we have not—but we do realize that there is so much to be done in other directions, and we call on and expect all sections of the people of Southern Rhodesia to work together to achieve a really strong economy." [17] This rhetoric did not satisfy the party, but Field himself was not prepared to consider seriously the possibility of UDI. He always believed that Rhodesia should act within constitutional channels. Maj. Gen. John Anderson, whom Field appointed as General Officer Commanding the Rhodesian Army on January 1, 1964, subsequently revealed that he had only agreed to take the post after Field promised him that no unconstitutional action was contemplated. [18]

The pressures leading to Field's ouster arose partly from his failure on the independence question, but also from other criticisms such as aloofness from the party organization, giving political appointments to non-RF members, autocratic methods, and hesitancy in restricting Joshua Nkomo, leader of ZAPU. In sum, the party thought Field was reluctant to move quickly on racial-political questions. His hesitancy was read as "moderation," and when the party confronted him with a direct challenge on the independence issue, Field refused to put a time limit on negotiations and balked over the possibility of UDI. He was compelled to resign on April 13, 1964; Ian Douglas Smith became the new prime minister—the first Rhodesian prime minister who had been born in Rhodesia.[19]

The removal of Field ranks with the Todd ouster of 1958 as an important step toward white isolation. Whereas Todd's removal ended whatever small chance there was of meaningful African-European dialogue and cooperation, Field's removal made the possibility of a British-Rhodesian settlement very doubtful. Field was essentially a UFP figure, and once said, "I am not a white settler reactionary . . . I am a somewhat conservative individual who does not like rapid change for the worse." [20] He basically shared the beliefs and orientations of Huggins, Whitehead, and Welensky that the British not only *had* to be dealt with but that they *could* be dealt with. All shared a deep skepticism toward many British ministers and officials, but all were prepared to deal with the British; except Huggins, all paid a substantial political price for their willingness. This point was not lost on Ian Smith as he assumed office.

Field's ejection marked a dramatic shift in the power alignment within the white community. Running the government with an inner cabinet (Smith, Clifford Dupont, and John Howman) until the first two deserted him, Field had showed little regard for the party structure or the caucus. In a manner reminiscent of Welensky and Huggins, he had ruled over, rather than through or with, the party. Nothing typified this procedure more than the decision to go to the Victoria Falls Conference. Nevertheless, when this type of leadership did not produce results, the RF activists made their move.

The central instigators of the Field coup were those on the back bench, but the idea was popular throughout the lower ranks of the party organization. Discontent fed on the criticisms mentioned earlier and was bolstered by the economic unease and white emigration which came with the end of federation. Frustration throughout the white community on a variety of economic, social, and political questions found its outlet in the change of prime ministers and the heightened demand for independence. When the flag of revolt was raised, the party, with the exception of Howman (the minister of internal affairs), fell into line. Power shifted from the hands of a strong but willful prime minister to a broadly based, party-oriented collective leadership headed by Ian Smith and closely attuned to the demands of the party organization.

Field was encouraged to stay on and fight the revolt by a wide variety of people, many from outside the party. However, on the grounds that his health was not good (which was true) and not wanting to fight for a job in which he was demonstrably disliked, Field quietly returned to his farm. The RF itself was fearful that Field might fight—or even worse, cross the floor. By taking only three RF MP's with him (certainly not an impossibility), Field could have created a new UFP majority or at least precipitated an election. Field remained loyal to the Rhodesian Front, however, and by April 1964 he had lost the will to fight.

The Forging of the Independence Issue

Question to Smith. What would be the main repercussion, apart from belt-tightening, if we declared our independence?
Answer. I don't think there will be any belt-tightening, when we are independent—the days of belt-tightening will be over. That's for sure. As far as the City of London is concerned, it might be a three-day wonder. For that reason I think a Friday afternoon would be a good time. By Monday morning all the excitement (if any) would be over.[21]

In the months preceding the ouster of Field, Ian Smith established himself as the leading spokesman for those pushing hard for independence. His "three-day wonder" prediction came in early 1964. This statement, combined with others, led Britain to warn the Rhodesian government privately about the dangers of UDI:

International reaction would be sharp and immediate. The issue would be raised at once in the United Nations; . . . Commonwealth and foreign governments, with one or two exceptions, would almost certainly refuse to recognize Southern Rhodesia's independence . . . Thus isolated, Southern Rhodesia would increasingly become a target for subversion, trade boycotts, air transport bans and other hostile activities, organised in other African states . . . The British government would be . . . under heavy pressure to withdraw Commonwealth's preferences and to reconsider Southern Rhodesia's membership of the Sterling area.[22]

This warning, however, did not deter pressure for independence, and shortly thereafter Field was replaced.

Smith's first action as prime minister was to reassign cabinet positions to correspond more accurately to power within the Rhodesian Front. William Harper and Clifford Dupont assumed the key portfolios of internal affairs, and justice, law, and order respectively. Nkomo was then re-restricted in an obvious move to demonstrate a new hard line. Most important, Smith immediately embarked on an extended tour of the country, addressing many meetings, with the intent of consolidating the European community behind the RF in its accentuated drive for independence. All the Smith speeches argued that independence was necessary for three reasons: to stop African nationalists from going over the heads of local white leaders to London for political redress, to end forever the possibility of British interference in Rhodesian affairs, and to establish the conditions for economic stability and growth.[23]

The clearest overall statement by Smith on African advancement came on May 10, 1964, over the African service of the Rhodesian Broadcasting Service. "If in my lifetime we have an African nationalist government in power in Southern Rhodesia, then we will have failed in the policy that I believe in." [24] Subsequently he stated that "if, for the normal span of life for a man my age we can stave this thing off, then I believe we may stave it off forever. And if, as a Government, we fail to do this, then I don't think we deserve to be charged with the responsibility of handling the affairs of Southern Rhodesia." [25] Smith could hardly be more explicit about the RF's long-range commitment to white rule.

There was little correspondence between the Rhodesian and British governments during the first months of Smith's tenure. Most Rhodesian efforts turned toward building a political consensus on independence on the European home front and toward curbing the African nationalists who were opposing one another and the whites. On August 26, 1964, the government declared a state of emergency in the Salisbury African township of Highfield, and the *African Daily News* was banned. By the end of August more than six hundred people had been detained, and the rival African nationalist organizations, ZANU and ZAPU-PCC, were in disarray.

With the home front consolidated, Smith flew to London for independence talks with Prime Minister Home.[26] The talks lasted from September 7 to 10, 1964, and largely consisted in Smith's efforts to convince Home that independence should be granted on the basis of the 1961 constitution. Home noted the British desire for expanded African representation, but Smith countered with the RF view that it was the chiefs who truly represented the African people. Home was in a difficult position. With an election pending, he wanted neither to inflame a sensitive issue nor to enter into agreements which he might not have time to fulfill. From the talks came a joint communique in which both governments averred their desire to see Rhodesia independent and agreed that independence must be based on general consent. Smith, however, "was convinced that the majority of the population supported his request for independence on the basis of the present Constitution and franchise," while Home "said that the British Government had as yet no evidence that this was the case." Home promised to "take account of any views which might be freely expressed by the population on the issues involved; but he must make it plain that the British Government reserved their position." [27]

The next two months in Rhodesia were filled with political activity associated with the intensified independence drive. These events included two important by-elections on October 1, an October *indaba* (traditional meeting) of chiefs and headmen, the removal of the head of the Rhodesian army, and on November 5, 1964, a referendum of registered voters on the question, "Are you in favor of independence based on the 1961 constitution?" The indaba and referendum sprang directly from Smith's September talks in London, while the importance of the by-elections emerged from the decision of Sir Roy Welensky to attempt a return to politics.

Welensky decided to stand at a by-election in opposition to the Rhodesian Front in the hopes that by winning he could breathe new life into the old United Federal Party (now renamed the Rhodesia Party) which had fragmented badly once out of power; he also hoped to prevent UDI.[28] Sir Roy stood in Arundel, a fashionable Salisbury suburb which had traditionally been a UFP-RP stronghold. His opponent was Clifford Dupont, the RF minister of justice, law, and order, who resigned a safe seat to take on Welensky. During the campaign the only important difference that emerged was on the question of UDI, which Welensky strenuously opposed. The campaign degenerated into a bitter battle and many of Welensky's election meetings were seriously disrupted. At one large meeting on September 21, Welensky was jeered as "a Bloody Jew, a communist, a traitor, and a coward." [29]

The RF worked relentlessly to defeat and destroy Welensky. Radio and television outlets were turned against him, and the Rhodesian Information Service issued a statement by Smith censuring Welensky for continuing "to meddle in the Independence issue." It added that "It had been made very clear to him [Smith] in London . . . that the British government found him to be the most forthright and tenacious protagonist of the Rhodesian cause with whom they had yet had to deal . . . They had also informed him that, from past experience, they had found Sir Roy Welensky . . . to be one of the weakest." [30] Unity was the key to independence, the Front proclaimed, and Welensky stood in the way of a "national approach" to the problem. Welensky was undercut on the UDI issue by Smith's statement that "I have no intention whatsoever of interpreting victory in the forthcoming by-elections here as being a mandate . . . for a unilateral declaration." [31] Liberty, security, opportunity, freedom, unity, independence, Smith, and the Rhodesian Front were all linked together in an intense drive to taint Welensky with the aura of weakness. The appeal having perhaps the greatest impact on the affluent homeowners of Arundel was published on September 28, under a half-page picture of a family watching television:

HOME MEANS EVERYTHING TO MOST WOMEN. It certainly does to me, and as I sit between Mike and the two boys in our comfortable home watching TV, I count my blessings. My sister Marge's husband was a coffee planter in Kenya and they were better off (or so it seemed) than we were. Then the political scene changed and they lost their beautiful farm with its lovely homestead, as a result of the Government falling into irresponsible hands. Now they have to start all over again in a strange country, and have lost their life's savings. [Mike and I] will support our Prime Minister and the Rhodesian Front Government who have done so much in such a short time to free us from worry, and to give us the freedom and security we so much want.[32]

The RF's effort to defeat Welensky was an unqualified success. In an extremely high poll of 75.9 percent, Dupont defeated Welensky 1,079 to 633.[33] In Avondale, in an accompanying by-election in another traditional Rhodesia Party seat, Sidney Sawyer, another former federal politician, was defeated by the RF candidate 1,042 to 416. The percentage swing to the RF from the 1962 election returns was 23.4 percent in Arundel and 27.8 in Avondale. The victory gave the RF a tremendous boost of confidence and devastated the RP. The Rhodesian Front could now be sure that a large majority of the European community was strongly behind it.

One of Smith's major efforts at the September London talks had been to convince the British government that the tribal chiefs spoke for the African people. A plan was already in the works to consult the chiefs and headmen on African opinion about independence, and Smith announced in his parliamentary statement reviewing the London talks that this consultation would take place (though without specifying its form).[34] Smith made no mention of the British government's total reservation of its position.

The RF strategy was to interpret the September communique as a promise of independence if Rhodesians could demonstrate their acceptance of the 1961 constitution. From the speed with which the indaba and then a referendum of registered voters on independence took place, it was evident that the Rhodesian government hoped to stampede the British government into giving way. As Smith said, "Let our united aim be—Independence by Christmas 1964." [35] The British government became aware of the indaba plan on October 14, 1964 (the day prior to the British general election) when Smith notified the British high commissioner in Salisbury of the indaba and asked the United Kingdom to send observers. The British declined, however, since the sending of observers "might be interpreted as implying a commitment on the part of the British Government to accepting your consultation as representing the opinion of the people as a whole." [36] This view, sent by British High Commissioner Johnston to Smith, was fully endorsed by Arthur Bottomley, secretary of state for commonwealth relations in the new Labour Party government, in a letter to Smith on October 19, 1964.[37]

Although the British reply angered the Rhodesian government, it went ahead with its plan and from October 21 to October 26, 1964, under conditions of strict military secrecy, some six hundred chiefs and headmen met at the Domboshawa school, 25 miles from Salisbury. The convocation of the indaba was not publicly revealed until it began; the area was ringed with military, and until the last day the area was sealed off to the public, press, radio, and even to opposition members of parliament. To guarantee that the chiefs and headmen would come, the army was mobilized and teams of at least three soldiers were posted to each chief's village. This was done in order to protect their property and families from African nationalists and others who objected to the role the chiefs were playing. The chiefs were not told where they were going and only a few trusted ones were allowed to speak. Finally on the last day of the indaba, an open meeting was held where the chiefs and headmen revealed that they unanimously supported the government's demand for immediate independence.

The verbatim record of this final meeting plus a sociological defense of this "decision-making . . . . according to . . . tribal custom and tradition" have appeared in a Rhodesian government White Paper.[38] The recorded speeches of the always-anonymous chiefs and headmen combine a strenuous defense of their own authority with a bucolic vision of the future under an independent RF government. The chiefs were collectively appalled by the activities of their "children" (the African nationalists) and by the disasters which had befallen the independent African countries to the north. "Let the strings be cut today; we, the African chiefs and headmen of Rhodesia, have made our decision . . . It is now up to the Europeans to support us and show that we all want this independence on the 5th of November." [39] This method of ascertaining African opinion was vigorously criticized by five University College of Rhodesia and Nyasaland sociologists and anthropologists—J. Clyde Mitchell, J. van Velsen, G. Kingsley Garbett, Hilary Flegg, and P. D. Wheeldon—in two privately circulated memoranda, parts of which appeared in the *Rhodesia Herald* on February 3, 1965.[40]

The flurry of independence activity was heightened by a new state of emergency declared in Harare, a Salisbury African township on October 7, and by the sudden removal of Maj. Gen. John Anderson as head of the Rhodesian Army on October 23, 1964. Although only 51, Anderson was retired "on grounds of age." In actuality, he was expendable because "he had accepted the job on conditions that there was no question of unconstitutional action," conditions acceptable to Field, who appointed him, but not to Smith.[41]

These events, coupled with the forthcoming referendum, created the suspicion in London and Salisbury that UDI was imminent.[42] With the atmosphere tense, Britain's new prime minister, Harold Wilson, released the text of a letter he had earlier sent to the Rhodesian government. This October 27 statement warned that "an illegal declaration of independence in Southern Rhodesia would bring to an end relationships between her and Britain; would cut her off from the rest of the Commonwealth, from most foreign Governments and from international organisations; would inflict disastrous economic damage upon her; and would leave her isolated and virtually friendless in a largely hostile continent." [43]

This stiff warning provoked an outcry in Rhodesia from opposition members of parliament and from business and commercial leaders. Smith, seeing he had pushed too fast, immediately sought to defuse the UDI implications of the forthcoming referendum (just as the RF had done in the Welensky by-election) by declaring that the RF would not consider a Yes vote at the referendum as a mandate for UDI.[44] Nevertheless, the RF appeal for a Yes vote made clear the linkage in its mind between independence and continued white domination. The RF noted:

> The African Chiefs have shown the way. They have braved the extremists, ignored intimidation, and even risked their lives in giving the Government a unanimous "Yes" vote. YOU CANNOT LET DOWN THESE HONEST AND COURAGEOUS MEN! A "No" vote can only mean a vote *for* a racialist Black Government.[45]

In a letter sent to all households, Smith saw Rhodesia's struggle in cosmic terms

> between the forces of good and evil. A struggle in which our established standards of politics, public and private morality, and integrity are pitted against expediency and selfishness. Unless we Rhodesians can unite to sever the strings which tie us to Britain . . . we have no hope of survival . . . I hope you will realise how absolutely essential the YES vote is. Without it, Rhodesia is surely lost; with it we will surely survive.[46]

With assurances given that a referendum Yes vote would not mean UDI, there was really little at stake. Both the RF and the RP supported negotiated independence on the 1961 constitution. In a 61.6 percent poll, 58,091 voted Yes, 6,096 voted No, and there were 944 spoiled ballots. Of those voting, 89.1 percent voted Yes.[47] The overwhelming vote clearly suggested that the white electorate was prepared to follow the RF's lead on independence.

Having survived October and November without UDI, the British government under Wilson slowly moved to take some heat out of the independence controversy. Wilson himself was highly suspect to Rhodesians, not only as a Labour prime minister, but even more because on October 2, 1964, just days before the British election, he had sent a personal letter to Dr. E. C. Mutasa, a Salisbury African doctor, in which he had stated that "the Labour Party is totally opposed to granting independence to Southern Rhodesia so long as the Government of that country remains under the control of a white minority." [48] This view, however, did not long survive his accession to power and on November 17 of the same year, Wilson wrote Smith that "I am anxious to take the matter out of the public controversy . . . We look forward to a peaceful transition to majority rule in Southern Rhodesia, but we do not seek ourselves to stipulate how this might be achieved or when that stage should be reached. I assure you that we have no preconceived plan that we wish to impose on your country." [49]

The British efforts were not really successful and no progress was made until Smith went to London for the funeral of Sir Winston Churchill. Smith saw Wilson on January 30, 1965, and on the basis of that conversation and subsequent correspondence it was announced that Arthur Bottomley, the commonwealth secretary, and Lord Gardiner, the lord chancellor, would visit Rhodesia. They would be allowed to see anyone in Rhodesia except those in jail under criminal offenses.

During their stay from February 21 to March 3, Bottomley and Gardiner spoke with people representing all segments of Rhodesian society and extensively toured the country. They privately revealed to the Rhodesian government the five principles on which the British government would have to be satisfied if they were to grant independence. These principles were as follows:

(1) The principle and intention of unimpeded progress to majority rule, already enshrined in the 1961 Constitution, would have to be maintained and guaranteed.
(2) There would also have to be guarantees against retrogressive amendment of the Constitution.
(3) There would have to be immediate improvement in the political status of the African population.
(4) There would have to be progress towards ending racial discrimination.
(5) The British Government would need to be satisfied that any basis proposed for independence was acceptable to the people of Rhodesia as a whole.[50]

Negotiations made little apparent progress, and in their departing communique Bottomley and Gardiner noted a "hardening of attitudes" in Rhodesia but expressed hope that negotiations would continue in a "sober search for ways by which current dilemmas can be resolved constitutionally and honourably and by which the common goal of independence can be achieved." [51]

The 1965 "Independence" Election

The first official communication following the Bottomley-Gardiner visit was a letter to Smith on March 29.[52] The next day, after cabinet and caucus meetings, parliament was dissolved and an election called. This decision was the result of several factors and not directly attributable to the new correspondence. The opposition Rhodesia Party was in near-collapse following the Welensky defeat, and the RF believed the time was propitious for decimating the white opposition. By thus demonstrating white unity, the RF hoped to improve its bargaining position vis-à-vis Britain. An election also gave Smith an opportunity to consolidate his position within the party and was a response to RF demands for action on the independence question. The election was set for May 7.

From the outset, there was no question as to why the RF called the election. In his opening campaign speech, Smith stated, "The main issue of this election IS Independence. Anyone who believes that Independence is not vital, and our first priority, is out of touch with reality and the considered views of Rhodesians . . . without Independence, we cannot achieve the economic expansion or political stability which is so essential for the survival of civilised government in this country." [53]

Victory in the general election, hopefully with an overwhelming mandate, was seen by the RF as another phase in its battle for independence and to this end it made its one clear request to the electorate—it asked for a two-thirds majority in the new parliament. This was desired both to put added pressure on Britain and to allow the RF to pass constitutional amendments without needing opposition-party support. At this time it was widely believed that the RF might introduce a controversial amendment (such as for preventive detention) and then, if the British government did not approve, use this as a pretext for UDI on the grounds that Britain was breaking the convention of noninterference in Rhodesia's internal affairs.[54]

The election was contested under the 1961 constitution. The racial breakdown of registered voters was as follows:

	Africans	European	Coloured	Asian	Total
A-roll	2,330	92,405	1,307	1,242	97,284
B-roll	10,689	587	181	120	11,577

The cross-voting provisions of the 1961 constitution were in effect but preference voting, crucial in the 1958 election, had been eliminated by the Rhodesian Front.

The RF contested all 50 A-roll seats, but the RP could find only 25 candidates; in three other constituencies the RF was opposed by independent candidates, making 28 seats in all where the RF encountered opposition. The RP leadership seriously debated a total election boycott. Those in favor argued that they could not win and that a crushing defeat would encourage the RF to UDI far more than would a meaningless uncontested election. (A precedent was the RF's boycott of the

1962 federal election.) Other RP leaders argued that they had a moral and constitutional obligation to provide the electorate with a choice; they also felt the RP could win most B-roll seats and enough A-roll seats to provide a vigorous parliamentary opposition to the RF. This tactical split became apparent when only 5 of the 13 RP constituency incumbents sought reelection.

The Rhodesia Party made no attempt to conceal its electoral difficulties. David Butler, the party's new leader, candidly conceded that there was "no ready belief in the country that it would be likely for us to form a government." [55] He also added prophetically that the greatest danger to the RP was in being wiped out on the A-roll and thus losing multiracial membership in the House (the RP had 12 African B-roll district incumbents). The maximum hope of the RP was to win the 15 B-roll seats and 7 A-roll seats, thus preventing the RF from attaining a two-thirds majority.

The first part of the campaign was listless. The RF hammered at the point that independence required white unity, while the RP struggled to condemn UDI without being termed a sellout to Britain and the Africans. This effort led the RP to offer the Rhodesian electorate "The Third Choice"—not (1) UDI, or (2) a nationalist handover, but (3) independence by negotiation. The Rhodesian Party platform embodied five key points: independence by negotiation, maintenance of standards, responsible government, economic prosperity, and racial harmony.[56]

The RP's problem was clear. Each point of its platform was fully accepted by the RF, only more so. The only difference between the two parties turned on the question of UDI. Because the RP refused to endorse this possibility, the RF subjected it to relentless attack: "The 'Third Choice' means a Black future for *all*. A COUNTRY CANNOT STAND STILL! It either progresses or declines. Look what happened to the Kenya farmers . . . the B.S.A. company millions . . . the massacre of white and blacks in Stanleyville. THIS IS WHAT THE 'THIRD CHOICE' MEANS." [57] The RP was never able to shed the image of advocating a "phased handover"; this was the RF's most bitter taunt.

Another small squabble developed over proposed constitutional amendments, an area of concern because of the possibility of generating a constitutional crisis. The new minister of law and order, Desmond Lardner-Burke, had released a list of six rather innocuous amendments on April 23—"the only amendments that the government was contemplating." [58] The RP countered with its own different list which it said Smith had privately revealed in March.[59] Most important, the RP list included the provision of introducing preventive detention, which Lardner-Burke and other RF ministers were known to favor.[60] Nothing much came of this controversy, and it was virtually forgotten once the government released its White Paper on the economic consequences of UDI.

The RP had had little success in finding an issue which would favorably distinguish it from the RF. There was still one point, however, on which the RP hoped to gain ground—the general apprehension within the community over the possible economic consequences of a UDI. The RP's hope was to publicize special reports prepared by major Rhodesian economic groups, estimating the consequences should Britain implement her threatened sanctions following a UDI. These reports were written following Wilson's statement of October 27, 1964, and by mid-January 1965, eight reports had been prepared and submitted privately to the government.[61]

As time passed it became apparent that the government was not pleased with the reports and was in no hurry to divulge their findings. One report, that of the Rhodesian Tobacco Association, had been released on January 25, 1965, and the government made no secret of its displeasure. Confining its analysis to the tobacco industry alone, this report declared that without the Commonwealth Preference, the London Agreement between British manufacturers and Rhodesian producers would be endangered and that if embargoes were applied, the agreement would be destroyed. The probable results would be that only about one-half of the tobacco produced could be sold, even at minimum prices; that the auction system would break down; and that Rhodesia would lose her place in the world market. Lord Graham, the minister of agriculture, immediately attacked the report by saying that to raise such "bogeymen" was a disservice and that Rhodesians would not take kindly to attempts to "blackmail them into deserting their aim that government here will remain in responsible hands." He saw the report as nothing more than speculation and crystal gazing.[62]

The RF reticence on the subject of the reports was understandable. On April 20, however, Smith said that the government would soon issue its evaluation of them, after which the organizations could issue the reports if they wished.[63] On April 26 the Government published its White Paper, and the controversy over UDI broke wide open. Just over 1,200 words, the White Paper made *no* mention of the contents of any of the economic reports. It alluded to their existence only in noting that they had been based upon the assumption that Britain would carry out her threatened sanctions, an assumption which the RF now sought to discredit.

The government's position was that Britain would not fully impose sanctions and even if she did, Rhodesia was sufficiently prepared. The White Paper observed *inter alia:*

> Economies in countries to the north could be crippled; Withdrawal of preference and trade was a two-edged sword; Rhodesia could redirect her trade for there is no sentiment attached to money; Britain would not attempt to destroy Rhodesia's economy and stable government when countries to the north give every indication of submitting to

Communist influences; An embargo on Rhodesian tobacco would give America a virtual monopoly; Rhodesia could repatriate foreign workers to Zambia and Malawi; Economic sanctions would hurt all races; Counter-measures had been prepared to protect Rhodesia's national interests, economic and otherwise; History has shown that sanctions will not work; and In the long run Rhodesians have nothing to lose but all to gain by accepting their responsibilities and becoming completely independent as a sovereign nation.[64]

The publication of the White Paper was coupled with a statement by Smith that publication of the memoranda "would be a disservice to the people and economy of Rhodesia." His justification was that "UDI is not an issue in this election." [65]

By attempting to prevent publication of the original memoranda, by shifting the question from the economic consequences of UDI to the Rhodesian Front's preparedness to retaliate, and by criticizing the reports for assuming severe economic sanctions rather than possible non-implementation of sanctions, the government brought a wave of criticism upon itself. More important, it elicited publication of the memoranda themselves.

In addition to the Rhodesian Tobacco Association, the following organizations published their reports before election day: the Rhodesian Institute of Directors, the Associated Chamber of Commerce of Rhodesia (ACCOR), the Association of Rhodesian Industries (ARNI), and the National Commercial Distribution and Office Workers' Association (NCDOWA). To avoid "getting involved in politics," the other organizations did not release their studies.

Of the four newly published reports, only the NCDOWA's assessment matched the optimism of the government. Drawing on many of the same points (Rhodesian retaliation, Communism to the north, the universality of the profit motive, and the historical failure of sanctions), the NCDOWA firmly associated itself with the quest for independence and suggested that Britain could not and would not implement her threats.[66]

But the other three reports—those of the Directors, ACCOR, and ARNI—representing all segments of Rhodesian commerce and industry, were clearly worried. In assessing the possible economic consequences of a UDI, their findings were largely complementary.[67] Trade and financial difficulties foreseen included withdrawal from the sterling area, diminishing foreign investment, the freezing of Rhodesian assets abroad, loss of entry to the London money market, withdrawal of Commonwealth Preference, loss of access to raw materials, and loss of Rhodesian export markets. Within Rhodesia a combination of these effects could lead to a credit squeeze, import and exchange controls, and probably devaluation. A serious fall in exports and internal sales was expected, which would inevitably lead to rising costs of production and higher costs of living. Large-scale unemployment for all races was also envisaged. The Institute of Directors, noting the frequent RF statements that capital was waiting to flow into Rhodesia as soon as independence was declared, drily commented. "It seems to us that their weakness is that they convince nobody outside this country." [68]

The Rhodesia Party attempted to capitalize on these reports. A typical RP advertisement stated: "STOP THIS MADNESS. UDI has been condemned by the Institute of Directors, the Chambers of Commerce, industrialists, RTA and the Tobacco trade. This is also the view of the RP . . . Twice already the RF has gone to the brink and then pulled back. THIS TIME IT IS NO BLUFF. If they get enough encouragement on Friday, there will be a UDI. You may have been content to go along with the bluff . . . YOU CANNOT AFFORD TO GO ALONG WITH THE REALITY." [69]

In the final days of the campaign the RF did not attempt to deal seriously with the questions raised by the economic reports. Instead it launched a counterattack to impugn the motives of the business community and to downgrade the possibility of UDI. The parliamentary secretary for information, P. K. F. V. van der Byl, second only to Smith as a prominent RF campaign speaker, commonly argued that only a small fragment of Rhodesian businessmen opposed UDI. His standard argument always included an historical treatment of the mistakes made by businessmen when they attempted to influence politics. Financial mining interests in Johannesburg had always financed the Progressive Party—distinctly a lost cause; great business names had supported Hitler—a clear political error; and finally, the Bolshevik Revolution was largely financed by American big business.[70]

The Rhodesian Front issued a press statement that "whilst not questioning the validity of the arguments raised it should not, of course, be forgotten that it was ARNI and other kindred bodies that foretold disaster and doom: (a) if the Federation was destroyed; and (b) if the RF was returned to power in 1962. Their assessment can, therefore, be treated with a modicum of reserve." [71] In attempting to dispel UDI fears, UDI became in the last week of the campaign a "United Drive [or Demand] for Independence" [72] and Smith repeatedly said that "not one of the RF candidates is for UDI." [73] Harry Reedman, a cabinet minister, called UDI "an Alice in Wonderland—a 1,000 to 1 chance against." [74]

Despite the RF's attempts to cloud the issue (just as it had in the 1964 campaigns), UDI *was* an issue and the only one dividing the European electorate. The RP's position was clear: "UDI is an unnecessary and disastrous step which would do irrevocable harm to our national and personal pockets. Rhodesia is virtually independent already and derives great strength from the legality of her constitutional position." [75] The RF's position was equally plain: "If, in the future, we find ourselves heading for a takeover by extreme racialists in our midst, . . . we [will] have no option but to take matters into our own hands. Should such an eventuality arise, you will find your Government will have taken the necessary precautions and will be well prepared for what may follow." [76]

This basic position had been echoed time and time again by RF candidates; no Rhodesian citizen could fail to take cognizance of the possible outcome of an RF victory. Smith succinctly summed up the position on April 20 when he said that if negotiations failed, Rhodesia would be forced "to take it, seize it, assume it, . . . call it what you will, the end result is exactly the same." [77]

Much of the viciousness which dominated the Welensky by-election bid had subsided because of the RF's confidence and the RP's lack of hope. Still, there was heavy RF heckling, and RP meetings were generally disrupted and often closed by three cheers for "good old Smithy." Question time, an important part of all meetings, generally ran smoothly although critics of the RF rarely found a receptive audience; most whites preferred to accept the RF viewpoint without question.

Unlike the A-roll campaign with its frequent meetings and intense feelings, the B-roll campaign was largely a phantom affair. Few meetings were held and there was uniform disinterest in all candidates. Both banned African nationalist parties urged all Africans not to participate.[78] Participation was limited to RP Africans plus a variety of African "independents"—many secretly financed and supported by the RF. Dr. Ahrn Palley, the white Highfield incumbent, was the best-known B-roll candidate.

For the RP, contesting the B-roll seats was a corollary to its desire for "moderate" African support for its white party. The RP's eight-page published policy statement, however, devoted only one paragraph to African matters; it simply noted that urbanization and detribalization was occurring and assured the Europeans that "the Party's realistic policies will guard against the real danger that such people will continue to become embittered nationalists." [79]

The RF's public position was nonsupport of B-roll candidates. The party, in direct opposition to the theory of the constitution and its cross-voting procedure, had come to view the B-roll as a guarantee of racial representation and felt these members should be free from the domination of a European party.[80] This position, however, more accurately reflected the RF's minimal support among Africans (all 15 RF B-roll candidates had lost in 1962) and its confidence about the A-roll results. In addition, not contesting the B-roll seats left open the possibility of bringing chiefs into parliament, since the RF would not be committed to elected party members on the B-roll. The RF did in fact secretly support "the more moderate and responsive" candidate in each district, not so much with victory in mind, but simply to confuse the issue and perhaps to cause a few RP candidates to lose.[81] Any "independent" Africans who supported the RF in parliament would be added insurance in case the RP made unexpected gains on the A-roll and would be useful if the RF could claim to Britain that it had support from elected Africans as well as chiefs.

The chiefs urged Africans to participate in the election and throughout the campaign, "prominent members of the Chiefs Council" (invariably unnamed) made strong press appeals to the African voters not to ignore the coming election. In the chiefs' view, "half a loaf was better than none," and they urged support for the government.[82]

On election day the RP was a party without a public (see Table 10). The Rhodesian Front won all 50 A-roll seats. Its majorities ran from 318 in urban Willowvale to 1,200 in rural Lomagundi. The average swing to the RF from the 1962 election was 28.9 percent.[83] If anything, the RP vote of 19.0 percent overvalued the party's actual strength. The 25 seats it contested included all those where it had incumbents. In Hartley and Lomagundi, where the RP tried to fight rural seats, the RF received 88.0 and 86.5 percent of the vote respectively.

Table 10. 1965 Rhodesian general election: summary of constituency results.

	A-roll	Percent	B-roll	Percent	Total	Percent	Seats won
Registered voters	97,284		11,577		108,861		
Registered voters in 28 contested constituencies	55,025		5,656		60,681		
Number voting and percent participation	35,506	64.5	719	12.7	36,225	59.7	
Rhodesian Front	28,165	79.2	206	28.6	28,371	78.3	50
Rhodesia Party	6,377	18.1	509	70.8	6,886	19.0	0
Independent	964	2.7	4	0.6	968	2.7	0

SOURCE: *Rhodesia Herald,* May 10, 1965; *SRLAD,* vol. 61 (July 21, 1965), 1215–1218; and *Central African Examiner,* June 1965. Computations done by the author.

As far as the electoral districts were concerned, the RP won 12 of 15 seats. The tiny group of African schoolteachers, ministers, government employees, nurses, and purchase area farmers who had been registered on the B-roll in 1961–1962 continued to support the nominal multiracialism of the RP. Table 11 compares B-roll voting patterns in 1962 and 1965.

Far more impressive than the RP's 12 victories was the almost uniform success of the B-roll boycott. Only 14.4 percent of registered voters in contested districts participated—a 10 percent drop from the already low 1962 poll. Nationalist pressure provides only a partial answer to the question posed by this African apathy. Although they called for a boycott, the nationalists really had little at stake in its success or failure. The difference between 10 and 50 percent B-roll participation was irrelevant when less than 1 percent of the African population was enfranchised at all. A more appropriate explanation was African rejection of the 1961 constitution. The blacks did not have to

Table 11. Electoral district B-roll voting in the 1962
and 1965 Rhodesian elections.

	1962 election			1965 election [a]		
	Votes	Percent	Seats won	Votes	Percent	Seats won
Registered B-roll voters	10,632			11,577		
Number voting	2,577	24.2		1,443	14.4 [b]	
United Federal Party— Rhodesia Party votes	1,870	72.6	14	754	52.3	10
Rhodesian Front votes	306	11.9	0	232 [c]	16.1	2
Independent	401	15.5	1	457	31.6	3

SOURCE: *Rhodesia Herald*, May 10, 1965; *SRLAD*, vol. 61 (July 21, 1965), 1215–1218; *Central African Examiner*, June 1965; and F. M. G. Willson, ed., *Source Book of Parliamentary Elections and Referenda in Southern Rhodesia 1898–1962* (Salisbury, University College of Rhodesia and Nyasaland, 1963), pp. 190–191. Computations done by the author.

[a] In 1965 A-roll voters cast a total of 31,036 votes in the districts, which devalued to 339 votes. In no district did the A-roll devalued vote alter the victor as determined by the B-roll votes.
[b] In thirteen contested districts. Two RP candidates were unopposed.
[c] In 1965 the RF votes refer to the independent candidates secretly supported by the RF. In three districts the RF-supported candidate was also the RP official candidate. These totals are included in the RP vote.

accept the nationalist brief to realize that their present representatives could do little for them. This attitude corresponded with the RF's desire to discredit the parliamentary and electoral process for Africans in order to accentuate the importance of the chiefs. Finally, lest we be tempted to read anything into the B-roll figures regarding African support for European parties, it is worth remembering that in a country of four million Africans, the difference between 754 and 232 votes is hardly significant.

Excessive racial fear and complete hostility to African advancement permeates every aspect of Rhodesian life. This is the only way to explain fully the crushing defeat of the RP—a party pledged to a restricted franchise, school segregation, maintenance of law and order in the Rhodesian manner, and substantial land apportionment.

The RF convinced the electorate that there was no "Third Choice." Either independence was achieved (in any fashion) or a black government was inevitable. Since the RP had no answer to the question, "What will you do if negotiations fail?," its attitude was seen as equivocal and weak-willed. The RP hoped that the economic memoranda would have an effect and that Britain would publicly announce proposed independence terms (which the RP tended to view as acceptable), but Britain was not prepared to show its hand until agreement was certain or found impossible. The RP's wildly flung charges—no useless bluffing, no censorship, no blank check, no one-party state—could not begin to hit home in the harsh political climate which it had done so much to engender.

For white Rhodesians there was no doubt that the Rhodesian Front had come to be seen as the party of hope. As unlikely as this might seem to outsiders, Smith and the RF had consolidated the white electorate. Rigid inflexibility was a stance equated with strength, and the RF self-righteously and self-confidently could now push ahead. Following the election the essential similarity of the two parties was conspicuously revealed when the RP disbanded rather than continue in operation under African parliamentary leadership.[84]

The Taking of UDI

The massive mandate for "independence without strings" set the stage for a unilateral declaration of independence. The six months between the election and the event itself were taken up by Rhodesian attempts to badger Britain into giving way and by various British efforts to ward off the inevitable. Following the election, Smith and his cabinet faced increased party pressure to get moving on the independence question. An inconclusive visit to Salisbury by Cledwyn Hughes, minister of state in the commonwealth relations office, sparked discontent over the possibility that party leaders were straying from RF principles in an effort to reach agreement with Britain. These fears were first voiced in *The Citizen,* an independent Salisbury weekly newspaper, which normally supported the most conservative elements of the RF.[85] Rumors reached such a peak that Smith had the RF chairman, Lt. Col. W. M. Knox, release the following statement:

> I called on the Prime Minister this morning and received his personal assurance firstly that the Government was not contemplating any action which could be construed as contravening the principles and policies of the RF, and secondly that independence, whether it comes through negotiations or not, would be—to use a colloquial expression —without strings.[86]

Smith defended the government's policy at the annual RF congress in August:

> If we had to take matters into our own hands 12 months ago, it would have proved disastrous. It would have failed miserably and it would have been the end of this Government and the Rhodesia we know. Even six months ago, while we had strengthened our case, it would still have been doubtful. I am pleased to tell you that today, if we were forced to resort to such action, not only can we carry this out with complete safety inside Rhodesia, as far as the external position is concerned we have far more sympathy and support and even a guarantee of official recognition as far as certain external countries are concerned.[87]

That Smith should feel compelled to release a statement asserting his fidelity to RF principles was indicative of heavy party pressure demanding a decision one way or another. The implication of this pressure, however, was not to free Smith for wide-ranging meaningful discussions with the British, but to tighten the lines of control between the party and its leaders. Once UDI was seen as an acceptable end to negotiations, there was little negotiating room. Any compromise formula would be termed a sellout, and no RF leader could have survived such a charge.

Following the Hughes visit negotiations quickly lapsed into a new round of mutual recriminations. During this July–August period the RF leadership apparently decided to take UDI if a last attempt at negotiations proved fruitless. This hard attitude was directly expressed to Bottomley on September 15:

> I [Smith] must make it very clear to you that if you do visit us for discussions those discussions must reach final decisions . . . No good purpose would be served by . . . further exploratory talks or general discussions without a mandate . . . The hardening of our views . . . is very real and serious . . . Our planting season, which affects our all-important agricultural industry, is upon us, and before planting, our farmers expect and are entitled to a decision on our independence.[88]

The discussion surrounding the proposed Bottomley visit soon collapsed and was replaced by a major Rhodesian mission to London for what the Rhodesian government insisted must be "final and conclusive" talks. Accompanying Smith to London were W. J. Harper, minister of internal affairs; D. Lardner-Burke, minister of justice; and J. J. Wrathall, minister of finance. Talks were held between October 5 and 11, 1965. Britain's five principles formed the basis for the lengthy discussions. The result was, as Prime Minister Wilson put it, that "on every one of the five principles the disagreement is almost total, absolute." [89] The Rhodesian government offered to establish a Senate composed of

African chiefs as its major concession to African political advance. It claimed it had already demonstrated that the majority of Rhodesians wanted independence on the 1961 constitution, and it refused to agree to repeal of the Land Apportionment Act.[90]

It was on the first principle (the guarantee and implementation of un-impeded progress to majority rule) that critical disagreement took place. Britain now considered it essential that Africans hold at least one-third of the House seats in order to prevent the RF from altering the A-roll/B-roll ratio. The Rhodesians adamantly refused to forego this important control over African political advance. They refused to set any time limits as to when an African majority would be achieved or to countenance any effort (such as massive aid to education) which would speed up the process of getting Africans onto the A-roll. Indeed the Rhodesian government openly and strenuously insisted that it must retain its prerogative to set the rules, regulations, and timing for the emergence of an African government. Brigadier Andrew Skeen, Rhodesian high commissioner in London during the months before UDI, wrote:

> We in Rhodesia . . . were determined to control the rate of African political advancement to power till time and education had made it a safe possibility. Moreover we wished to have the power to retard it, should that advancement outstrip the capability of the African to govern wisely and fairly . . . We could not say five, ten, fifty or a thousand years. It could not be forced, it had to develop in accordance with the character and nature of the African and his hitherto unproved qualities of democratic behaviour.[91]

The Rhodesian position was unrelenting.

The British had two responses to the Rhodesian demands. The first was punitive. Wilson stated again and again, publicly and privately, that the British government would not stand idly by if Rhodesia declared independence. To little avail, Britain attempted to explain how its world role would not allow Rhodesia to go unpunished. Yet the threat of sanctions was not enough to deter the Rhodesian government; with 75 years of British concessions to white interests behind them, it is not surprising that the RF was skeptical of British threats.

The second British response was to make concessions. It is fair to say that negotiations were spun out for so long only because the British continued to yield ground. By the time the London talks were over, Britain was prepared to offer independence to a minority government with only a slim one-vote margin in the legislative assembly to guard against retrogressive amendments. She was ready to forego land apportionment changes and the release of political prisoners and restrictees within Rhodesia. There was to be no change in A-roll qualifications. Literally the only strong point which the British retained lay in the fifth principle—that the independence proposals be acceptable to the people of Rhodesia as a whole. Despite these major concessions, the two sides could not reach agreement. A joint communique on October 11 stated, "No means have been found of reconciling the opposing views. No further meeting has been arranged." [92]

The stage was clearly set for UDI, and Smith said in a final London press conference, "Having considered all the problems most carefully, in the end we came to the conclusion that if we have to go down—get out of our country—we would rather go fighting than go out crawling on our hands and knees." [93] Wilson was reduced to pleading, "I beg you yet again, . . . for the sake of your country, for the sake of Africa and for the sake of future generations of all races, to pause before bringing hardship and misery, perhaps even worse, to your own people and to countless others . . . who have no power to influence your decision but whose lives may be gravely affected by it." [94] Nevertheless, the RF went ahead inexorably with preparations for a unilateral declaration of independence set for October 25 or 26.[95]

In a final desperate effort to ward off UDI, Prime Minister Wilson flew to Salisbury for more discussions. The Rhodesian government stood firm on its London terms and once again no agreement was reached.[96] Wilson, in an unexpectedly candid statement, finally admitted that the heretofore sacrosanct 1961 constitution *could* impede progress to majority rule.[97] The talks ended with Britain suggesting a Royal Commission to review the acceptability of the 1961 constitution to all Rhodesians. This marked another concession, for it meant indirect, rather than direct, consultation with Africans on independence. The two governments, however, could not even agree on the Royal Commission's terms of reference.

Apart from negotiations, Wilson pursued two other objectives in Rhodesia. He spent considerable time with the African nationalist leaders, trying to reconcile them to working together within the constitutional framework.[98] He also appealed over the head of the RF to white Rhodesians in an effort to convince them that nationalist rule or UDI were not their sole alternatives. These efforts were bluntly summarized in a parting news conference:

> I have had to tell them [the African nationalists] . . . and it was a bitter pill for them to swallow, that their demand for Britain to attempt to settle all Rhodesia's constitutional problems with a military invasion is out . . . A thunderbolt in the shape of the Royal Air Force . . . will not be coming . . . The British government . . . does not believe in the present and tragic and divided condition of Rhodesia, that majority rule can or should come today or tomorrow. A period of time is needed, time to remove the fears and suspicions between race and race . . . and the time required cannot be mea-

sured by clock or calendar but only by achievement. There are others who feel that Rhodesians can take the law into their own hands . . . I want you to realise, we have a responsibility for Rhodesia, which we cannot escape or evade . . . In financial terms, in economic terms —for I have said we forswear the use of military force—we would have to do everything in our power to restore constitutional rule.[99]

Following this appeal Wilson returned to Britain, the African nationalists refused to merge, and the Rhodesian Front moved resolutely to UDI.

Fear and mistrust prevented the two governments from reaching a settlement on independence. The Smith government's hard line was an outgrowth of its belief that only negotiating weakness and lack of resolve had prevented Welensky, Field, and even Huggins from achieving independence at an earlier date. Smith and his ministers also reflected the RF's demand for independence without strings. All of the RF ministers were too busy looking over their shoulders at the party militants to accept the massive concessions which Britain was prepared to offer. This stance prevented the RF from joining Britain in a serious bargaining effort.

Wilson faced an equally complex dilemma. The British government had shouldered full responsibility for Rhodesia without having any means of enforcing or implementing her will. The Rhodesian police, army, and civil service all reported to the local government. Thus, no matter how principled Britain's five points were on paper, their substance was of little worth unless fully acceptable to the Rhodesian government or enforced by the British government. With Britain promising at every opportunity not to use force against Rhodesia, it was clear that the British position was built on sand.

Leaving aside Rhodesia's free hand internally, the weakness of the British position was apparent in September 1965 when Britain was unable to prevent a Rhodesian diplomatic mission from being established in Lisbon despite intense pressure on the Portuguese government.[100] Wilson's trump card was not what he could threaten to do to Rhodesia, but that he could offer her such generous terms. It was clear that Wilson was prepared to forego some commonwealth support and accept the possibility of a left-wing Labour Party revolt in order to divest himself of the onerous Rhodesian problem. He could always count on Conservative votes to support any settlement. All that Britain demanded in the end were the verbal niceties of compromise and the solemn diplomatic sounds of concession and agreement. But the Rhodesian government was too blinded by its slogans about standards, civilization, and the Land Apportionment Act to distinguish between victory and defeat.[101] It preferred the uncertainties of UDI to Britain's minimal terms for settlement. The RF had convinced itself and its public that UDI was the only choice if Britain did not accede to its demands. Since the only alternative envisioned was a "racialist black dictatorship," it is perhaps not surprising that this choice was made.

The timing was carefully considered. The October–November period came just at the end of the tobacco-selling season. Full revenues for 1965 were in, and in the event of tobacco sanctions Rhodesia would have four full months, a maximum time period, to make selling adjustments before her major export again came up for sale.[102] Further, UDI was scheduled to occur in the middle of the day, when African population at work in the urban centers was widely dispersed and not together in the townships where trouble would be more likely to break out. Finally, in perhaps unconscious realization that UDI might not be the "three-day wonder" that Smith had predicted, it was set for a Thursday, not a Friday.

The Rhodesian government justified UDI as a step needed to achieve political self-respect and to erase economic uncertainty. Independence was seen as the only way African nationalists could be forced to cease their direct lobbying of the British government for political redress; the implication here, of course, was that under local jurisdiction the African nationalists could be permanently contained.[103]

The decision for UDI was a cabinet one—fervent party support was well established and the only remaining question was that of timing. The most reliable breakdown of votes within the cabinet seems to have been six for UDI immediately (Dupont, Lardner-Burke, Lord Graham, Mussett, Rudland, and van Heerden) and six against (Ian Smith, A. P. Smith, Harper, Howman, Mclean, and Wrathall).[104] Ian Smith then cast a deciding vote for UDI. In the end he preferred to opt for UDI rather than expose himself to party criticism (and possible ouster) for being afraid of Britain.

The single consideration that overrode all the fears about UDI was the endlessly-given British pledge that force would never be used against Rhodesia.[105] How serious Britain was about sanctions was a subject of deep disagreement and even worry, but if the RF deprecated the reports on the economic consequences of UDI, at least it had the information at hand. Even though it disdained world opinion, it did know that hostility was likely. The fact that clearly emerges is that the RF was confident that it could survive sanctions and ride out the political storm.

In the final days before UDI, the government restricted Garfield Todd (the former prime minister) to his farm for one year, withdrew Reserve Bank statistics from publication, gave the police a pay raise, instituted wide-ranging import curbs, and declared a nationwide state of emergency. The emergency declaration allowed for sweeping controls covering all aspects of political, civil, and economic life including full police powers of 30-day detention (without access to legal guidance) and total censorship of everything published within Rhodesia. The governor, Sir Humphrey Gibbs, signed the emergency proclamation on November 5 because he was guaranteed that UDI was not in the offing.[106] Six days later, on November 11, 1965, Ian Douglas Smith began droning over the Rhodesian Broadcasting Corporation:

> Whereas in the course of human affairs history has shown that it may become necessary for a people to resolve the political affiliations which have connected them with another people and to assume amongst other nations the separate and equal status to which they are entitled . . .[107]

With all its attendant perils and hopes, UDI had come. It remained to be seen whether Rhodesia's strategy was correct and that "civilised standards" were thus assured or whether UDI had in reality opened the way for new political pressures on Rhodesia—pressures which might be more determined than Britain to break the 75-year control of Rhodesia by whites.

5

The Rhodesian Front:
Political Power in
Contemporary Rhodesia

A unilateral declaration of independence was possible only because of the firm support given the Rhodesian Front by the white population. The party led Rhodesia to UDI and since then has successfully resisted the wide variety of pressures designed to break its control within Rhodesia. The RF is the first Rhodesian party to mobilize whites into an effective political organization and involve them in public policy decisions. Huggins, Welensky, Whitehead, Todd—none of these prime ministers ever built (or even tried to build) a party organization that lasted more than a month or two before and after elections. Once elected, all (to somewhat differing degrees) felt free to make nearly any political decision without reference to anyone, except perhaps a few senior colleagues. The style of Winston Field, the first RF prime minister, in many ways followed these earlier practices. He did not, however, reckon with the party organization that had been created. It removed him with ease and brought in Ian Smith. This change in 1964, far more than the political party shift in the 1962 election, constituted the real internal revolution in white Rhodesian politics. Decision-making within the white community became more complex and more inflexible.

Little is known about the internal politics of the RF, the organization that has been built, or the way it makes its decisions. Without this knowledge it is difficult to make informed judgments about the actions taken by the party. That we lack this information is not surprising; the party is secretive and hesitant about opening its doors to strangers. Nevertheless, this door must be pried at least partially open if we are to have any idea of how Rhodesia is really governed.[1]

The Rhodesian Front Organization

The dominant internal struggle within the RF since its formation has been the effort by the party rank-and-file to gain effective control of the decision-making apparatus, and through this control to make its will as binding as possible upon the RF governing leadership. Through the party organization the members have endeavored to narrow the limits within which the leaders could maneuver regarding the implementation of RF principles and policies. In organizational terms, this has meant that the party rank-and-file have demanded constant intraparty communication, a strong party machine with close ties to the government, and, in effect, weak rather than strong ministers. The RF organization is a product of this jockeying for influence and bears witness to the success of the party members in building their strength within the party and vis-à-vis the government.

The Rhodesian Front experienced rapid growth at its inception. From an initial "foundation" membership of less than a thousand, the size of the party has increased as follows: March 1962—1,000; December 1962—9,000; May 1965—15,000; and December 1968—18,000. Membership has fallen off somewhat since then but remains between 10 and 15 percent of the European electorate. Membership figures need not mean very much. While the former United Federal Party boasted large party enrollments, its organization came to life only to fight elections. The RF, on the other hand, from its inception encouraged the participation of white Rhodesians in party activities. At its founding the party named itself a "Front" in an effort to underline its interest in embracing as many participants as possible. The reasons for its success are manifold, but the critical one is that the RF articulated the right program at the right time, thus providing an initial focus for widespread discontent, and then retained the people it attracted by making good on its promise of participation and consultation.

In the early days anyone could become a member simply upon application, as long as two party members supported the applicant. Even this minor condition, however, served to give a note of formality to the joining process that was new in Rhodesian politics. Electoral success made party membership more important. The perquisites of power passed to the RF; patronage, nominations, and access to the decision-making process opened to those who were active in the party. Suddenly, to have been a "foundation" member of the RF meant something.

The major surge of membership came in two waves—during the 1962 election campaign and just following the RF victory, and in 1964–1965 following the defeat of Sir Roy Welensky. The latter event (October 1964) confirmed to everyone's satisfaction that the RF was firmly entrenched in power; the UFP-RP disintegrated rapidly. There was a consequent onrush of people eager to join the RF for essentially careerist reasons, much as many people had once perfunctorily belonged to the United Federal Party. The older RF members reacted coolly toward these newcomers, and membership regulations tightened in 1965. Applications for party membership were altered so that each application had to be countersigned by the constituency council chairman, the branch chairman, and one other party member of at least two years' standing. Further, no person joining the party after March 1, 1965, was to be eligible for election to national office for three years if he had previously belonged to another Rhodesian political party and for two years in any other case. Finally, all new applicants were required to be both citizens and registered voters. This last provision was inserted to exclude people who live permanently in Rhodesia but found it convenient to retain citizenship and passports from other countries.

All party members belong to a branch, and it is at this level that most party members participate in the RF organization. A branch is established whenever twenty or more party members come together; most branches are much larger. Geographic proximity generally governs the size of the branch. In tightly knit urban constituencies there is often a single branch which doubles as the constituency council; in outlying rural areas there are generally several branches per constituency. Overall there are approximately 165 branches, an average of three to four per constituency.[2]

Each branch has officers and a branch committee made up of party members not in the government (that is, not members of parliament). This reservation of jobs and responsibilities for nongovernmental party activists is repeated at all levels of the party and is a unique and important feature of RF organization. The entire branch must meet at least once annually, generally in May prior to the annual divisional and national congresses. Branch committees are supposed to meet at least quarterly. Branches finance their own activities, keep their own membership rolls, and generally handle party business within their own area. The party secretariat attempts to keep track of branch activities through copies of branch minutes, which are forwarded to party headquarters, and through branch subscription fees of five pounds per month payable to the national headquarters. Branches that fail to maintain their dues can find their membership altered from full to interim status, which precludes them from voting at party gatherings or proposing members for party offices.

There are several reasons why RF branch organizations have proved a viable focal point for local political activity. One must remember the miniscule size of the European community in Rhodesia and the real sense of *national* access one can get through local participation. Rhodesia Front members of parliament (MP's) represent, on the average, only about 1,500 voters. Thus any active RF member is certain to know his MP and may easily know many others, simply through run-of-the-mill party activities. The RF MP's generally have been eager to sustain RF branches as a part of their own political base. Many meet frequently with the branch committee, and this promotes a feeling of participation and sustains branch interest. In rural areas where there are many more branches, there may be less direct contact with the MP himself, but this is compensated for by the greater social dimension of party activity and by extensive rural representation at the national level of RF policy-making.

The party has also endeavored to institutionalize the branch as a sounding board for all grievances. Branch chairmen have direct access to the national executive and national standing committee whenever the branch desires. From the annual general meetings of the branches flow the resolutions debated at the annual national congress where each branch is directly represented. By giving branches local authority for party activities and by providing regular and meaningful access to all levels of party decision-making, the RF has succeeded in building the first stable party structure in Rhodesian political history.

The national congress is the sovereign governing body of the Rhodesian Front. It meets annually after the month of July, following the earlier party meetings at branch, constituency, and divisional levels. Congresses have met rather faithfully in either September or October. The only year in which a congress has not been held was 1964, a year of such political turmoil both within Rhodesia and in her international relations that the party congress, planned for October, was postponed until early 1965.

The national congress is composed of the ten party office holders, all RF MP's, members of the party executive, and delegates appointed by the branches on the basis of one delegate per branch for the first twenty members and thereafter one delegate for each ten members with a maximum of three per branch. Observers appointed by branches and the party executive may come and speak, but not vote.

The national congress alone can change the constitution, principles, and policies of the RF. The first two require a two-thirds vote for alteration, the policies require only a majority. In practice there have been few important changes. At the 1963 congress a major restructuring of party bodies was approved, reflecting thereby the demand of party activists to play a larger role in all party undertakings. Six divisional congresses were established and interposed between the branches and the national congress. With the proliferation of branches, the early pattern of branch resolutions going directly to the national congress had become unwieldy. One function of the new divisional congresses was to filter branch resolutions before they reached the national congress. Although in some ways the divisional structure slowed the direct access of branch demands to the top, concomitant changes significantly increased lower-level access to top decision-making bodies. The six divisional chairmen were placed on the national standing committee and substantial divisional representation on the party executive was assured.

The 1965 special congress voted additional constitutional reforms. New membership regulations were adopted and numerous party positions (the six divisional chairmen, two vice-presidents, and the party chairman and his deputy, among others) were thereafter reserved for party activists outside the government. Each of these changes served to strengthen and consolidate the power of nongovernmental members.

The party principles remained unchanged from 1962 until 1967, when another special congress approved a new draft of the principles. In fact, little was changed except that references to loyalty to the Queen were deleted and replaced by "loyalty to the independent country of Rhodesia." A slightly stronger wording was given to the principle recognizing the government's right to provide separate facilities for the different racial groups. For all practical purposes, however, the RF's central principles—permanent establishment of the European in Rhodesia; maintenance of "civilized" government; continuation of segregated neighborhoods and social facilities; and preservation of European land tenure, employment, and wage privileges—remained constant.

Policies adopted at congress serve only as guidelines to governmental action. In practice it is accepted that party policies need not be implemented immediately if the government holds other considerations paramount. This flexibility has allowed the party leadership to hold the line against the more egregious resolutions that invariably come forward at each congress. The party accepted this type of delay because it usually gets what it wants; it has understood the need for tactical delay in policy implementation in the interest of Rhodesia's negotiation strategy vis-à-vis Britain, both before and after UDI.[3]

The national congress fulfills a few other functions. It sets the annual subscription fee for members (generally one pound per year) and elects the party's ten national officeholders: president, two deputy presidents, four vice-presidents, chairman, deputy chairman, and honorary treasurer. Originally there were no particular requirements for any office, but since 1965 these ten positions have been evenly divided between men in and out of the government. The officeholders are members of both the national executive and the national standing committee, the two primary party administrative bodies.

The senior administrative body of the RF is the party executive. It derives its authority from, and is responsible to, the national congress. It is empowered by the congress to act in its stead and conduct the affairs of the party between annual congresses. It establishes the administrative procedures by which the national standing committee and the party secretariat conduct the day-to-day business of the party. The national executive normally meets at least quarterly. It is composed of the 10 officeholders, all the RF MP's, and the 50 divisional representatives (not MP's).[4] At the time of this writing the executive has 105 members: the 50 RF MP's, the divisional representatives (effectively one per white constituency), and the 5 officeholders who are not MP's. The composition yields a majority to party members not in the government and it should be noted that as presently constituted, the government's share of the executive (50 of 105) is the highest percentage it could possibly have, since the RF presently holds all the parliamentary seats that it contests.

The importance of the executive has varied. Until around mid-1963, the original officers dominated party affairs to the exclusion of nearly everyone else. During Winston Field's tenure as prime minister, however, a series of events led to the formation of an intraparty coalition of caucus back-benchers and nongovernmental party activists. This coalition was directly responsible for forcing through the major 1963 party reforms, and later for the removal of Field himself. These reforms represented a critical victory for the party rank-and-file. They achieved massive representation on all party bodies and direct access to all governmental figures. In the absence of any serious parliamentary or political competition, the party organs have become the only places where the government can find itself articulately challenged on its handling of policy matters.

The National Standing Committee (NSC) is a smaller and more workable replica of the executive. Like the executive, the composition of the NSC represents a wedding of senior government ministers with the most powerful nongovernmental party leaders. It is made up of the ten officeholders, the six divisional chairmen, the chairman of the party finance committee, and four MP's selected by the caucus. Again the composition guarantees a majority to nongovernmental activists. The NSC is responsible to the executive for the day-to-day running of the party; it meets at least monthly. It is important as a point of frequent contact between the ministers and the divisional chairmen, who have emerged during the life of the RF as the most critical liaison figures between party and government. As with the executive, easy access is guaranteed to branch, constituency, and divisional representatives simply upon notice being given to the party secretariat.

The Party Finance Committee (PFC) is responsible to the executive for the management of the RF budget. It comprises the treasurer, as chosen by the congress, and six other members appointed by the executive. The committee then elects its own chairman. For nearly the entire life of the party, the PFC chairman has been D. C. ("Boss") Lilford, a party vice-president, and perhaps the wealthiest farmer in Rhodesia. Since the party annually runs on a budget exceeding 20,000 pounds per year—a figure that goes higher in election years—the PFC has considerable responsibility for raising, allocating, and investing party funds.

The executive has established permanent subcommittees, made up from the nongovernmental executive members, which parallel all governmental ministries. These executive subcommittees form a direct liaison with caucus subcommittees on all matters affecting RF policies and governmental legislation. The executive subcommittees have the power to co-opt outside experts onto their committees and have succeeded in establishing direct access to the minister on any matter within his purview. They act as a powerful vehicle through which the party keeps tabs on the various ministries. In addition, both the executive and the NSC occasionally establish ad hoc subcommittees for special projects, particularly such controversial ones as information policy, RF participation in local government, and the feasibility of UDI.

A word must be said in conclusion about the party secretariat. The RF maintains a national office in Salisbury and several regional offices. From Salisbury, under the direction of the executive and the NSC and under the on-going management of the party chairman, the party runs its affairs. As the membership of the party has expanded and the members have become more aware of their ability to influence government policy, the running of the party has become more complex. Lt. Cmdr. F. W. Bradburn was employed as a full-time general secretary from early party days until his accidental death in December 1967. In 1968 his job was split and an administrative secretary and a political/public-relations secretary hired. To date the secretariat has simply fulfilled administrative duties and not become a political force in its own right. The secretariat has no patronage or appointive powers to reshape the party in any particular image. Instead it has found its major responsibility in organizing and sustaining party branches, in keeping open channels of communication between party and government, and in moderating conflicts between party factions when they have broken out.

Power within the Party Organization

It is difficult to say with precision who are the most powerful men in the Rhodesian Front or which committee or party body has the most influence. Personnel change over the course of time and influence varies with different issues. Nevertheless, some characteristics of the RF have remained stable for a sufficient length of time to be recognized as permanent organizational attributes. Similarly, some individuals and groups have so influenced the shaping of events through their RF activities that they should be briefly mentioned.

It has been a traditional practice in Rhodesian electoral delimitation to overweigh rural representation. The constitution requires that at least 18 of the 50 electoral constituencies be rural, but this has proved difficult to do and still keep constituences at roughly the same size, because the European population is substantially urban. The dilemma is currently resolved by calling two Salisbury suburban constituencies rural. This legerdemain gives an official breakdown of 31 urban and 19 rural constituencies, a breakdown that still conceals the predominantly urban cast of much of the electorate in other "rural" constituencies (particularly Wankie, Victoria, and Shabani).

A realistic appraisal of the 50 electoral constituencies would give a total of 33 urban (66 percent) and 17 rural (34 percent). This is not too far from the national breakdown, which classifies the European population as about 76 to 77 percent urban. These urban-rural ratios are not even remotely duplicated by RF branch organizations, for the urban areas maintain 63 branches and the rural areas 102 (see Tables 12 and 13).

It is readily apparent that rural representation within the RF far outweighs its numerical proportion of the population. The rural constituencies have far more branches, and therefore far more voting weight, than the urban areas. In fact, the single division Mashonaland Rural (which surrounds Salisbury and contains Rhodesia's richest tobacco and maize farmlands) has more than one-third of the party's branches and voting strength, even though it has only 15.7 percent of the European population. The rural divisions uniformly have more branches per voter than the urban divisions. Overall, the 17 rural constituencies have 25,108 European voters and 102 branches (one per 246 voters), and

Table 12. Rural-urban breakdown of Rhodesian
Front party organization, 1967.

Rhodesian Front division (location)	Rural constit- uencies	Rural branches	Urban constit- uencies	Urban branches
Manicaland (east)	2	19	2	3
Mashonaland Rural (near Salisbury)	8	57	0	2
Salisbury East	0	0	9	21
Salisbury West	0	0	10	18
Midlands (central)	4	15	2	4
Matabeleland (near Bulawayo and west)	3	11	10	15
Total	17(34%)	102(62%)	33(66%)	63(38%)

Table 13. Party branches per Rhodesian Front division
and European voter, 1967.

Division	No. of European voters[a]	Percent	Party branches	Percent	Voters per branch (average)
Manicaland	5,551	7.1	22	13.3	1 per 252
Mashonaland Rural	12,354	15.7	59	35.8	1 per 209
Salisbury East	15,361	19.5	21	12.7	1 per 732
Salisbury West	17,136	21.8	18	10.9	1 per 952
Midlands	8,414	10.7	19	11.5	1 per 443
Matabeleland	19,832	25.2	26	15.8	1 per 763
Total	78,648	100.0	165	100.0	1 per 476

[a] *SRLAD,* vol. 67 (May 19, 1967), 1143–1144.

the 33 urban constituencies have 53, 540 European voters and 63 branches (one per 834 voters).

Part of this disproportion results from valid organizational considerations. Rural constituencies often incorporate huge areas where it would be impractical for all RF supporters to constitute a single branch. Therefore branches are established in small rural centers which service the surrounding farms or ranches. In urban areas, however, an entire constituency may only incorporate a few dozen square blocks and a single large branch can easily suffice. Another important reason for the rural bias is that the party's early base was in rural sections of the country where its rigid defense of land apportionment was particularly popular. A third reason might well be that all party chairmen so far have had close ties to the farming community and farmers have always been the most prominent party financial supporters.

The rural bias is repeated in all other sectors of the party. Representation in the party executive closely follows the constituency breakdown, that is, about one-third rural. The caucus has been heavily weighted toward farmers and ranchers. Eighteen of the fifty MP's elected for the RF in 1965 came from this occupational category, far in excess of their proportion of the total European population. Finally, both RF prime ministers have been farmers: Winston Field was one of the most prominent tobacco farmers in the country, and Ian Smith, though primarily a politician all his life, maintains a ranch near his home in Selukwe.

It is difficult to determine the political or policy implications of this systematic overweighting of rural interests, because rural interests do not differ greatly from urban ones in the context of Rhodesian politics. The Rhodesian political system sustains itself by uniting whites along racial lines against all foes rather than splitting itself along class or social lines. Nonetheless, Rhodesian Europeans in rural areas have always led resistance to any internal or external compromises that would threaten European control of the political system. The thrust of most resolutions from the branches mirrors this rural determination to resist any threat to their narrow and well-defined goals. Party policy since 1962 has reflected these demands by the increasingly stringent enforcement of land segregation and by tightening controls over other areas of interracial contact. UDI was nothing if not the ultimate act in defense of these policies. It is inconceivable that the RF would continue in its present form if rural residents were not convinced that the party and its leadership were serving their specific interests.

A group invariably at the center of all party decision-making is that comprising the ten national officeholders. They are elected each year by the congress in elections which, aside from the president, are often hotly contested. There has been considerable continuity in high party office, as seen in Table 14. Ian Smith, Lord Graham, and D. C. ("Boss") Lilford have held positions since the inception of the Rhodesian Front. Several other figures have held positions for a number of consecutive years. Largely through the guidance of these officers, the party functions between congresses; and substantially because of the good working relations that have evolved, party and government have maintained close and stable relations.

The party chairmen have played an important role. The first chairman, Clifford Dupont, was without question one of the two or three most important men in the RF until UDI. At that time he became the "Officer Administering the Government" (thus assuming the functions of governor for the rebelling regime), and his subsequent party activities have been less prominent. As chairman in 1962, however, he was responsible for building the early party organization, designing campaign strategy, and providing the verve necessary to convince a somewhat ragged band of perpetual losers that they could win. Dupont became Field's deputy prime minister and held other important portfolios until UDI. Many consider Dupont the real instigator and driving force behind independence.

The second chairman was Fred Alexander, Rhodesian-born and the most prominent cotton grower in Rhodesia. He took on the chairmanship when Dupont entered the cabinet. Alexander's tenure was less successful than Dupont's, and in 1965 he was eased out and given a parliamentary seat. Discontent with Alexander arose from a variety of personal and political factors that need not be related here. Most important about his tenure was his advocacy of party activism and his willingness to support the various party reforms already described. In a speech delivered at the 1963 party congress, Alexander told the congress (and implicitly warned Field and the other ministers) that the party must guard against the head taking complete control of the animal and sup-

Table 14. Rhodesian Front officers, 1962–1971.

	President	Deputy President	Deputy President	Vice-President (MP)	Vice-President (MP)
1962	Winston Field	W. Cary	Ian Smith	Lord Graham	None
1963	Winston Field	W. Cary	Ian Smith	Lord Graham	J. Gaunt
1965[a]	Ian Smith	Clifford Dupont	William Harper	Lord Graham	W. Cary
1966	Ian Smith	Lord Graham	William Harper	John Wrathall	W. Cary
1967	Ian Smith	Lord Graham	William Harper	John Wrathall	W. Cary
1968	Ian Smith	Lord Graham	John Wrathall	Desmond Lardner-Burke	W. Cary
1969	Ian Smith	Lord Graham	John Wrathall	Desmond Lardner-Burke	D. Smith
1970	Ian Smith	Lord Graham	John Wrathall	Desmond Lardner-Burke	D. Smith
1971	Ian Smith	Lord Graham	John Wrathall	Desmond Lardner-Burke	D. Smith

	Vice-President (non-MP)	Vice-President (non-MP)	Chairman	Deputy Chairman	Treasurer
1962	D. C. Lilford	None	Clifford Dupont	D. Tanner	Unknown
1963	D. C. Lilford	I. McLean	Fred Alexander	C. Phillips	Unknown
1965[a]	D. C. Lilford	S. N. Eastwood	W. M. Knox	C. Phillips	Unknown
1966	D. C. Lilford	S. N. Eastwood	W. M. Knox	Ralph Nilson	D. McAllister
1967	D. C. Lilford	S. N. Eastwood	W. M. Knox	Ralph Nilson	D. McAllister
1968	D. C. Lilford	O. Robertson	Ralph Nilson	W. de Kock	Unknown
1969	D. C. Lilford	G. Rudland	Ralph Nilson	W. de Kock	Unknown
1970	D. C. Lilford	G. Rudland	Ralph Nilson	W. de Kock	Unknown
1971	D. C. Lilford	Ralph Nilson	Desmond Frost	H. Coleman	Unknown

[a] No congress was held in 1964. The requirement that two vice-presidents, the party chairman, and the deputy chairman not be members of parliament was instituted in 1965.

pressing any expression by the tail. He added that "if the Party is to carry out its proper functions and to succeed in keeping control of the Government, here at congress is the place to allow full scale debate and, it is imperative that the Prime Minister, the Cabinet, and the MPs take heed of the matters resolved." [5] Finally, Alexander's dedication to the farmers of Mashonaland should be noted. During his chairmanship branches sprouted up much faster in Mashonaland Rural constituencies than elsewhere. This remains a prominent legacy of Alexander's work.

The third chairman, Lt. Col. W. M. Knox, ran the party in a much different way than his two predecessors. Less a political figure, Knox tended to be Smith's man at the helm of the party. This relationship, which might have been awkward in some circumstances, worked well because the building of the party had largely been accomplished by Dupont and Alexander and the party was prepared to accept consolidation following the 1965 election triumph. The circumstances surrounding UDI and the resulting sanctions war also made it imperative, from the party and the government's perspective, to avoid internal dissension if possible and to conceal it when it occurred. Knox's close ties to Smith and broad personal acceptance by nearly all party members made stable relations possible despite some quite trying times. Knox was particularly instrumental in smoothing over party discontent following the British-Rhodesian constitutional talks in December 1966. This discontent was revealed in an internal party memorandum which insinuated that Smith was selling the party out and that senior ministers were using UDI as an excuse to avoid intraparty consultation and the implementation of RF policies.[6] In 1968, when the party divided over the new constitutional proposals, Knox eased himself out and he is now Rhodesia's top diplomat in Lisbon.

Ralph Nilson, chairman from 1968 to 1971, and Desmond Frost, the current chairman, resemble Dupont and Alexander more than Knox. Both are Mashonaland farmers with a long history of party activism. Both are men of strong views and were less likely than Knox to be a moderating influence if serious disagreements broke out within the party. At the 1970 party congress, Nilson did not hesitate to warn the government against "complacency, intolerance of criticism and departing from laid down party policy." [7]

The six divisional chairmen should be mentioned. Their prominence developed gradually until, throughout the 1968–1969 crisis within the party over the new constitution, they played an absolutely critical role in shaping the new proposals and in keeping the party together despite substantial disagreement. Both Nilson and Frost were promoted from divisional chairman to party chairman, so there is every likelihood that the new prominence of the divisional chairmen will continue.

The parliamentary caucus is an important body in RF activities. All caucus members sit on the party executive and nine of their number are on the national standing committee. In addition, from their ranks, which number only 50, are drawn the entire cabinet and government of Rhodesia. In practice around 20 caucus members (40 percent) are either ministers, deputy ministers, or parliamentary officers.

Considerable solidarity exists among the members of the caucus, particularly the back-benchers. They meet regularly, both with and without their ministerial colleagues, whenever parliament is in session. Almost without exception the back-benchers consider themselves influential as a group, and substantial evidence justifies their assertion. The back-benchers derive much of their importance from the close personal and organizational ties which most have established with the party organization and with the activists within their own constituencies. Most RF MP's have local roots in the party organization before they are even nominated, as the party pays considerable deference to local constituency council wishes regarding nominations. Few MP's fail to maintain local organizations once they are elected. These close ties were most convincingly revealed in 1964 when the back-bench (overwhelmingly supported by party activists in and out of the executive) forced the cabinet to remove Winston Field. The implications of this incident still shape most aspects of intraparty relations.

Because the RF lacks parliamentary opposition, it may be useful to profile briefly the full caucus as a way of suggesting further some of the biases of the RF organization. Like most political organizations the Rhodesian Front attempts to find candidates who represent most important aspects of local life—within the white community, of course. Inasmuch as the European population is most distinguishable by its homogeneity, this is not too hard to achieve. Although the white population is over 80 percent Protestant, the RF still manages to include Catholic and Jewish candidates. The Afrikaners and Greeks, as small nationality subgroups, are also represented.

As far as occupational background is concerned, the caucus reflects a rural bias. Table 15 compares the economically active European population and the RF candidates at the 1962 and 1965 elections. This table should be used as a rough guide only, because many RF candidates are successful (and even occasionally unsuccessful) in several fields of occupational endeavor, but have been listed for only one occupation. Professionals, administrators, and farmers comprise the overwhelming majority of RF candidates. Even though the party draws heavy support from white artisans and laborers, few candidates have come from this occupational sector. Women also are underrepresented; there has never been a female RF MP, although one woman, Olive Robertson, was a candidate in 1962 and was elected a party vice-president in 1968.

Rogers and Frantz found in their study of racial attitudes in Rhodesia that the longer Europeans live in Rhodesia, the more conservative they become in their attitudes toward race relations.[8] While this generalization need not hold true for MP's, nonetheless RF MP's tend to have

Table 15. Occupational structure of Europeans in Rhodesia compared to
Rhodesian Front candidates in 1962 and 1965.

Occupation	European working population		RF candidates 1962		RF candidates 1965	
	Number	Percent	Number	Percent	Number	Percent
Professional, including engineers, teachers, and accountants	14,535	15.1	13	26	16	32
Managers and directors	10,466	10.9	10	20	9	18
Clerical	25,828	26.9	0	0	0	0
Sales	8,291	8.6	2	4	0	0
Farmers-ranchers	8,066	8.4	18	36	17	34
Labor, transport, communications	20,795	21.6	2	4	2	4
Other	8,136	8.5	5	10	6	12
Total	96,117[a]	100.0	50	100	50	100

SOURCE: *1961 Census of the European, Asian and Coloured Population*, pp. 51–61.

[a] This total comprises 65,342 males and 30,775 females. The vast majority of the females are engaged in clerical work, teaching, nursing, or sales.

been in Rhodesia longer than the overall European population, far more than half of which has either been born or arrived in Rhodesia since the end of World War II. Table 16 compares the MP's elected in 1965 with the rest of the white population by length of time in Rhodesia.

The remaining seven members of the RF caucus were born in Rhodesia. Their percentage of the caucus (14 percent) cannot be fairly compared with the percentage of the European population born in Rhodesia (77,453 or 35.0 percent), for the Rhodesian-born population is largely made up of children. If the percentage of Rhodesian-born Europeans over the age of 29 is compared with the percentage of Rhodesian-born MP's, however, we find again that the caucus overrepresents Rhodesians who have been longest in the country. Only 5.6 percent of the Rhodesian-born white population is over 29 years of age.

These figures are interesting, but it is hard to demonstrate their usefulness in explaining the pathology of Rhodesian white politics. To say that professionals are more liberal than farmers, or that old-timers are more conservative than newcomers, is relevant only if it can be shown that the two categories (liberal-conservative) are substantively different in the context of Rhodesian white politics.[9] In fact, the regimentation of African life and the repression of African politics is at the very heart of

Table 16. Residence in Rhodesia for immigrants born
outside the federation and Rhodesian
Front members of parliament.

Arrival date	European population		RF MP's elected in 1965	
	Number	Percent	Number	Percent
1952–1961	68,115	49.8	12	28.0
1942–1951	42,140	30.8	13	30.2
1932–1941	8,921	6.5	8	18.6
Before 1932	15,998	11.7	10	23.2
Unknown	1,747	1.2	0	0.0
Total	136,921	100.0	43	100.0

SOURCE: *1961 Census of the European, Asian and Coloured Population*, p. 13.

all white politics. In these critical areas the RF has, with minor modifications, simply used legislation and practices passed on from previous governments. If there is a choice within white politics, it is simply over language (for instance, white rule forever versus white rule for the foreseeable future) or over the best strategy to preserve a commonly accepted goal—the maintenance of the white-dominated political system.

Decision-Making by Party and Government in Rhodesia

In the years that the Rhodesian Front has governed Rhodesia, a few decisions stand out as critical to both party and country: the removal of Winston Field; UDI; the decisions in 1966 and 1968 to reject potential settlements with Britain; and the constitutional decisions taken in 1968–1969. On the surface each seems to deal with a different matter, but all link together as part of the Rhodesian Europeans' endless quest for political independence and with it the right to order their internal affairs as they see fit.

The history of white Rhodesian actions to achieve this end and the principles and policies which the RF is dedicated to uphold make the parameters of RF dialogue and conflict extremely confining. There simply are not many ways to defend the system beyond those already used. The conflicts and choices are essentially over the best strategy to preserve the system, not over how to liquidate it least painfully. Still, conflicts over strategy and tactics often become heated and personal because when there are no principles at stake, decision-making comes down to choosing between one person's strategy or another's. The notion of conflict and the appearance of faction conveys to the uninitiated the impression that real change is possible. Given the present constellation of forces and personnel represented within the RF, however, it is impossible to conclude that any choice made by the party would willfully further the destruction of the system that the members are elected to preserve.

The Rhodesian Front formed in 1962 as an amalgam of previous political groupings. It is occasionally asserted within Rhodesia that these prior affiliations continue to have relevance. The general tenor of this type of comment would be to the effect that the old Dominion Party members are harder-tougher-firmer on the question of white resistance and that the former United Federal Party members are more inclined to compromise, even sell out, the white population.[10] These prior affiliations are charted in Table 17, but it is difficult to demonstrate that they have any ongoing relevance.

Table 17. Rhodesian Front caucuses and cabinets
by prior political affiliation.

Affiliation	Caucus		Cabinet		
	1962 election	1965 election	1/63 (Field)	11/65 (UDI)	12/68 (*Fearless*)
Dominion Party	21	30	6	8	7
United Federal Party	11	12	2	4	7
None	3	8	0	0	0
Total	35	50	8	12	14

In the aftermath of the RF's surprise election victory in 1962, it fell to Winston Field to become prime minister and form the first Rhodesian Front cabinet. As neither he nor any of his new ministers had had any previous ministerial experience, there were no party traditions on how the cabinet and government should be run. Partly out of personal instinct and partly because "it was the way it had always been done," Field easily slipped into the almost dictatorial pattern which had been established for a generation in Rhodesia under Huggins and Welensky. Field exiled his chief party rival, William Harper, to an unimportant ministry; gave other ministers appointments only if they promised to resign without question when asked; and then generally proceeded to run things with little reference to party, caucus, or cabinet. His personal decision to go to the July 1963 federal breakup conference at Victoria Falls without getting ironclad guarantees from Britain on Rhodesia's independence particularly infuriated many ministers and party members.

One major complaint was that Field ran the government without paying any attention to the party. His brusque manner often offended MP's and cabinet members. This was true, even though Field would have been justified in noting that ministers' demands to be consulted were generally in inverse proportion to their ability as ministers. Field emulated the style of Welensky and Huggins—the very style the RF was determined to end. He could not carry it off. He did not have the favorable times or the vast political skill and prestige of his predecessors. The party organization came to feel that Field was acting outside party guidelines on the independence issue, and he neglected to communicate his intentions to party members. When one of the ministers finally contrived to have a showdown between himself and Field, there was no contest. One minister stood with Field. There was no question of factions at all; Field had completely lost touch with the party at all levels. His replacement by Ian Smith was accomplished with ease and precision within the party.

The lesson of Field's removal was not lost on Smith. Partly because he had always been a cautious political figure and partly because it was the price the party demanded for his appointment, Smith designed his new government and its mode of operation along lines almost wholly new to Rhodesian politics. He made ministerial changes which reflected closely the real distribution of power within the RF and took the unprecedented step of clearing his appointments with the caucus.[11] He breathed new life into the caucus subcommittees and the party subcommittees which parallel all ministries, and gave the party assurances that its views would be heard not only through these subcommittees but through all other party bodies.

Smith has always moved with extreme caution. Following the RF's massive electoral triumph in 1965, a victory which one might have expected to accentuate Smith's personal power, it took him fully two weeks to arrange the removal of his two most criticized and undistinguished ministers, and even then he could only manage by giving them top diplomatic assignments. In choosing to be this cautious type of prime minister, Smith has inevitably conceded considerable authority to other groups within the party.

The decision to take UDI was undoubtedly the most important choice made by the RF, if not the most momentous political decision in Rhodesia's history. It was thoroughly canvassed within the party for over a year prior to the final decision; particularly following the 1965 election, the party activists and the back-bench were unwavering supporters of the UDI idea. As was suggested earlier, Smith and many of his ministers were more cautious—but once a majority was prepared to act, Smith went through with the decision.

Much the same pattern seems to apply to the RF decision in 1966 to reject the British proposals for a settlement. It is indicative of the party's strength that Smith was clearly instructed not to make any decisions alone, but to refer all proposals to the party and cabinet in Salisbury. The available evidence suggests that Smith once more tended toward a compromise solution but that the cabinet, strongly backed by the caucus and party activists, again overruled him. The deciding vote on rejecting the 1966 proposals was thought to be eight to five. Both this decision, and that for taking UDI, found the cabinet split; but in neither case does previous party affiliation help us much in defining internal factions.

The enactment of UDI has given Smith a degree of authority that was not his during his early days as prime minister. This is because he has inevitably been thrust into the limelight as the symbol of white determination and resistance. If Smith were forced to resign, it would be an indication to Rhodesia's external foes and to all Rhodesian citizens that there was deep disagreement within the RF. Thus a paradoxical situation has in a sense developed, whereby Smith is a prisoner of well-established practices of intraparty consultation on all major decisions, while the party is Smith's captive in that any showdown with him would be interpreted (rightly or not) as a sign of internal party weakness.

There is some indication that these factors played a part in 1968 developments. Two long-time senior party ministers and national office-holders (William Harper and Lord Graham) were removed from the cabinet because of policy disagreements relating to the new constitutional proposals. This was the first major shakeup since the Field ouster. Later in the year Smith went out of his way to force the party congress to adopt constitutional proposals that he favored; he prevailed by only 11 votes. These actions seemed to indicate that Smith was prepared to act much more forcibly to assert his control over the party. However, the aftermath of both controversies suggests a return to a much less forceful Smith role. Although Harper left parliament, Graham remained and was reelected as a national officer. More important, by the time the constitutional proposals came before the electorate in June 1969, they had been substantially modified to meet the many party criticisms evinced during more than a year of polling, interviewing, and consulting. When Smith returned to negotiations with Britain aboard the warship *Fearless* in October 1968, he again arrived with no mandate to deal alone; only back in Salisbury, with the party chairman by his side, did Smith once more reject the compromise proposals.

As long as UDI remains the ultimate action in defense of white interests, there is little likelihood of factional splits breaking apart the RF. The clear priority of seeing UDI through mediates against disruptive splits arising out of any other disagreement. The party's reaction to events in 1968 would seem to support this judgment. William Harper, more than any other party figure, was the symbol of the old Dominion Party, yet his removal from the cabinet and resignation from the party did not spark any exodus to his side. Two other well-known party figures (Len Idensohn, Salisbury East divisional chairman, and Chris Phillips, former deputy chairman) resigned in 1968 and formed a new party which claimed to be more militant than the RF. Yet at the Gatooma by-election in September 1968 for Harper's old seat, Phillips, standing for his new party against the RF, lost the election 870 to 65; in the 1970 general election this party did not win a seat. The dispute over the shape of the new constitution was heated and prolonged, but once the decision was taken, most of the losers did not leave the party. Instead, they stayed to fight from within and in the end were quite successful.

Undoubtedly in time the Rhodesian Front will dissolve and a new governing party will take its place, but this will probably only occur within the context of the resolution of UDI. If the whites are successful in their resistance to Britain, the UN, and internal foes, factions will probably emerge along the lines of the South African white system; if they are unsuccessful, a Kenya pattern may emerge for the short run but will last only until the Africans take power. Until the independence issue is finally resolved, however, it is difficult to imagine that white unity will not be substantially maintained.

Every important decision made in Rhodesia since December 1962 has been hammered out first within the closed confines of the Rhodesian Front. This fact alone justifies taking a careful look at the party organization. Moreover, the Rhodesian party system has developed no viable alternative government (and none seems likely, given present conditions). In the absence of internal decay the RF finds itself without substantial political opposition over how to maintain the present system.

The RF has arrived at this dominant position as a result of both its program and its style of organization and decision-making. The party has established solid linkages to the whole white community. This extensive organization is probably both the RF's strength and its weakness. It has so far derived overwhelming popular support from the white electorate because its actions have embodied the collective will to resist political change. On the other hand, the considerable counting of noses that must go into any significant party decision does not make for flexible and imaginative leadership. The political system is designed to resist change, and the party apparatus developed by the RF accentuates this tendency. If the leadership wanted to rescind the prerogatives which the rank-and-file have so carefully developed over the years, the stage would be set for a calamitous party row. However, given the political goals of the white Rhodesians, success can probably best be measured in terms of rigidity. As long as this is so, the RF is likely to remain the party and government of the whites and continue to be a formidable political foe for all who seek change in Rhodesia.

6

Isolation and Survival:
White Rhodesia under
International Sanctions

Rhodesia's unilateral declaration of independence was promulgated on November 11, 1965, and Britain, as threatened, implemented a policy of economic sanctions to force the Rhodesian Front to return to constitutional government. Britain's efforts were supported by the United Nations, which attempted to isolate Rhodesia economically and politically. Today in 1972, nearly seven years after UDI, not one nation has formally recognized Rhodesia; on the other hand, sanctions have failed to induce her to change political direction. White Rhodesia's continuing ability to circumvent sanctions and maintain itself in power has led the British government into repeated efforts to settle the dispute via negotiations. A tentative accord was finally reached in November 1971, but it was later rejected by Britain after a commission sent to Rhodesia reported that the agreement was unacceptable to the African population. The position of Rhodesia thus remains as it has been since UDI—the white government in firm control but isolated, with external and internal pressures for change continuing, however ineffectively.

Sanctions and the Rhodesian Economy

Once UDI was declared, Britain's bluff had been called and she had little alternative but to implement sanctions.[1] Britain's original actions in November 1965 were to expel Rhodesia from the sterling area, end commonwealth preferences on Rhodesian goods, remove Rhodesia from the commonwealth sugar agreement, ban the import of tobacco and sugar to Britain, make all trade with Rhodesia subject to exchange control, freeze 9 million pounds worth of Rhodesian reserves in London banks, and abolish export credit guarantees to Rhodesia. Many of these steps were followed by other commonwealth countries. Britain's hope was that by showing Rhodesia that it was serious about sanctions, Rhodesian white leaders would quickly forego their rebellion.

When initial efforts failed, Britain turned to the United Nations for assistance. Since 1962 the General Assembly, the Security Council, and the Special Committee on Colonialism (the Committee of 24) had actively tried to put pressure on Britain to alter the situation within Rhodesia.[2] In June 1962 the General Assembly supported a Special Committee recommendation that Rhodesia be declared a nonself-governing territory. The following October the General Assembly passed a resolution calling for Britain to suspend the Rhodesian constitution, cancel the upcoming elections, convene a new constitutional conference, and install a one-man one-vote franchise.[3]

Britain never had an easy time with the Rhodesian question at the United Nations. In October 1962 (during the debate just mentioned) the British representative on colonial questions, Sir Hugh Foot, actually resigned because he could no longer support the British position on Rhodesia.[4] The British held that Rhodesia was *both* a British dependency and a self-governing state and therefore it should not come under the purview of the Special Committee. Simultaneously, Britain denied that she had any administrative authority within Rhodesia. She was right on both counts. Rhodesia was self-governing and Britain exercised no administrative authority within the country. Yet in claiming that Rhodesia was still a British dependency, Britain was effectively saying that Rhodesia was her responsibility and that she had no authority to deal with the very situation that had brought on UN pressure—the rule of Rhodesia's white minority. Britain thus acted as a buffer and a shield for white Rhodesia from all outside pressures. Rhodesia knew and expected this support, and when Sir Hugh Foot (now Lord Caradon) was appointed British Ambassador to the UN after the Labour Party victory in 1964, Ian Smith declared that if Britain failed to support Rhodesia at the UN, that would be grounds for UDI.[5]

United Nations pressure grew. In September 1963 Britain vetoed a Security Council resolution which called for her to oppose the transfer of the Royal Rhodesian Air Force to the Rhodesian government at the end of federation. In April 1965 the Security Council adopted another resolution calling upon Britain to prevent UDI and upon all states not to accept such a declaration. In October the General Assembly adopted a resolution urging Britain to take "all possible measures" to prevent UDI, and in November (six days before UDI) a General Assembly resolution passed asking Britain "to employ all necessary means including the use of military force" to avert UDI.[6]

United Nations' involvement with the Rhodesia question has gone through three distinct stages in the years since UDI. Initially sanctions were selective and optional; then in December 1966 selective mandatory sanctions were voted; and finally in May 1968—for the first time in UN history—full mandatory sanctions were voted by the Security Council. Sanctions were implemented in these gradually escalating steps at the request of the British government, which has largely defined and controlled the extent of UN involvement. In a very real sense, Britain's ability to control UN action over Rhodesia operated to the benefit of the rebel regime, for Britain protected it from the wrath of many members eager to vote more stringent measures.

In days immediately following UDI both the General Assembly and the Security Council passed resolutions condemning UDI and calling on all states not to recognize the rebellion. A week later the Security Council passed another resolution urging states to "refrain from any action which would assist and encourage the illegal regime and, in particular, to desist from providing it with arms, equipment and military supplies, and to do their upmost in order to break all economic relations with Southern Rhodesia, including an embargo on oil and petroleum products." [7]

The call for an oil embargo was an important early step, affirmed by an April 1966 Security Council resolution which permitted Britain to begin a blockade of Rhodesia's nearest port of Beira, Mozambique, where oil normally was unloaded into a pipeline for the Rhodesian refinery at Umtali.[8] Oil supplies, however, were quickly shipped to Rhodesia by other routes. Initially South Africa sent road shipments; now Rhodesia's oil comes mostly via rail from the Mozambique refinery at Lourenço Marques. Britain has made no effort to extend the blockade.

The oil embargo revealed the obstacles to effective sanctions against Rhodesia. As long as sanctions were limited to Rhodesia, and her neighbors were prepared to ignore them, Rhodesia had a very good chance of survival. Britain continued to hope that sanctions would work, however, and in December 1966 (following the failure of the talks with the Rhodesian government) Britain went back to the UN and received selective mandatory sanctions against the principal Rhodesian exports—asbestos, pig iron, tobacco, copper, chrome, iron ore, meat products, sugar, hides, skins, and leather. Exports to Rhodesia of oil products and arms were also banned.[9] This marked the first time that the UN had voted the use of enforcement measures under chapter 7 of the UN charter. Even so, Britain had to struggle to defeat requests asking her to use force if sanctions failed and to extend sanctions to South Africa and Portugal if they did not observe the Security Council resolution. A year and a half later (in May 1968) Britain returned to the UN again, asking for and getting a Security Council resolution calling for compulsory mandatory sanctions against Rhodesia.

In turning to the UN repeatedly, the British government has not sought to relinquish her responsibility for Rhodesia; indeed, it is her position that she still retains sole legal authority. The tacit admission of failure in each new attempt to escalate sanctions, however, must bring wry smiles to Rhodesian whites who remember Prime Minister Wilson's famous remark that "economic and financial sanctions might well bring the rebellion to an end within a matter of weeks rather than months." [10] Sanctions simply have not brought the success Britain desired. In turn, Britain has been under increasing pressure from the Organization of African Unity and the Afro-Asian bloc at the United Nations either to use force or to broaden sanctions against all white Southern Africa. Britain has resolutely refused to go along with either proposal. In March 1970, when the Security Council was finally able to get a majority to pass a resolution condemning Britain for not using force to overthrow the Rhodesian government, Britain joined the United States in vetoing the resolution. In February 1972 Britain vetoed yet another Security Council resolution—this one calling for a rejection of the November 1971 settlement and asking Britain to recall the Pearce Commission which had gone out to assess Rhodesian opinion. [11]

Despite the fact that sanctions have not achieved their political goal, they have had some economic impact. It is difficult to be precise because the data are limited and not fully reliable. There was an almost complete statistical blackout in Rhodesia from November 1965 to early 1967. Since then limited data have been issued but, for instance, detailed trade statistics have been completely withheld. Nevertheless, some general effects can be summarized: the tobacco and sugar industries have been hit hard, but other exports (meat, chrome, asbestos, nickel, copper, gold) have held up well; imports have been reduced to stay within the bounds of reduced foreign-exchange earnings; the gross domestic product has grown steadily after an initial slump; the balance-of-payments position has remained strong; and the overall development prospects have been hindered by lack of foreign investment. Table 18 shows some of these effects.

The primary success of sanctions has been to cut Rhodesian exports, primarily tobacco. After World War II the tobacco industry became Rhodesia's major foreign-exchange earner and one of the keys to Rhodesian growth and prosperity. [12] In 1965, the year of UDI, Rhodesia produced 25 percent of the non-Communist world's exports of tobacco,

Table 18. Selected economic indicators for Rhodesia, 1964–1970.
Figures are given in millions of pounds.

Indicator	1964	1965	1966	1967	1968	1969	1970
Gross domestic product at factor cost	326.3	351.8	345.7	369.6	398.9	449.7	485.4
Exports[a]	140.6	164.7	103.9	100.6	97.4	120.0	137.1
Imports	110.0	119.8	84.7	93.5	103.5	110.0	117.5
Balance of payments[b]	1.4	15.0	0.9	−9.4	−26.8	1.8	−7.4

SOURCE: Rhodesia, *Monthly Digest of Statistics; Quarterly Summary of Statistics;* and *Economic Survey of Rhodesia,* 1965–1970. The figures for 1969 and 1970 are estimates.

[a] Including reexports.
[b] On current account.

and the foreign-exchange earnings to Rhodesia from tobacco exceeded 46 million pounds. Since UDI, all tobacco sales have been secret and the government has steadily reduced the annual crop. In both 1964–1965 and 1965–1966, Rhodesia produced about 250 million tons of tobacco; in comparison, the government's projected crop for 1970–1971 and 1971–1972 is 132 million tons. The sale price is also sharply lower. Reliable estimates hold that between 1965 and 1969 Rhodesia produced 714 million tons, of which 413 million tons were sold at rock-bottom prices and 301 million tons were stockpiled.[13] John Wrathall, Rhodesian finance minister, revealed in his 1970–1971 budget address that through June 30, 1970, the loss to the government through the subsidizing of tobacco farmers was 24.5 million pounds and he estimated an additional 9.5 million pound loss for 1970–1971.[14]

Tobacco has been the easiest target for sanctions, because Rhodesia alone among Southern African countries has a substantial tobacco industry. It is impossible to disguise the country of origin of tobacco, as is done for other Rhodesian products. Approximately one-half of Rhodesia's four thousand white tobacco farmers now have either gone out of business or diversified into crops such as wheat, maize, or cotton; others are raising beef. These crops are all easily grown in Rhodesia. Though not as profitable as tobacco, they are more easily exported.

Another major impact of sanctions has been to shift Rhodesian trading patterns. While lack of statistics made it impossible to be explicit, two major trends stand out: Rhodesia's trade with Britain and Zambia —her two leading trading partners prior to UDI—has been dramatically curtailed, and her trade with (and more importantly, through) South Africa has sharply increased.

In 1965 Zambia (formerly Northern Rhodesia) was the leading buyer of Rhodesian exports (45.9 million pounds) and Rhodesia's imports from Zambia were so few (4.3 million pounds) that the relationship was almost entirely to Rhodesia's advantage.[15] Zambia's copper was exported through Rhodesia; the coal for the Zambian Copperbelt came from Rhodesia, as did the power from the Kariba Dam, controlled from the Rhodesian side of the Zambezi. All of Zambia's oil came through Rhodesia. Since UDI, Zambia has been in the forefront of nations pressing for sanctions against Rhodesia. Zambia's oil now comes from other routes; its dependency on Rhodesian coal has in part been lessened by the opening of new mines within Zambia; and a project to dam the Kafue River within Zambia (which was vetoed in favor of the Rhodesian-controlled Kariba project in the early days of federation) is now in the planning stages. Zambia has also found new suppliers for imports. In 1966 Zambia's imports from Rhodesia were off 35 percent and in 1967, 55 percent; by 1970 they were under 10 percent of what they had been in 1965.

Britain's break with Rhodesia has been severe. Two years after UDI, British imports from Rhodesia were under 1 percent and exports to Rhodesia only 3 percent of pre-UDI figures. These figures are fairly accurate, but with a British trade boom with South Africa in progress, it is highly probable that some British-Rhodesian trade is concealed in the South African figures.

Sanctions have not achieved their objective of forcing Rhodesia to renounce UDI, largely because of the support furnished Rhodesia by South Africa and Portuguese Mozambique. Oil has been supplied by both countries and South Africa's Central Bank has freely exchanged South African rand for Rhodesian pounds. This has helped Rhodesia maintain its credit position and freed Rhodesian foreign exchange for goods South Africa could not supply. South African businessmen have established dummy corporations whose only function is to conceal the Rhodesian origin of exports and destination of imports. What limited evidence is available suggests that Britain, the United States, and Zambia have done the most to implement sanctions, but that West Germany, France, and Japan (among major trading nations) have been less than scrupulous in limiting their Rhodesian trade. In late 1971 the United States position changed when Congress attached an amendment to the Military Procurement Bill allowing U.S. firms to import Rhodesian minerals in violation of the UN boycott. This law, signed by President Nixon, took effect on January 1, 1972, and the United States thus joined with South Africa and Portugal as the major public violators of the UN resolutions. The U.S. action was an important victory for the Smith regime.[16]

The Rhodesian economy has also survived because of its inherent strength. It is based on a large number of crops and minerals and is self-sufficient for food and many other items. Manufacturers diversified quickly to supply many products previously imported. Mineral exports have risen in value from 32 million pounds in 1965 to 49.4 million pounds in 1970. Sanctions could stifle growth in some sectors, but could hardly force the government into submission.

The piecemeal and gradual application of sanctions also helped Rhodesia. Problems could be solved one at a time, and each new success bolstered the whites' confidence. The skill and resourcefulness with which sanctions have been fought can hardly be overestimated. Businessmen and government officials (whatever their previous attitude toward UDI) worked closely together to circumvent sanctions. They were linked together because when forced to make a choice, nearly all white Rhodesians preferred UDI with the Rhodesian Front to the uncertainties ahead if UDI failed. Using the authority granted under the permanent state of emergency, the government issued regulations to control foreign exchange, imports, and employment conditions for whites. The balance-of-payments position was helped by Rhodesia's repudiation of her foreign debts and by blocking the exports of any dividends, interest, or profits to Britain by British firms operating in Rhodesia.

The thrust of internal effort has been to shield the politically crucial white population from any harmful or demoralizing effects of sanctions. The government guarantees employment to any white losing his job as a result of sanctions and similarly guarantees jobs to new white immigrants. The tobacco farmers have received direct subsidies. Incentives have been introduced to turn farmers to marketable crops and manufacturers to import-substitution items. It is likely that this forced economic diversification both on the farms and in the cities will in the long run help the Rhodesian economy.

One interesting aspect of UDI is that the whites most directly hurt by sanctions—the tobacco farmers—remain the backbone of the RF. The farmers' capital is in their land; without a political system that protects their right to this land, their financial worth and political strength would vanish. Thus they support UDI. The urban white community also strongly supports the Rhodesian Front. Although they may forego some luxuries, their jobs have been maintained and many have had an economic windfall from the expansion in internal manufacturing and construction. Normalcy for Rhodesia is the maintenance of high white standards of consumption; this has been successfully sustained despite sanctions, and therefore the will of the whites to resist has not faltered.

A final factor mitigating the effect of sanctions is the fact that the 1968 resolution calling for compulsory mandatory sanctions is unenforceable.[17] Britain has no interest in pushing sanctions any farther; the UN committee established to monitor violations has no executive authority. Furthermore, no one with power or authority is prepared to confront South Africa and Portugal over the Rhodesian situation. As long as this is the case, it can only be concluded that the Rhodesian economy is in no danger of collapse.

Sanctions have not achieved their objective. The RF remains firmly in power, and despite some dislocation the Rhodesian economy appears strong. No one would argue that sanctions have not harmed the Rhodesian economy; clearly optimum growth can hardly be achieved when Rhodesia's primary export crop is halved and when international trade must be carried on secretly. Nonetheless, the absence of immediate detrimental effects gave the RF confidence that white Rhodesia would survive. It is in this context that Rhodesia has shaped its relations with other states since UDI.

Britain and the "Rebels"

A blunt step which openly revealed the meagre nature of British authority within Rhodesia, UDI was a plain and unadorned assertion by white Rhodesia that it was fully competent to handle its own affairs. It did not want British supervision, however infrequently that supervision was attempted or accepted. It was also a blatant challenge to Britain to assert its proclaimed authority. In not being able to regain any semblance of control within Rhodesia, Britain has been forced to admit its inability to do anything about the Rhodesian rebellion, at least within the limits of action it considers acceptable.

Britain's relations with Rhodesia since UDI have gone through several phases. In the early days of the rebellion, Britain was angry, arrogant, and confident that Rhodesia would soon be forced to forego independence. Prime Minister Wilson denounced UDI as "an act of rebellion against the Crown" [18] and said sanctions would be "quick and effective measures . . . to bring Rhodesia at the earliest possible moment back to the paths of constitutional government." [19] As these hopes did not materialize, Britain gave up its fierce posturing and opened negotiations. Under the Labour government these talks reached high points in December 1966 and October 1968 when Prime Minister Wilson had direct discussions with Smith. Neither meeting proved successful, because Smith saw no reason to compromise and Britain still wished for the sign (if not the substance) and some contrition on white Rhodesia's part. In June 1970 a Conservative government under Prime Minister Edward Heath came to power in Britain. Discussions were resumed with the Rhodesian Front, resulting in a tentative accord announced on November 24, 1971. This agreement accepted Rhodesian independence and guaranteed white rule at least until well into the twenty-first century, barring unforeseen developments. The accord represented Britain's final admission that its influence over Rhodesian affairs was nil and was indicative of the eagerness with which the Tories wished to terminate Britain's responsibility for Rhodesia.

Through these different phases, Britain's great ambivalence toward

Rhodesia has been evident. Just after UDI, Britain instructed the governor (who remained loyal to British authority) to issue the following statement:

> I call on the citizens of Rhodesia to refrain from all acts which would further the objectives of the illegal authorities. Subject to that, it is the duty of all citizens to maintain law and order in the country and to carry on with their normal tasks. This applies equally to the judiciary, the armed services, the police, and the public service.[20]

This was paralleled by Wilson's statement in the House of Commons that "it is the duty of public servants to carry on with their jobs, to help maintain law and order . . . [and] they must themselves be the judges of any possible action which they might be asked to take and which would be illegal in itself or illegal in the sense of furthering this rebellious act." [21]

The contradiction implicit in the two statements is obvious. How could one carry on with normal tasks without furthering the objectives of the illegal authorities? It was essential to the RF that normalcy be maintained in the aftermath of the rebellion, and British statements clearly helped. No encouragement was given to those within Rhodesia (black or white) who might have resisted UDI.

The limited goal of sanctions further emphasizes British ambivalence. They were not utilized for the express purpose of furthering the political cause of the African people of Rhodesia, though it is possible (but far from certain) that this would have resulted if sanctions had worked. It is crucial to note that the object of sanctions was always to get the RF to renounce UDI and return to legal, constitutional rule. *This is not the same as renouncing white rule.* As we have seen, Britain has lived comfortably with a white government in Rhodesia for a long time. Sanctions were applied to get the RF to revert to the political pattern existing on November 10, 1965 (or to agree to some other form of negotiated settlement), *not* for the express purpose of radically altering the Rhodesian political system.[22]

Whatever hope Britain had for success was based on three erroneous assumptions: that sanctions would be effective, that there was the possibility of getting Smith to split with the RF in order to reach an amiable accord with Britain, and that internal opposition to UDI would materialize.

The sanctions policy has already been examined and found lacking. As far as Smith is concerned, nothing known about his position within the Rhodesian Front suggests that he is likely to break decisively with the party. Still, British propaganda often pictures him as an honest but misguided man "who is a prisoner of some very racialist and Fascist-minded people." [23] Shortly after UDI, Wilson stated that "I was speaking in the early hours this morning to a confused and unhappy man. He has been under intolerable pressures from some of his colleagues and from the unreasoning extremists of the Rhodesian Front." [24] Unfortunately this "liberal" interpretation of Ian Smith is quite without factual base. Furthermore, there can be no certainty that Smith could break with the RF and be sure to carry the country with him. In judging the British position on Smith, one must choose between two explanations: either Britain really believed Smith might ditch the RF (an explanation that shows no understanding of Smith as a leader or his relationships within the RF) or that Britain had no confident strategy for bringing change to Rhodesia and this was just another shot in the dark.

In the absence of sanctions working or the RF splitting apart, Britain could only rely on the growth of internal opposition. This was perhaps the weakest reed of all. The African nationalists remained divided among themselves and subject to harsh internal repression. On the European side (where Britain actually expected to find internal allies), nothing occurred. Whites who opposed UDI had no substantial political base in the society. They had no seats in parliament and Britain's direct instructions to the judiciary, armed services, police, and public service inhibited any resistance growing in these quarters. There was no reason for poeple to risk their careers in the name of constitutional legality or loyalty to the crown when the crown promised them nothing and asked nothing from them.

The position of the judiciary merits special comment. In accordance with the British government's express wish, the judges carried on their normal activities and took no initiatives against the rebellion. It was not until September 1966 that the justices had to rule on the legality of the rebellion. Then in a notably "diplomatic" decision, justices Goldin and Lewis ruled that the 1965 UDI constitution was not lawful and that the government was thus illegal, but that since the government was the only effective one Rhodesia had, the courts should continue to allow such measures, both legislative and administrative, as had been or could be taken under the 1961 constitution.[25] Since the 1961 constitution had not inhibited any actions the white government deemed critical, this ruling was hardly a slap in the face of the regime. To be called illegal meant little when the judiciary continued to administer the country's legal system as if nothing had occurred. The justices may have remained verbally uncommitted to the Smith regime, but in their actions they were serving the ends of the rebellion very nicely.

During 1968 a series of new cases led the Appellate Divison of the Rhodesian high court to rule that the Rhodesian government was legal under the 1965 constitution. In doing so the high court turned its back on its 1966 decision which had wavered on the question of the Rhodesian government's de jure control of the state. With judicial support the regime then proceeded to hang several Africans over the express and explicit appeal for clemency issued by the Queen.[26] Later rulings rejected the proposition that the Judicial Committee of the Privy Council had any power of review of Rhodesian cases (which had been its role under the 1961 constitution). During 1968 two justices resigned, but their action was far too late to have any political significance.[27]

In the absence of internal pressures seriously affecting the dominance of the Rhodesian Front, the British government had no option (if it wanted to seek a settlement) but to deal directly with the government of Ian Smith. Wilson's early blustering that "we cannot negotiate with an illegal regime" and "we cannot negotiate with these men, nor can they be trusted, after the return to constitutional rule, with the task of leading Rhodesia in the paths of freedom and racial harmony" were quietly forgotten.[28] Various fictions were devised by Britain to suggest its continued colonial control, the most common being that the governor, Sir Humphrey Gibbs, was at all times said to be the intermediary in discussions between the two governments. This was nonsense, and the two governments bargained openly because each had something it wished to attain which it could not get without the other. Rhodesia obviously wanted sanctions lifted, but only if white control was maintained. Britain wished an end to the rebellion so as to get out from under a political situation that was causing great disquiet in the commonwealth, harming Britain at the UN, causing unease in its important ties with South Africa, and giving no British politician or government comfort at home.

All talks centered on the same five principles that had guided pre-UDI negotiations. To these five Wilson added a sixth in January 1966: "The need to ensure that, regardless of race, there is no oppression of the majority by the minority or of the minority by the majority." [29] When the Tories returned to power, this principle was dropped. In each negotiation phase, Britain has attempted to bring Rhodesia to political agreement, largely through the offering of concessions. When these concessions have met with Rhodesian rebuff as not being sufficient to guarantee white rule and meet all Rhodesian demands, Britain has withdrawn in anger and made dire threats, only to return within a few months to offer ever more advantageous terms to the white Rhodesians. Britain has had no alternative to this pattern, since its commitment not to use force or to confront South Africa and Portugal over sanctions left it without credible weapons with which to challenge Rhodesia. Britain's dilemma was that to impose real change in Rhodesia was to countenance methods deemed unacceptable, while to concentrate on a "return to legality" was to risk achieving no change at all.

In addition to countless informal meetings through both government and private emissaries, three major sets of talks were held. The discussions between Smith and Wilson in December 1966 and October 1968 are commonly called the *Tiger* and *Fearless* talks—each name deriving from the British warship on which the talks were held. The last meetings occurred in November 1971 when Sir Alec Douglas-Home, foreign secretary in the Heath cabinet, journeyed to Salisbury and reached a tentative accord with Smith.[30]

The *Tiger* and *Fearless* talks were long, tedious, loaded with false drama, and fruitless. The impetus toward the *Tiger* talks was given in a promise made by Prime Minister Wilson to the September 1966 Commonwealth Prime Minister's Conference that set a time limit of November 30, 1966, for a settlement. If an agreement was not reached, Wilson promised to withdraw all previous offers of independence before majority rule and to go to the United Nations for selective mandatory sanctions.

At the *Tiger* talks held December 2–4, 1966, Wilson went farther than ever before in offering Smith the political control he demanded. The two leaders and their advisers prepared a "working document," which outlined specific changes to be made in the 1961 constitution to meet the six principles. The working document ostensibly met British conditions, although it provided for independent white rule under the Rhodesian Front subject to all the vagaries of the 1961 constitution outlined earlier and notwithstanding the RF's perspectives on African political advance.[31] Both Smith and Wilson signed the working document without commitment and returned home to consider it more carefully.

Back in Salisbury the Rhodesian Front found many parts of the working document unacceptable. The major provision it disliked was the transition period before a "return to legality." While during this time the RF would have remained in power, legal authority would nominally have rested again with the governor. Through this period final constitutional proposals were to be carried forward, but the Rhodesian government considered that it "would be extremely foolish were they to abandon the substance of their present Constitution for the shadow of a mythical constitution yet to be evolved." [32] The RF was unprepared to take any step that would look as though Rhodesia were backing down from independence. For this and other reasons the working document was rejected on December 5, 1966.[33] It was clear that pressure on Rhodesia would have to grow far more intense before the Rhodesian government would be prepared to make any concessions.

Following the talks Wilson kept his promise to the commonwealth prime ministers by calling for selective mandatory sanctions at the UN and by publicly declaring that henceforth British policy toward Rhodesia would be governed by a new standard, NIBMAR—no independence before majority rule.[34] This new policy was entirely in contradiction to Britain's continued adherence to the six principles as a basis for a settlement, for it had long been abundantly clear that Britain could be satisfied without the RF having to forego independent white rule.

On the *Fearless* in October 1968, it became readily apparent that NIBMAR was a dead issue, if in fact it had ever had any credibility.[35]

Renewed discussions between the two governments again failed because of Rhodesian fears of British trickery. Britain openly abandoned NIBMAR and proposed a transition to majority rule that was certain to take a generation or more, with contingencies so numerous that the proposals in reality had little long-term meaning other than their formal recognition of white domination within Rhodesia. Still the RF refused to make even a verbal commitment to the possibility of eventual majority rule, standing fast behind its demand for total internal control over the pace of African political advance. In so doing it unwaveringly backed long-time RF principles and confounded the British experts who expected that at some stàge Rhodesia would make a deal with Britain, even if only to rip it up the next day.

Between the *Fearless* talks and the 1970 British election, there were few contacts between the two governments. During this period Rhodesia declared itself a republic, thus severing its remaining ties with Britain. Britain withdrew its residual diplomatic mission from Salisbury. Except for South Africa and Portugal, all other governments followed the British lead, as they had remained in Salisbury only under the guise that they were still officially accredited by the British government from pre-UDI days.[36] Rhodesia thus became more isolated than ever.

The Conservative victory in the British general election led to renewed efforts to resolve the Rhodesian dispute. Foremost in his eagerness to reach a settlement was Sir Alec Douglas-Home, the new foreign secretary, long a friend of white Rhodesia. Indeed, Home's own government in 1963 and 1964 had conducted early discussions with the Rhodesian Front, which had terminated with the Tory defeat in October 1964. And the five principles had been originally formulated by Home.

Throughout 1970 and 1971 numerous private discussions were held between Smith and various emissaries of the British government. The most prominent British intermediary was Lord Goodman, who made repeated trips to Salisbury in an effort to find a way of satisfying British adherence to the five principles without asking for more than Smith was prepared to concede. This was not easy. Smith felt no compunction in noting in the midst of the Goodman visits that the five principles "are no longer of any consequence to Rhodesia." [37] Nonetheless discussions continued and in November 1971 Home traveled to Salisbury for high-level negotiations.

After a week of intensive discussions, Home and Smith formally announced their agreed proposals for a settlement. The proposals were enormously complex and shrouded in such ambiguity and uncertainty that it is impossible to be utterly precise about them. Certain fundamentals, however, are clear. Britain offered to grant Smith's government independence and lift sanctions; in exchange the Rhodesian government agreed to proposals which satisfied the British interpretation of the five principles. The terms reflected British weariness with the entire issue, and potentially the settlement was a tremendous victory for the Rhodesian Front. Britain's interpretation of the first four principles made a mockery of language and was little more than a smoke screen for its capitulation to the RF.[38] Only British willingness to adhere to the fifth principle when faced with overwhelming African opposition prevented the agreement from being consummated.

The first principle of unimpeded progress to majority rule was dependent upon a rather remarkable sense of the term "majority rule." A new African higher roll was to be established with the same income, property, and education qualifications that applied to whites. As more Africans attained these higher roll qualifications, additional parliamentary seats would be created. The eventual goal was parity between the 50 seats now held by Europeans and 50 African seats (8 elected by the current African lower roll, 24 indirectly elected by the chiefs, and 18 elected on the new African higher roll). At the point of parity (perhaps fifty or a hundred years away, no one really knew), [39] an elaborate process would occur leading toward the establishment of 10 common-roll seats to be elected by African higher-roll voters and Europeans. Thus "majority rule" would be attained. It should be noted that, at best, this would be the majority rule of very rich Africans (certainly less than 10 percent of the African population). Moreover, Africans would always be limited to no more than 60 of 110 parliamentary seats. This is something less than the common interpretation of majority rule.

The second principle, guaranteeing against regressive constitutional amendments, was dependent upon the assumption that more than half the African members of parliament would always hold firm against European pressure. This was possible but far from certain, since African members indirectly selected by the chiefs are particularly vulnerable to government pressure, and other members may be as well.

The third principle of immediate improvement in the political status of the African population was met insofar as "the African population" is equated with the groups (chiefs and rich Africans) that the British government and the RF are prepared to consider "civilised." Lowering the qualifications for the African lower roll is really irrelevant, since this group can never elect more than 8 of 50 African members.

The fourth principle of progress toward ending racial discrimination was all but ignored. Nothing was done about land apportionment, and the rewritten Declaration of Rights was as lacking in substance as that in the 1961 constitution. The government's right to preventive detention was explicitly written into the declaration. Extant legislation was not affected and Home publicly concurred that discrimination would be acceptable if the Rhodesian government discovered "overriding" reasons for it. These reasons no doubt would have included getting reelected.[40]

The fifth principle, that Britain must be satisfied that the agreement was acceptable to the people of Rhodesia as a whole, was the only point where African views potentially could be heard. The test of acceptability was to be carried out by a British commission visiting Rhodesia. The check would be by consultation, since the Rhodesian government would not allow a referendum on the subject.

In parliament, Home defended the agreement as "a chance of setting the Rhodesian Constitution and the protection of the individual Rhodesian on a new course." [41] With considerable intensity he reviewed the five principles and explained how they were met, and he used the lame threat from prefederation days that unless the agreement were accepted, Rhodesia would drift irrevocably into the South African sphere.[42]

Lord Goodman was more forthright in presenting the British case.[43] He frankly admitted that there was much about the settlement that was sad, but that the terms were the best that could be attained given the circumstances. He spoke directly to the question of Britain selling out the Africans and pointed out:

> The African had been sold out long before. This happened during the long years of British Colonial administration which notwithstanding our reserved powers, accepted discriminatory legislation against the black man, preferred constitutions that entrenched discrimination at least to its then point of development, and ultimately remained infirm and supine at the seizure of power by a handful of desperate men determined to assert that the black man would never be fit to rule. It is necessary to recognise that it is against this background of constant moral capitulation by every shade of government that the terms we negotiated, scratched out of a wall with bare fingers, have to be set.[44]

This statement both accurately summarizes the history of British involvement with Rhodesia and conveys the hopelessness of the British negotiating position. It was a settlement couched in honorable words, but it rested on an impregnable base of historical indifference and moral expediency.

Smith's speech to his own parliament reflected the RF achievement:

> For six years now, we have held out not only against world opinion but also against sanctions which escalated into a savage economic war with tremendous odds loaded against us. Few people outside Rhodesia would have been prepared to venture a wager on our chances of seeing the operation through . . . [yet] the task entrusted to your Government was to ensure the control of Rhodesia was retained in civilised hands . . . It has been a long haul to reach the position in which we now find ourselves.[45]

From within and outside the Rhodesian Front, there was almost uniform white acceptance of the proposals and hope that the British commission would find the proposals acceptable to all Rhodesians.

The British commission to test Rhodesian opinion was headed by

Lord Pearce, a retired high court judge. Three deputy chairmen were also named. They were assisted by 20 commissioners (many with long years of experience in Africa with the British Colonial Service). The commission's mandate was straightforward: "to ascertain by direct contact with all sections of the population whether the people of Rhodesia as a whole regard these proposals as acceptable as a basis for independence; and to report to the Foreign and Commonwealth Secretary accordingly." [46] The commission was not asked to assess whether the proposals *ought to be* acceptable to the people of Rhodesia. Rather the proposals were seen as a package deal which had to be accepted or rejected on the merits of the bargain itself. The commission spent two full months in Rhodesia, from January 11 to March 11, 1972.

In Rhodesia the commission found overwhelming European acceptance of the proposals.[47] The dominant reason for acceptance was that an agreement would end sanctions and lead to the return of foreign investment and greater Rhodesian prosperity. The settlement was also seen as "the best means of preserving a familiar and pleasant way of life and of reducing the risk of violence." [48] Other reasons for acceptance were occasionally articulated and a few Europeans opposed the accord, but the commission found no difficulty in reporting conclusively that "the Proposals are acceptable to the great majority of Europeans." [49] Given the terms of the settlement and the Rhodesian Front endorsement, this was hardly a surprising finding. The tiny Asian and Coloured communities were also found to be broadly in favor of the settlement. The real crux came in evaluating the response of the Africans—the overwhelming majority of the entire population of Rhodesia.

To do this, the Pearce Commission took several lines of inquiry. Pairs of commissioners were assigned to seven provinces in order to assess African opinion in the reserves and on European farms. Other commissioners took responsibility for the two large urban centers of Salisbury and Bulawayo, while the sole woman commissioner separately inquired about female opinion. Many meetings, both announced and unannounced, were held in rural and urban areas. Overall the commission reported that it had met with 114,600 adult Africans—approximately 5.8 percent of this population group. In addition, the commission took written evidence from 124 African organizations, received written views from an additional 51,000 Africans, and took direct oral evidence and memoranda from key African groups such as the chiefs, African members of parliament, detainees, trade unionists, and the African National Council (the primary organization that arose in opposition to the settlement).[50]

The Rhodesian government deeply opposed the entire idea of a test of African opinion. They believed the two governments, having agreed on terms, should simply go ahead and implement the settlement. Africans were viewed as either not having the capacity to understand and make a reasonable judgment on the terms or subject to intimidation to such a degree that any judgment rendered would be so suspect as to be useless. When widespread disorders occurred during the early days of the Pearce Commission's stay in Rhodesia, the Rhodesian government's view was summed up in Smith's angry statement on January 21 1972: "Those responsible for all this barbaric destruction have, ironically, played right into our hands. What greater proof could anyone have of their lack of maturity, lack of civilisation, their inability to make any constructive contribution?" Smith hoped to have it both ways. In the same address he declared, "Let me say to the broad mass of our decent African people that it would be tragic if history recorded that they were so bemused, so susceptible to intimidation, that they rejected an offer which is obviously so much to their advantage, an offer to advance the position of the African in every way—politically, economically, socially." [51] As usual, Smith and the Europeans were prepared to accept the validity of African opinion when it concurred with their own views, but not when it differed.[52]

For a short time there was some concern that African unrest would prevent the commission from carrying out its mission. During January a few meetings were cancelled, but a combination of stern governmental action and African willingness to protest peacefully quieted the situation and the commission continued its work. After two months in Rhodesia and ten additional weeks assessing its data, the commission reported that "the majority of Africans rejected the Proposals" and that "in our opinion the people of Rhodesia as a whole do not regard the Proposals as acceptable as a basis for independence." [53]

The commission found that the reasons for African rejection "were broadly speaking the same whether given privately, in groups, at mass meetings or in writing . . . Mistrust of the intentions and motives of the Government transcended all other considerations . . . This was the dominant motivation of African rejection at all levels and in all areas." [54] The Africans who opposed the settlement believed that as soon as independence was given and sanctions lifted, the government would simply tear up any terms of the settlement disliked by whites or be thrown out in favor of a government that would. There were many complaints as well about specifics of the agreement—the limited franchise, the indefinite wait for so-called majority rule, the complete absence of any African consultation on the proposals themselves, the irrelevancy of the Declaration of Rights, the continuation of preventive detention, and the perpetuation of racial discrimination and land apportionment. In sum, most Africans realized that the settlement promised them nothing but a guarantee of perpetual oppression—an oppression they were now asked openly to accept—and they took advantage of this sole opportunity to express their outrage at the accord.

Africans from all walks of life and all areas of Rhodesia rejected the proposals. The unity of African opinion was most firmly articulated by the African National Council (ANC), which emerged in December 1971 as a new African organization expressly to oppose the settlement. Led by two ministers, Bishop Abel Muzorewa and the Reverend Canaan Banana, the ANC quickly became the most active African organization to emerge in Rhodesia since 1964. The commission found that the ANC within four weeks had successfully disseminated information opposing the proposals to many parts of the country. In summarizing the analysis of African verbal opinion (at public meetings and in groups of more than 20), the commission found 97,800 rejections and 670 acceptances. In groups of under 20, the figures were 9,509 opposed and 2,264 in favor.[55] The commission found strong opposition even in remote rural areas where political meetings had been banned since the late 1950's.

Despite their long-time use by the RF as spokesmen for African opinion, the chiefs too were found to be divided on the question. The 26-man Council of Chiefs told the commission it unanimously accepted the proposals, yet when separately interviewed in their home areas 8 of the 26 members rejected the proposals. (Two of these chiefs subsequently told the commission that they personally did support the settlement but were unwilling to publicly express that opinion.) [56] Furthermore, 184 of Rhodesia's 245 chiefs were polled. Of this group 44 accepted, 87 rejected, and 53 gave no answer or abstained. In addition, the 8 Rhodesian members of parliament elected indirectly by the 1,400 chiefs, headmen, and elected counsellors in accordance with the 1969 constitution all rejected the proposals.[57] The failure of the chiefs to support the government fully once their actions were exposed to public scrutiny was a blow to the government's ten-year effort to establish that the chiefs both spoke for the African people *and* supported the Rhodesian Front government. The 7 African members of parliament from the small multiracial Centre Party also rejected the proposals, despite the firm support given them by the Centre Party's white leadership.

The Rhodesian government prepared an extensive dossier for the commission, which argued that the Africans had been so intimidated by the troubles of mid-January and the presence of a few nationalist politicians recently released from detention that the mass of the African people had been afraid to support the settlement. The Pearce Commission examined this proposition in meticulous detail in the longest chapter in its report. After examining all the evidence, including that submitted by the Rhodesian government, the commission stated:

We do not accept that there was ever a moment when a majority on reflection and with some understanding of the Proposals would have answered "Yes" to our Commission . . . . We found it improbable if not impossible that with such a tight security system as that which has existed in Rhodesia for several years, a minority could dominate a majority by intimidation in a few weeks. We have grounds for belief that the African National Council itself was surprised at the extent of its success. We do not think that the ANC would have obtained so great and so swift a response had they not met a potential desire among a majority of the people for leadership in a rejection of the terms and in a protest against the policies of the last few years . . . We ourselves have no doubt from all the facts and circumstances and our own observations that, in spite of the incidents of intimidation, the Africans' rejection by a substantial majority was a genuine expression of opinion.[58]

The commission also rejected the ANC charge of governmental intimidation of chiefs by district commissioners, of African employees by their employers, and of the Africans generally by the presence of police and special branch officers at African meetings.[59] Although some of this occurred, it was generally felt the Africans had sufficient opportunity to express their views freely.

In the aftermath of the Pearce Commission report, the situation today continues as it has since UDI. A saddened Sir Alec Douglas-Home reported to the British Parliament that sanctions would be maintained and that an indefinite period of time would now have to elapse to wait for a change of heart in Rhodesia. Home held out the dim hope that Africans and Europeans in Rhodesia "will decide to choose the way of compromise and work together for orderly political change." [60] But what chance is there for a change of heart in Rhodesia? An enraged Ian Smith called the Pearce Commission findings "naive and inept" and gave his countrymen assurance that "we shall govern firmly and that we shall not tolerate any attempt to disturb the peace and harmony . . . the country has returned to since the departure of the Pearce Commission." [61] He pledged Rhodesia's determination to carry on with its own 1969 constitution, and in early June 1972 he told his parliament that there would be "no more negotiations" because the British government "has lost the will to settle with us." [62]

No doubt Britain and Rhodesia one day will again attempt to resolve their differences by negotiation. Unless sanctions prove far more effective than they have been in the past, however, there is little reason to expect that the RF soon will be prepared to offer concessions to the Africans any more promising than those already rejected. Thus, to settle, Britain will have to find a way to abandon the fifth principle. Home seemed to allude to this possibility when he stated in parliament that "Any new proposals must be within the five principles. I would not like at this stage to commit myself exactly to the method that will be used with the fifth principle in the future when we are looking at the matter entirely new and completely blind . . . On this we will keep a completely open mind." [63]

As all negotiations since UDI have demonstrated, it is impossible for Britain and Rhodesia to turn the clock back to before that act. It may now be true that there is no way to go back to the position before November 24, 1971. Although it was a great disappointment to both the Rhodesian and British governments that the accord was unacceptable to the Africans, the fact remains that the two governments in power did come to an agreement. This appears to have had a detrimental effect on the international sanctions campaign; clearly American willingness to defy the UN was based in part on the belief that the dispute was all but over. Other nations too may now take a more open line in defiance of the UN. Rhodesia's unilateral declaration of independence is an accomplished fact, and the proposed settlement admitted this. With sanctions weakened, it is hard to foresee growth in Britain's ability to induce concessions from white Rhodesia. The unknown quantity of the entire Pearce Commission exercise is what effect this African success will have on African politics within Rhodesia and on the liberation forces challenging the white government. This it is too early to tell.

Rhodesia and Its Neighbors

Rhodesia's relations with all of its neighbors were complicated by UDI. Even its two friends, Portugal and South Africa, have been unwilling to grant Rhodesia full diplomatic recognition, while black-governed states have been torn between their political desire to help Rhodesia's Africans and the reality of their limited ability to challenge Rhodesia.

These relations with surrounding countries by and large can be understood as a function of two criteria: the race of the particular government in question and the degree of dependency of that government on Rhodesia or of Rhodesia on that government. The reaction of black Africa to UDI was generally very hostile. Through the Organization of African Unity, through African participation in the commonwealth, and through African pressure applied at the United Nations, these countries sought to oppose the white regime.[64] Their attitude over time has moderated to the degree that they have realized that African influence on the situation is limited and that nothing would have forced Britain to take steps she was determined to avoid.

In the immediate aftermath of UDI, African states, through the Organization of African Unity, called for a complete severing of diplomatic relations with Britain. This call grew out of a general belief, voiced by President Nyerere of Tanzania, that UDI "represents an advance by the forces of racialism, fascism, and, indeed, colonialism in Southern Africa." [65] The OAU call for action, however, had a limited response, as only 9 of 36 African nations severed their ties with Britain. This response to a call for collective action openly revealed fissures within Africa over Rhodesia, at least insofar as African countries were prepared to align their actions with their professed concern. In analyzing this early period, R. Cranford Pratt has noted that the African states were "intemperate and extreme in their demands, inept in their diplomacy and irresolute in their actions." [66]

Since this early period, African states have concentrated their actions in two ways. At the UN they have constantly supported efforts to escalate the sanctions battle, not only against Rhodesia but against South Africa and Portugal as well. They have also, without success, urged British or big-power military intervention to break the Rhodesian rebellion. The second goal of Africa, much more moderate but equally elusive, has been to tie Britain to her NIBMAR pledge. Thus at commonwealth prime ministers' conferences and in discussions generally, African leaders have foregone hopes of any early resolution to the Rhodesian crisis or of any rapid transition to African rule; instead, they have stood by the argument that the fight in Rhodesia was "about the principle of majority rule first, then independence; not about timing." [67] In this framework almost any arrangement would be acceptable except the granting of independence to Rhodesia prior to majority rule. As Nyerere has written, "independence means power," and to expect that any pledges would be honored by white Rhodesia once it achieved independence and sanctions were lifted would at best be uncertain.[68] As the terms offered by Britain to Rhodesia reveal, however, even to get Britain to honor NIBMAR was impossible.

One other aspect of black Africa's relations with Rhodesia are Rhodesia's ties with its two former partners in federation, Zambia and Malawi (the name since 1964 for Nyasaland). Zambia has been in the forefront of African nations seeking more rapid action against Rhodesia and has been very involved in implementing sanctions. Its efforts have been substantial; no nation in the world has had its political and economic life so disrupted and dominated by the Rhodesian crisis. Zambia moved quickly to find alternative sources of imports and new export routes. This was not easy, for nearly all its ties prior to the middle 1960's had been southward. When the new Tan-Zam railroad is completed sometime in 1975, linking Zambia northward to Tanzania, many of its continuing ties with Rhodesia may be broken. Until then, however, Zambia has no alternative but to exist uneasily as Rhodesia's northern neighbor, still tied uncomfortably to Rhodesia and the white south in ways developed and institutionalized long before UDI.

Malawi, on the other hand, has been one of the African countries least concerned about the Rhodesia crisis. Malawi has parted ways with most of Africa on the question of possibly using force against white Rhodesia and has refused to comply fully with mandatory sanctions against Rhodesia. Its position toward Rhodesia is governed in part by the fact that many migrant laborers go to Rhodesia each year, but more significantly by the decision (taken by President H. Kamuzu Banda, the one-time nemesis of white-dominated federation) that Malawi's future interests can best be served by entertaining close ties with the white states of Southern Africa. Rhodesia is a part of this, although Malawi's ties with South Africa and Portugal are far more important. The lack of stridency toward Rhodesia is a source of minor satisfaction to the RF, even though Malawi's trade and political ties with Rhodesia are so limited that its stance does not really much affect either the success of failure of UDI.

This lack of influence hardly applies when we consider Rhodesia's relations with its white neighbors—Portuguese-controlled Mozambique and South Africa.[69] As we have seen, these two states have assisted Rhodesia in blunting the effect of sanctions. Their willingness to support Rhodesia arises out of common racial bonds of white governments trying to preserve control in black Africa and out of an interest in showing the ineffectiveness of economic sanctions, lest sanctions one day be turned against themselves.

So far Portugal and South Africa have succeeded, but this success does not come without some degree of ambivalence about what they are doing and about the Rhodesian government that has so obviously forced their hand. Portugal's position with regard to Rhodesia is really of minor importance compared with South Africa's, both because Portugal's relations with Rhodesia are far more limited and because in many ways Portugal's relations with South Africa are analogous to Rhodesia's relations with South Africa. Both Rhodesia and Portugal are weak white states compared to South Africa, and to an increasing extent in both states South African financial, political, and military power is being used to underwrite their white governments.

South Africa has come to Rhodesia's aid for the reasons mentioned previously and because its own white citizens would probably not have allowed white Rhodesia to be overcome without a fight. On the other hand, the Nationalist Party leadership in Pretoria has always had deep reservations about the leadership of the Rhodesian Front. South Africa considered UDI a senseless act. Like Rhodesia's black and white critics within, South Africa realized that Rhodesia's white government had effective independence prior to UDI. There was no need to seize independence and thus precipitate an international crisis. To the South African leadership, UDI was unnecessary and stupid and needlessly gave black Africa an excellent issue to build international pressure against white Southern Africa. South Africa has always tried to run her external affairs with scrupulous attention to legality, and the Rhodesian action was the complete antithesis of this. South Africa's main concern was that its important relations with Britain would be affected by the

Rhodesian imbroglio. Britain, however, made it clear publicly and privately that she would do nothing to escalate the Rhodesian issue. The continuation of UDI saw an easing of South Africa's fears that it was being drawn into a situation where it had something less than complete confidence or complete control.

Despite reservations, South Africa has been able to have its way in Rhodesia. The financial costs of helping Rhodesia survive as a white state are clearly tolerable to Pretoria, and South Africa's support of Rhodesia has not harmed its relations with the West. What has happened is that South Africa has supplanted Britain as Rhodesia's link with the rest of the world (South Africa has always been Rhodesia's model for internal policies), while exercising—like Britain before her —only a limited ability to affect Rhodesian policies. South Africa, like Britain, could choose to exercise the massive force at its disposal to insist on fundamental changes within Rhodesia, but at present this possibility is unlikely. South African influence in Rhodesia is certain to expand, particularly now that the Rhodesians have decided to build a direct rail link. Nonetheless, the strong internal position of the Rhodesian whites continues to be a major trump card against any nation seeking influence over them.

In the long run (say by the end of this century) other developments may occur. Incorporation of Rhodesia into South Africa as a fifth province is an outside chance. It is not inconceivable that South Africa might one day sponsor a "moderate" African government for Rhodesia at the expense of Smith (or more likely his successors). South Africa presently is eagerly seeking friends in black Africa and may one day feel that its own white government can best be protected by underwriting and dominating compliant black governments on its borders rather than by supporting white governments such as the Rhodesian Front. At the moment, however, these possibilities are remote and it appears certain that South Africa will give white Rhodesians whatever assistance they need to continue to rule Rhodesia.

7

Internal Politics and Control
since the Unilateral
Declaration of Independence

Familiar themes have dominated Rhodesian political life since the unilateral declaration of independence. Within the white community, unity
has been stressed as a primary goal in order to ensure victory over internal and external foes. The conflicts that have arisen have been over
tactical questions related to the possibility of a settlement with Britain
or of Rhodesia irrevocably going it alone. With regard to race relations,
there has been constant white pressure to tighten controls over Africans
in all fields of social, economic, and political activity. Changes have
evolved slowly and for the most part have been limited to minor elabo-
rations and refinements of well-established practices. The major new
problem the government has faced is the emergence of guerrilla incursions from Zambia by supporters of the two banned African nationalist
parties, ZAPU and ZANU. As could be expected, the government has
responded vigorously because of the serious threat armed conflict poses
for the small white population.

White Politics, the 1969 Constitution,
and the Rhodesian Republic

The united white support for the Rhodesian Front has not changed since UDI. In the April 1970 general election (the first since UDI) the RF repeated its 1965 sweep of all European seats in parliament. The pressures to resist white conflict have been great because of the particular circumstances of post-UDI Rhodesia. The whites feared that open fighting among themselves would suggest both to those implementing sanctions and to the Africans within Rhodesia that sanctions were working and that they were vulnerable.

As time passed, however, and it became apparent that the white community could survive sanctions indefinitely, the intense pressure for unity eased. Within Rhodesia different conflicts emerged. One involves the very meaning and purpose of UDI. Some white Rhodesians saw the split with Britain as a family quarrel that would soon blow over—a tempest that would quickly run its course and be forgotten in the greater unity of racial solidarity, British imperial traditions, and long-time trade and political links. Others such as Brigadier Skeen conceived of UDI in far more grandiose terms—as a major Western stand against the forces of Communism and totalitarianism, a stand necessary to the preservation of the Western tradition.[1] Depending on which of these perspectives was accepted, very different answers arose as to whether Britain was the enemy or only a misguided friend, and whether or not to seek a settlement.

A second source of white conflict is ideological and centers on whether to maintain the segregated society on its present basis or to formalize segregation (as in South Africa) with explicit apartheid legislation. While there is little disagreement on indefinite European political control, there is mixed feeling about full-scale apartheid. Pragmatic considerations such as cost and the small size of the European community militate against full-scale apartheid, as does an enduring sense of Rhodesian white nationalism that does not embrace Afrikaner thinking and in less precarious times might chafe at the growing South African presence in Rhodesia. This issue was drawn on the question of whether or not to retain any Africans in the Rhodesian parliament.

A third conflict arises out of the differing effects of sanctions. Many business and financial leaders, as well as some farmers, even though they were quite prepared to work for the success of UDI, did favor a settlement. Part of the small ongoing white opposition to the RF is identified by its desire to return to a situation like that prevailing before UDI; others urged a settlement on the *Tiger* or *Fearless* terms.

The pattern of these white disagreements is clear. Throughout the history of Rhodesia debate has arisen over the tactics for best preserving the white system. After UDI, conflict erupted over proposed new legislation and over specific administrative actions that were (or were not) taken. Perhaps with greatest intensity, conflict arose over a new constitution. None was possible without clear decisions involving the lessons of Rhodesia's past and the shape of its future. Though agreement on ends still prevailed, different strategies suggested themselves depending on the values party members chose to emphasize. Some favored a settlement as the best way for white Rhodesia to achieve international recognition and internal prosperity; others favored the declaration of a republic and territorial partition as the optimum means to the same end. The ideologically minded Rhodesian committed to apartheid found to his surprise that South Africa, in its eagerness for a settlement, had little interest in Rhodesian apartheid and that one of the weapons the RF could best use abroad was continuation of the multiracial university and parliament. This lack of consensus offered Prime Minister Smith and the government a certain degree of leeway, but only within the narrow confines of RF principles and European dedication to indefinite political control.

The decision to write a new constitution arose from the feeling that white independence would not be "real" until Rhodesia had a document not previously negotiated with Britain. Some whites felt it necessary to do away with minor constitutional impediments to white rule and to eliminate the slight chance that Africans might come to have more influence within the political system. A new constitution would also serve as a useful foil in the continuing negotiations with Britain. These were not urgent needs and it was not until the aftermath of the *Tiger* failure that the first steps were taken.

In April 1967 a constitutional commission was appointed under the chairmanship of William R. Whaley, a prominent Rhodesian Front member and a close personal friend of Ian Smith. The five-man commission included two Africans who were well-known government backers and two other Europeans including Stan Morris, a former chief native commissioner and at that time head of the Public Service Commission. The Whaley Commission's terms of reference were as follows:

> To advise the Government of Rhodesia on the constitutional framework which is best suited to the sovereign independent status of Rhodesia and which is calculated to protect and guarantee the rights and freedoms of all persons and communities in Rhodesia and ensure the harmonious development of Rhodesia's plural society, having regard to the social and cultural differences among the people of Rhodesia, to the different systems of land tenure and to the problems of economic development.[2]

The commission reported a year later and startled nearly all the whites in Rhodesia (except for leading RF officials who were in on the details) by advocating the eventual possibility of political parity between blacks and whites in Rhodesia. The commission wrote: "We see the fundamental objective of any new constitutional framework for Rhodesia as being . . . the removal of suspicion and misgivings among Rhodesians of any one of the main races or ethnic groups that they may be permanently dominated by one or more of the other main races or ethnic groups." [3] Because of the immense complexity of the constitutional arrangements suggested, it would clearly take a very long time (dozens of years, hundreds of years—as with the 1961 constitution no one could predict with certainty) for parity to be reached; nevertheless, the mere idea provoked an outcry that led to a struggle within the party for most of 1968 and into 1969.

When the report was published, an elaborate set of procedures were announced whereby the RF and then the country would express opinions on the proposed constitution. Two important party committees were established, one a subcommittee headed by Minister of Justice Lardner-Burke and the other composed of the six RF divisional chairmen. The Lardner-Burke committee was responsible for appraising parliamentary sentiment, and the divisional chairmen were to talk to the party regulars. From this broad sampling of opinion the two committees were to bring a joint recommendation to the party executive, which would then recommend a final constitutional draft to go before the RF National Congress for approval. Only after this extensive party scrutiny would the white electorate be given an opportunity to consider the proposal.

It was immediately evident that almost the entire party was deeply suspicious of the principle of eventual parity. The line in the Whaley Commission report stating that "we do not envisage permanent polarization of political forces along racial lines" [4] seemed to many RF members a direct repudiation of all they had worked for and a return to the hypocrisy they had always associated with the Welensky-Whitehead era. The party secretariat found antagonism so strong that it circulated (within the party) the evidence it had presented to the Whaley Commission in order to reassure party regulars that the original RF position had not advocated parity.

The two party committees struggled to find an acceptable formula that would command substantial party support. In July 1968 they published their recommendations (known locally as the Yellow Paper) for an elaborate two-stage system of representation. The first stage, to last for five years, retained the idea of parity but guaranteed European control for those years. The second and final stage would abandon parity in favor of a nationwide parliament and three racially segregated (two African and one white) provincial councils. The national parliament would remain racially mixed, with representation proportionate to the amount of personal income tax paid by each race; at present levels of income tax receipts, the Africans would have been limited to one seat.

Despite the fact that the Yellow Paper emasculated the Whaley Commission plan for parity, the new proposals also met with opposition. A group led by Minister of Internal Affairs William J. Harper and Minister of Defense and External Affairs Lord Graham drafted a constitution calling for racially separate national chambers. Heated party discussions ensued. Supported by Smith, other RF ministers, and the divisional chairman, the Yellow Paper proposals narrowly survived votes in the caucus and the party executive when opposed by the Harper-Graham proposals.[5] At the critical National Congress of the party in September 1968, Smith was forced to use his full prestige to save the Yellow Paper proposals from those who sought a constitution having fixed racial proportions in the national parliament of 50 Europeans, 4 Africans, 1 Asian, and 1 Coloured. The Yellow Paper survived by a narrow vote of 217 to 206.[6]

Behind this infighting lay the usual question of the best strategy to preserve white control. Those favoring the Harper-Graham proposals or the 50-4-1-1 constitution had given up on a settlement and wanted Rhodesia to move forward on her own. They feared that Smith intended to use the Yellow Paper proposals as the basis to try for a settlement and that the second stage would never be implemented. It was uncharacteristic of Smith to stand so firmly against party pressure, but he apparently had become convinced that Britain was prepared to grant Rhodesia independence and end sanctions once he had shown resistance to "extremist pressures"—something he felt he had demonstrated by his commitment to parity and by the removal of Harper and Graham from his cabinet during this hectic period. Just after the RF National Congress, Smith had his meeting with Wilson on the *Fearless*. As seen, this conclave came to nothing and in the aftermath, new constitutional steps were taken.

Early in 1969 Smith announced in a nationwide broadcast that his constitutional experts had found it impossible to draft a two-stage constitution and therefore the Yellow Paper proposals were being dropped. In their place a new draft constitution appeared. It was approved by the RF national executive, by the electorate in a referendum on June 20, 1969, and ultimately by parliament.[7] This constitution later became the basic document for the proposed 1971 settlement.

The 1969 constitution centered all political power in a dominant lower house called the House of Assembly. The initial membership of this body was to be 50 Europeans and 16 Africans. This ratio (only slightly different than the 50 to 15 A-roll/B-roll ratio of the 1961 constitution) would remain fixed until the African population paid at least 24 percent of the national revenue raised by direct income tax. Then, as the African percentage of the national income tax surpassed 24 percent, African representation would slowly increase to a maximum of 50, that is, parity.

In reality Africans were likely to maintain only 16 seats. Income tax revenues from Africans generally run about 0.5 percent of the national whole. In the year ending June 30, 1968, for example, Africans paid a total of 64,744 pounds of a total income tax collected of 28,560,000 pounds.[8] The chance of the African share of the direct income tax rising to 24 percent or more is miniscule. The scheme was nothing more than an efficient way to guarantee permanent white rule.

The method for selection of African representatives was also altered. Eight seats were to be elected by an African lower roll.[9] The other eight African seats were to be filled by chiefs selected and approved by the chiefs, headmen, and African rural councillors. This group totals about 1,400 men. Both the eight elected Africans and the eight African chiefs were to be equally proportioned between the Shona and the Ndebele, despite the fact that the Shona population is more than twice the Ndebele.[10] Other electoral changes were to include the elimination of cross-voting and the requirement that each race only vote for and be represented by a member of his own race; this latter change would effectively eliminate Dr. Ahrn Palley, the white independent, from parliament.

The proposed 1971 terms simply added the African higher roll on top of the base of eight directly elected Africans and eight selected by the chiefs. In addition, the income tax method of determining the rate of expansion of African representation was withdrawn in favor of the growth of the African higher roll as the determinant. Both Home and Smith cited this change as a major Rhodesian concession to British demands. In fact, both schemes were phony. Neither the 1969 Rhodesian constitution nor the proposed 1971 settlement was designed to promote African political opportunities beyond a narrow range. It is hard to take seriously a choice between two possibilities that may occur sometime in the next century.

The constitution established a new body, the Senate, comprising 10 Europeans elected by the European members of the new House of Assembly, 10 more African chiefs, and 3 representatives selected by the president, himself the new head of state. The Senate was to have minor delaying powers on some bills and come into play on constitutional amendments. There are numerous ways, however, in which the House of Assembly can circumvent the Senate, and it is hard to see this body as anything but a resting place for aging white politicians and another sinecure for "loyal" chiefs.

The new constitution eliminated the Constitutional Council and made the Declaration of Rights nonjusticiable. It expressly permitted discriminatory legislation "if such treatment is fair and will promote harmonious relations . . . by making due allowances for economic, social or cultural differences." [11] Protection from search and entry remained limited, an individual no longer could refuse to give evidence at his own trial, preventive detention and restriction were formally authorized in the interest of national defense and public order, and regulations were introduced for far stricter censorship.

The RF carried out a strenuous campaign in support of these new proposals. Smith and his senior ministers argued as usual that a vote against the RF would create a crisis that would help Rhodesia's enemies and lead to majority rule. Just as he had promised with UDI, Smith claimed in a May 7, 1969, speech that the new constitution "sounded the death knell of the notion of majority rule. We have created a yardstick where merit is the criterion. This constitution enshrines European control on merit. No one can undermine it." [12] Party ads could have been used in any election of the past twenty years: "A NO vote would mean a further period of waiting and wishful thinking, of relying on Britain and the UN for the planning of *our* destiny"; and "Vote YES for a secure future for *all* Rhodesians, for a Rhodesian constitution drawn up by Rhodesia, for a Republic and the benefits which will follow, for continuing economic stability and long-term prosperity, for continuing our independence." [13]

In opposition to the RF stood the Centre Party, formed in August 1968 from the various remnants of previous white opposition groups. It urged a NO vote, for fear that accepting the new constitution would foreclose the possibility of a settlement with Britain; the Centre Party favored the *Fearless* terms.[14] One surprise supporter of the Centre Party was Maj. Gen. Sam Putterhill, commanding officer of all Rhodesian armed forces from October 1965 to October 1968—from UDI through the first years of African guerrilla incursions. Putterhill argued that under the new constitution the Africans would have no hope for the future politically and thus would inevitably turn to more militant action. He argued that success against the guerrillas had been achieved because of the army's African support, and he felt that the new constitution would provide a fertile ground for guerrilla recruitment.[15] Smith attacked Putterhill's remarks as "despicable" and reassured the electorate that the government had always known of Putterhill's "extreme leftist views!" [16]

The Centre Party made only a minor impact, and the vote on the new constitution was 54,724 affirmative (73 percent) and 20,776 negative (27 percent).[17] Smith was pleased: "I was hoping for a strong majority as a message to the outside world as to the mood in Rhodesia today, and how determined we are to get on and attend to the affairs of our country ourselves." [18] The new constitution then was brought before parliament, where it was debated and finally passed on November 17, 1969. In introducing the debate, Minister of Justice Lardner-Burke indicated that the government had been "searching for a constitutional solution which will minimize racial influence in politics and will, at the same time, retain the principle of equality of opportunity and reasonable participation in the affairs of the nation by members of all races." [19] He went on to add that the constitution had been "tailored entirely by Rhodesians to meet the needs of Rhodesia . . . it is the first truly Rhodesian Constitution." [20] It was evident that to "minimize racial influence" in politics meant to minimize African influence and that to "meet the needs of Rhodesia" meant to guarantee white control.

One of the many anomalies of Rhodesia's rebellion has been the way in which, despite its bitterness toward British policy, the Rhodesian government has tried to maintain emotional ties to the queen, and thus indirectly to Britain as a whole. Just prior to UDI the entire RF cabinet sent a letter to the queen pledging its continued fidelity, and only in April 1967 did the RF amend its own constitution to pledge dedication to the "independent country of Rhodesia" rather than to the queen. It was not until 1968 that Rhodesia abandoned the Union Jack, and "God Save the Queen" was played at movie houses and sporting events long after UDI.

Despite these lingering imperial connections, there has been strong support for Rhodesia to become a republic. This step (taken by South Africa in 1961) is closely associated in the minds of many Europeans with notions of "true independence" and was seen as a necessary step for Rhodesia if it ever was to convince the world that it was really free of Britain.

The reservations within the RF about becoming a republic, like the earlier question of UDI, have not turned on its long-term desirability, but on the question of proper timing. Rhodesia benefited from the fact that not until two and one-half years after UDI did the British government finally go to the UN for compulsory mandatory sanctions; the British previously went to great lengths to assert official responsibility for Rhodesia. If Rhodesia had declared itself a republic at the time of UDI, for instance, Britain would have had no credible claim of continuing responsibility and the UN might have acted much sooner. Another reason for delay was to put off any showdown with the Rhodesian judiciary and other groups with pre-UDI pledges of loyalty to the queen. By 1969 everyone had found one reason or another to support UDI and the next step made little difference.

Following the *Fearless* talks, the RF decided to put the issue of a republic before the Rhodesian electorate at the same time as it voted on the 1969 constitution. It was massively supported; 61,130 voted yes (81 percent) and 14,372 voted no (19 percent).[21] The vote for a republic ran about 7,000 votes ahead of the vote for the new constitution. This was commonly attributed to the fact that more people opposed the constitution because it allowed Africans to sit in the same parliament with whites.

In the wake of this overwhelming vote the Rhodesian governor, Sir Humphrey Gibbs, submitted his resignation to the British government and it was accepted. At Britain's request, Gibbs had remained in Government House in the long years since UDI even though the regime had appointed its own Officer Administering the Government and Gibbs had had his staff and other official amenities withdrawn. Gibbs was a symbol of Rhodesia's past ties with Britain, and he attended the *Tiger* and *Fearless* talks at the insistence of the British government. Once the decision on the republic came, however, Gibbs retired to his farm. Britain's response was to close its residual mission in Rhodesia on July 10, 1969, and Rhodesia House in London shut officially four days later. On March 1, 1970, parliament was dissolved and a republic declared. In the aftermath of this declaration, most foreign countries closed their offices in Salisbury.[22]

The first election under the new constitution was held in April 1970—just a few weeks after the declaration of a republic and the withdrawal of foreign missions from Salisbury. No apparent lack of confidence on the part of the white electorate emerged. The RF again won all 50 European seats against insignificant opposition from the Centre Party and the Republican Alliance, a small dissident group who wanted all Africans out of parliament and who advocated strict and explicit apartheid.

The RF's principles, published for the election, contained all the traditional guarantees of white defense and included the assertion that "Rhodesia has achieved the unique distinction of being the first country in the world to win the first decisive round in its encounter with communist aggression." [23] The campaign was desultory and amounted to little more than a referendum on RF rule. The only lively moment came at an election meeting attended by African students from the university, where Prime Minister Smith "greeted" them by singing an Afrikaans song, "Bobbejaan, klim die berg" (Baboon, climb the hill). At another election meeting Smith commented, "Sixty years ago Africans here were uncivilised savages, walking around in skins. They have made tremendous progress but they have an awful long way to go." [24] Many RF candidates were returned unopposed; no candidate came close to losing. Within the structure of the white political system, the Rhodesian Front remained as impregnable as ever.

In retrospect it is clear that the 1968 struggle within the RF was really over whether to try again for a settlement with Britain. Smith stood by the Yellow Paper proposals (with their dim prospect of parity) because both the Graham-Harper and the 50-4-1-1 proposals undoubtedly would have been rejected by Britain. After the *Fearless* failure, Smith saw no further prospect of negotiating with Wilson and Rhodesia accordingly moved on to establish the 1969 constitution and become a republic. Both of these steps were favored by those in the party who had supported the Graham-Harper and 50-4-1-1 proposals. Thus the party was reunited. After 1970, Britain had no option but to accept the reality of Rhodesia's independent republican status. This was one reason why the 1971 proposals garnered substantial white support. The proposals for African "majority rule" scarcely raised an eyebrow, since the prospect was so distant that it posed no threat, even to this group of fearful and suspicious whites.

Trends in Race Relations and African Administration

Since UDI, the overall tenor of RF legislation and administrative action has been slowly to broaden white control over a variety of African activities. The goal has been to narrow the areas in which Africans and Europeans interact except on the basis of master and servant. There have been no dramatic developments—UDI was taken to preserve, not to alter, most Rhodesian racial practices. Still, some changes should be noted as suggestive of the way the RF perceives race relations over the long run.

The most important developments have been the introduction of the new constitution and the passage of the Land Tenure Act. The constitution defines the nature of African political representation and (by introducing the chiefs into parliament for the first time) marks the increasing RF commitment to the chiefs as prime spokesmen for the African people. In addition to political representation in the parliament and Senate, the chiefs have been given higher salaries, new land allocation powers, bodyguards and guns, and new criminal court powers to which their African subjects are liable.[25] The constitution has explicitly introduced tribalism into Rhodesian politics by equally dividing all African representatives between the two major African ethnic groups. This accords both with traditional European myths about African tribal conflict before the arrival of the whites and with contemporary needs of dividing the African population to make European control easier.

The Land Tenure Act of 1969 replaces the Land Apportionment Act of 1940, which had been the cornerstone of racial segregation within Rhodesia. The new Land Tenure Act (LTA) achieves the same goals but has a few new twists. The LTA permanently divides the land into two "equal" portions: 45 million acres for five million Africans and 45 million acres for less than one-quarter million Europeans. Henceforth alterations in land allocation are limited by the proviso that the variation between the two racially defined areas can be no more than 2 percent. This rigid formula was introduced to eliminate insecurity among the Europeans "who feel that their land may be taken away from them for use by the rapidly increasing number of Africans." [26] As he introduced the LTA in parliament, Minister of Lands Philip van Heerden echoed the theme of the old two-pyramid policy: "The main objectives of the Bill are to divide the major portion of the land in Rhodesia into two equal areas, in one of which the interests of Europeans, and in the other of which the interests of Africans, will be paramount." [27]

Although each race is supposed to have an area where its own interests are paramount, the LTA contains all the loopholes necessary for European exploitation of African land. Provision is made for "nonracial" residential and industrial centers in the African area, where Europeans presumably will reside as mineral finds are exploited. Opportunities for Africans in European areas except in rigidly defined roles naturally are excluded.

The LTA embraces many provisions which could be used to make Rhodesia a country with full apartheid. One allows the minister to make different land arrangements for different classes of Europeans or Africans, thus paving the way for legislation along the lines of South Africa's Group Areas Act. The government probably will bring forward legislation that will segregate Asians and Coloureds from the European population in urban areas.[28] The same type of provision could be used to group the African population as Shona and Ndebele, or indigenous and nonindigenous, or any other combination the government sees fit.

Finally the LTA has provisions which will enable the minister in charge of the act to exercise almost total control over the movement of all Rhodesian citizens through enactment of the comprehensive permit system to regulate how persons of one race occupy land reserved for the other race. This in effect makes all African urban workers (and even African university students) mere holders of permits which can be withdrawn at the minister's discretion. In this way, any dissident can be forced out of the urban into the rural areas. Furthermore, the minister is empowered to define what constitutes occupation of land. This power, combined with the permit power, gives the minister comprehensive power over entry and exit not only from land, but also from buildings or anything he defines as "land."

Other recent actions should be mentioned briefly. The Rhodesian Front has moved to close off small areas of interracial contact that were the legacies of the UFP's middle-class African strategy; it has refused to renew licenses for multiracial hotels; and small urban schools established by Europeans for their servants' children have been closed.

The Municipal Amendment Act of 1967 was an important piece of permissive legislation which opened the way for all Rhodesian local municipalities to authorize racially separate amenities for parks, public places and recreation, sports and athletic grounds, swimming pools, and public conveniences. This act has not been utilized much because segregation generally has always been practiced, but it lays the groundwork for more explicit apartheid legislation that may come in the future.[29] Recent evictions of African trade unions, businessmen, and professionals from the run-down section of European Salisbury (where they had long had offices) suggests a tightening up on land use.[30]

African education is another area in which the RF has made modest adjustments. Since shortly after UDI, spending for this purpose has been pegged at no more than 2 percent of the gross national product.[31] This is an important move, because the African population is expanding rapidly while the economy is making only modest gains. In 1969, to cut back on African education costs, primary school was reduced from eight to seven years.[32] In 1970 the government announced a 5 percent cut in its payments to missionary primary schools.[33] The purpose of these various moves is to decrease African education expenditure and force the Africans to pay more of the overall costs, despite the fact that government expenditure for each European pupil per annum is more than ten times the amount spent on each African student.

At the top of the education ladder, only a tiny fraction of African pupils go to a secondary school or university. Those that do find few employment opportunities when they graduate. African university students are all but forced to be teachers, since a combination of government regulations and social practices excludes them from other employment opportunities. In 1970 the government announced that the University College of Rhodesia, the only institution in the country ever integrated in any meaningful sense, would sever its connection with the University of London—perhaps the first step toward segregation of university education in Rhodesia.

The RF's legislation since UDI has not brought any dramatic departures for the simple reason that the central mandate of the party is to preserve the old order in Rhodesia, not to move to a new one. Yet a minor trend has developed which suggests that the RF may be laying the groundwork for more systematic segregatory legislation along the lines of that practiced in South Africa. It would be erroneous, however, to make too much of the new provisions of the Municipal Amendment Act or the Land Tenure Act. Rhodesia has always been a highly segregated society. Methods for shaping its segregation have changed with the times, and it should not surprise us that as South Africa's presence and influence within Rhodesia grows some of her practices (in a more specific ideological sense) may be adopted. Still, it would be entirely wrong to suggest that somehow this constitutes a change in the essential character of Rhodesia society. Rhodesian whites have always insisted on a segregated way of life and they still do. All white governments since 1890 have met this demand. Changes since UDI are those of nuance, not substance.

Internal Security and the Beginning of
Guerrilla Warfare

The political position of the Africans within Rhodesia has changed little with UDI. The broad array of security legislation discussed earlier has continued (with scarcely any modification) to supply the government with the legal and administrative weapons necessary to curb dissident political activity. These controls have been augmented by emergency regulations, which give the government additional authority to do almost anything it desires. The government believes that it has so thoroughly infiltrated the nationalist movement both within the country and in exile that it is all but impossible for anything politically important to happen without its knowledge. Government figures certainly suggest the decline in political activity by African nationalists. Table 19 summarizes government-released data on security measures since 1964. All but a tiny handful of those affected have been Africans.

Table 19. Use of selected security legislation in Rhodesia, 1964–1969.

Year	Restriction orders	Detention orders	LOMA prosecutions[a]	UOA prosecutions[a]	EPA prosecutions[a]
1964	650	1,670	2,017	200	0
1965	369	113	726	147	52
1966	361	179	248	66	323
1967	59	45	177	44	148
1968	2	56	48	40	72
1969[b]	0	14	11	8	n.a.

SOURCE: *SRLAD,* vol. 76 (November 12, 1969), 1231–1234, and vol. 76 (January 28, 1970), 1568–1576.

[a] LOMA = Law and Order (Maintenance) Act;
UOA = Unlawful Organizations Act;
EPA = Emergency Powers Act.
[b] Through November 11.

The situation internally for African nationalist activity has been harsh. Nearly all the leading nationalist figures from the period prior to 1964 are still either in detention or restriction within Rhodesia, or in exile. The security forces have spent much of their time in recent years keeping tight control over the entry of Africans into urban areas. It is a fundamental principle of the government's security strategy that a tight net must be kept over the urban areas and that anyone without a job or entry permit must return to the rural areas. The government regularly conducts unannounced sweeps through the African townships in order to round up anyone without proper papers. From 1965 to 1969, prosecutions under the Africans (Registration and Identification) Act have averaged well over 12,000 per year and prosecutions under the African

(Urban Areas) Accommodation and Registration Act have averaged over 6,000 per year.[34] While these prosecutions (nearly all of which result in conviction) are not directly related to specific African political activity, they must be understood as preventive actions against the possibility of African discontent building in the urban areas.

On the basis of available evidence, the conclusion is inescapable that strong government security measures have largely succeeded in stifling internally generated political unrest within Rhodesia. In one celebrated case since UDI, the ZANU leader the Reverend Ndabaningi Sithole, who has been detained in a Salisbury prison, was charged with having attempted to incite the murder of Ian Smith and two of his ministerial colleagues. Sithole allegedly had secretly passed coded instructions to followers outside the prison to commit the assassinations. In his closing statement to the court, Sithole stated: "I wish to disassociate my name in thought, word and deed from any subversive activities, from any terrorist activities and from any form of violence." [35] Sithole was convicted and sentenced to six years hard labor—a conviction that left him just where he long had been, in a Salisbury prison.

The only exception to this general picture is the short period of disorders and rioting that coincided with the arrival of the Pearce Commission in January 1972. Over a period of about fifteen days, riots occurred in several Rhodesian towns and security forces killed at least 14 Africans and wounded many more in subduing the unrest. Large numbers of arrests were also made. Figures supplied by the government to the Pearce Commission stated that in the two months the commission was in Rhodesia, 1,736 persons were arrested and detained under Emergency Powers regulations.[36] This was the most trouble the government had faced since UDI, but it was by no means as sustained as the African political activity of earlier days. That there had been any trouble at all deeply irked the government, for it helped turn the Pearce Commission against the settlement terms and demonstrated during a period of considerable international interest in Rhodesia that the RF's bucolic picture of Rhodesian race relations was perhaps suspect.

The government blamed the African National Council and former nationalist politicians for the trouble, but by the middle of 1972 it still had not banned the ANC or restricted its leaders, Bishop Muzorewa and the Reverend Mr. Banana. This surprised many observers who expected stern governmental retaliation, but it can perhaps be explained by the government's interest in not taking new security actions before the Pearce Commission had reported. The government has forbidden the ANC to issue membership cards and in an effort to avoid an early banning the ANC now deliberately calls itself an organization instead of a political party. However, it certainly follows a nationalist line in claiming "no more than to be heirs to the people's struggle which has ceaselessly been waged since the imposition of alien rule in 1890 . . .

and [to be] the sole voice and instrument of the African masses of Zimbabwe and all peoples of good will, in their just and normal struggle for national emancipation from the yoke of racist and oppressive minority rule." [37] There can be little doubt that the government will strike firmly at the ANC if it attempts to translate this talk into action.

The disturbances of early 1972 suggest the potential for racial unrest within Rhodesia. Occasional instances of violence can generate publicity and momentarily reveal the sham nature of the government's propaganda, but this is far from saying that such episodes really threaten white power. Much more sustained, determined, and directed efforts are needed before the security forces will be brought to their knees.

Because of the harsh internal climate, the major focus of African nationalist activity has been in exile, where the leadership has begun to plan and implement a strategy of guerrilla warfare.[38] ZANU and ZAPU call this new phase of their struggle against the settlers *Chimurenga*, the Shona name for the 1896–1897 rebellions. Both the *Zimbabwe News* and the *Zimbabwe Review* from Lusaka regularly exhort their followers "to return to the spirit of 1896, when our forefathers Shona and Ndebele, faced the common threat of white settlement." [39] Although it is hard to get reliable data, many guerrilla attacks have occurred and this strategy has replaced all others as the way in which Rhodesian nationalists now expect to attain political power.

The first reported guerrilla attack took place in Rhodesia in April 1966. Since then, except during 1969, fairly substantial attacks have come every few months, in a wide variety of places. Generally the guerrillas enter Rhodesia secretly from Zambia, by crossing the Zambezi River, and then fan out through the Zambezi Valley and try to make their way to the high plateau where most white Rhodesians live. The battles that we know about presumably have occurred when the guerrilla bands are discovered by the security forces. The fact that major battles have taken place in the Sinoia, Karoi, and Banket areas, as well as the most dramatic battle of all in Wankie area in August 1967, indicates that guerrillas have some success in entering the country safely and moving inland without being quickly discovered.

All figures concerning the number of guerrillas, the number of battles, and the number of casualties either sustained or inflicted are at best imperfect. One estimate put guerrilla casualties at about two hundred by October 1968, and indicated that the guerrillas had killed 13 Rhodesian soldiers.[40] After actually going into Rhodesia with liberation forces, Russell Warren Howe estimated that there are about two thousand African guerrillas engaged in combat.[41]

Planning and implementing a guerrilla insurgency campaign against Rhodesia is not easy, and it can be fairly said that Rhodesian nationalists have only begun to fight. Some of their difficulties are entirely of their own making. The two nationalist parties remain divided. Thus

ZAPU (under the current exile leadership of James Chikerema) and ZANU (under Herbert Chitepo) continue to compete in Zambia and around the world for potential recruits, for offers of guerrilla training and education, for weapons, and for money. This situation has utterly exasperated President Kaunda of Zambia, President Nyerere of Tanzania, and most of the members of the Organization of African Unity Liberation Committee. They have tried endlessly to get the Rhodesian nationalists to patch up their quarrel, but to no avail. There is much animosity between the two groups and they have engaged in several Lusaka battles.

There were reports emanating from Lusaka and Dar es Salaam at the end of 1970 and again in early 1972 that the two parties were having serious negotiations and were likely to unite under the leadership of Robert Mugabe, a ZANU member.[42] Other reports suggested a willingness to link military operations while retaining separate party structures. Nothing more has been forthcoming, however, and the parties still remain sharply divided. ZAPU appears to have the edge so far in gaining international support and in engaging Rhodesian forces on the battlefield. In 1967 ZAPU entered into a formal military alliance with the South African nationalist party, the African Nationalist Congress.[43] The two parties now claim that they are firmly joined together to liberate both Rhodesia and South Africa for African rule; they also have close ties with FRELIMO, the Mozambique liberation movement, whose successes in the Tete province of Mozambique (bordering Rhodesia) in 1971 and 1972 caused more concern to the Rhodesian authorities than anything generated by Rhodesian guerrillas.[44]

So far the repercussions on the white side from this announced ZAPU-South African ANC alliance are more interesting and important than any African military gains. In August 1967, when the ZAPU-ANC forces engaged the Rhodesian army in a month-long action centering on the Wankie area in western Rhodesia, a South African police contingent entered Rhodesia to help the Rhodesian security forces. It is still in Rhodesia helping with border patrol and generally gaining experience in counterinsurgency tactics. This move has gone a long way toward cementing a military alliance between these two white-governed states.[45] A long, drawn-out conflict between whites and blacks throughout Southern Africa has begun.

The official white reaction to guerrilla warfare has been twofold. On the one hand the whites have attempted to play down the importance of the guerrillas and assure their white constituents that the security forces are fully capable of dealing with any eventuality. The quarterly addresses of Lardner-Burke (Rhodesian minister of justice), made with each renewal of the state of emergency, invariably have combined appeals to white determination and unity with confident statements that everything was under control. (Since April 1969 states of emergency can be declared for a year at a time so there are fewer speeches, though probably no less confidence.)

The information service of the government regularly publishes booklets and handouts which repeat this type of message. *No Hide-Out,* a pamphlet on guerrilla infiltration, makes the following statement:

> The terrorist campaign has been, by and large, a dismal failure. The sturdy unity of Rhodesian people of all races has reduced it to just what it is—the infiltration of gangs of louts who are cleaned up one after the other as fast as they cross the border into Rhodesia. Far from being welcomed as liberators, however, they find that the local Africans detest and despise them and make no bones about giving them away to the security forces as quickly as possible.[46]

Despite these self-assured proclamations, the government has not hesitated to bolster the security forces. Compulsory military training for all Europeans has increased from 4½ to 12 months. The focus of police and army training is now on counterinsurgency techniques. The Law and Order (Maintenance) Act and the Emergency Powers Act have been amended to cover activities specifically associated with guerrilla warfare such as foreign training, recruitment, possession of various arms, and harboring of guerrillas.[47]

The entry of white South African police into Rhodesia may be understood as a sign of white Rhodesian weakness in the face of guerrilla activities, but there can be no doubt that white Rhodesia received a great boost of confidence from the entry of South African forces. By moving forces into Rhodesia (legally a British colony), South Africa was signaling to Britain and the world that she had interests of her own to serve in Rhodesia. Few white Rhodesians believe that this can mean anything but the maintenance of a friendly white government in Salisbury.

South Africans notwithstanding, the guerrillas are the only force with the potential to upset white Rhodesia's plans for indefinite political control. This is not true because of important military successes, for the insurgents still have not been able to sustain active military pressure for any consistent length of time. If they develop this capability, however, hard choices will soon face white Rhodesia and her protector, South Africa. The reason why things could change rather quickly derives from the simple fact that the white population of Rhodesia is tiny. While less than a quarter of a million whites can dominate five million Africans in a situation of little overt conflict, this would not be true if a guerrilla insurrection began in earnest. Rhodesia's army has but 3,400 men; as a supporting paramilitary force there are approximately 6,400 active members of the British South Africa Police (only one-third of whom are white) and 28,500 reserves (three-fourths white).[48] In comparison, Portugal (drawing on her metropolitan population of about ten million) is already fielding an army of 130,000 or more to fight liberation forces in her three African colonies. White Rhodesia does not have this kind of manpower; if trouble comes, it would have to look for outside assistance. South Africa may be prepared to help now that costs are low and the guerrillas weak, but if saving white Rhodesia were to look like a long-term, or perhaps endless, drain on South African money and manpower, she might seek a different solution.

Rhodesian whites are not unaware of this possibility, which explains why the security apparatus is well funded and well armed. The government knows that its best chance for survival depends on its ability to prevent anything from getting started; as long as trouble and unrest occur only occasionally, it feels it can maintain the status quo indefinitely.[49]

Much of what happens in Rhodesia is simply a reflection of racial confidence. By taking UDI and making it stick despite both British and international pressure, the confidence of the whites in their government and in their ability to hold power continues to be high. By the same token, Africans are dispirited. Many Africans favored UDI, not because they were certain that it would be to their advantage, but because it seemed as likely to aid their cause as anything else on the horizon. R. B. Sutcliffe has rightly argued:

> If UDI had not occurred it is very hard to see that the political position of Africans would be better now than in fact it is. If the British Government has had insufficient power to end a rebellion, it seems very doubtful that it would have had sufficient power to produce an improvement in the political status of Africans without the provocation of that rebellion. Certainly it seems inconceivable that economic sanctions would have been applied with this purpose if UDI had not occurred.[50]

The fact remains, as Africans now realize, that only through their own efforts is political change likely to come to Rhodesia. Such change is what the guerrilla strategy is designed to induce.

Conclusion:
Past Policies and Future Politics

Rhodesia is a country where much seems to happen but nothing seems to change. In the 1890's major African rebellions posed a massive challenge to the ability of a tiny handful of whites to survive in the interior of Africa. The decision to opt for responsible government, against the wishes of both Britain and South Africa, set Rhodesia on a unique constitutional course which had much to do with its later ability to defy both Britain and the internal African nationalist challenge. Rhodesia's audacious seizure of independence in 1965 and its ability to make it stick despite great international pressure is merely the most recent in a series of events that confirm white Rhodesia's ability to do the unexpected and survive.

The dominant question that this book has considered is how and why this tiny white minority has been able to retain power during a period in which colonial rule has been disappearing and ideas of racial superiority have become increasingly unfashionable. To answer this question, we have explored three different sets of interactions (which together define the nature and shape of political power within Rhodesia): the Rhodesian government's relations with the Africans and particularly the African nationalist movement, the group that has most seriously challenged the white elite for power within Rhodesia; the Rhodesian government's relations with the British government, the nominal colonial power over Rhodesia; and the internal conflicts within the white community itself.

There have been many different types of disputes within these patterns of interaction. Whites and Africans have struggled regularly over the question of access to the political system, over the distribution of economic goods (land, jobs, opportunities), and over the system of administration and control. Britain and Rhodesia have disagreed on the shape of African administration, the nature of various Rhodesian constitutions, and the question of Rhodesian independence. The whites themselves have fought over what strategies best facilitate their continued control. None of these conflicts has been easily settled, and the issues involved are quite profound. Still, the outcome of Rhodesian conflict has always been the same—the local whites remain dominant. This dominance has continued because the whites have been highly motivated and because, from a very early period, they have controlled the Rhodesian political system and thus could legislate the regulations needed to maintain control.

Since 1890 the position of the white population in Rhodesia has been marked by a determination to distribute the wealth produced within Rhodesia (and for a time the wealth produced in Northern Rhodesia as well) in such a way as to guarantee its entire European population a high standard of living. This level has invariably been far higher than that open to almost any African in the country. Since World War II these standards have approached, if not equaled, an average unmatched anywhere else in the world. Despite economic sanctions, the standards have been maintained.

The Rhodesian government since 1923 has had virtually complete internal autonomy and has used its authority to defend, protect, and sustain this privileged European position. The Land Apportionment Act, the Industrial Conciliation Act, and the Native Affairs Act became the cornerstones of thorough and systematic white domination over land, employment, and administration. Although the system was severely challenged by the African nationalist movement and forced to adjust its methods of control and administration to take into account population growth and demographic changes (particularly the urbanization of both racial groups), its fundamental character remained unaltered.

New pass laws and urban control measures have carefully delineated the rights and obligations of Africans in urban areas. Land regulations have been revised constantly to open opportunities for new European immigrants and to narrow options for indigenous Africans. A vast new web of security legislation has evolved that has effectively curbed all

African political activity except in very narrow channels. These acts—the Law and Order (Maintenance) Act, the Unlawful Organizations Act, the Preventive Detention (Temporary Provisions) Act, and many others—have been the bastion from which the white settlers have moved to crush the nationalist movement.

The system is completely authoritarian. For much of the decade of the 1960's Rhodesia was governed under emergency regulations which gave the government sweeping powers totally outside parliamentary or judicial control. There is absolutely no legal way for opposition to arise that in any fundamental sense challenges the basis of white rule. Those parties that have tried have quickly found themselves under surveillance and ultimately banned; the "opposition" that continues either shares the fundamental values of the government or acts (like the chiefs) as a European-controlled mouthpiece for the Africans.

Over time a variety of theoretical defenses have justified and explained the Rhodesian political system. In the earliest days of white settlement (indeed even up to World War II) there was little need to justify white rule except on the commonly accepted ground that the whites were civilized and the Africans were not and therefore the whites had the right, even the obligation, to rule. In the period of federation and after, the Europeans brought considerable new sophistication to their arguments. Civilized standards, advancement on merit, parity, partnership, and defense of Western civilization against Communism are but a few of the slogans around which the Europeans have rallied in the past generation. It is crucial to realize, however, that these slogans have always been given far more credence externally than in Rhodesia. One of the achievements of the white political system has been its ability to adopt the rhetoric of racial progress for the sake of its British mentors while internally retaining the mailed fist as the real symbol of its concern for Africans.

There is one significant aspect of Rhodesia's ordering of race relations that should be emphasized, namely that Rhodesia has managed to perfect its system of segregation and control without adopting the ideological baggage that accompanies the apartheid system in South Africa. This is curious, for the two systems have a great deal in common and much of Rhodesian law in the administrative, labor, employment, and security fields is based on South African statutes. One must remember, however, that there has been a traditional animosity between Afrikaners and English-speaking Europeans in southern Africa for generations. This enmity has inhibited the English-speaking whites from adopting apartheid, although in practice their approach to race relations is often almost indistinguishable from that of the Afrikaners. Secondly, Rhodesia has not been an independent country and therefore has had other constraints on its ability to implement apartheid. Since UDI, Rhodesia has been edging toward more formalized separation of the races in some areas, but for the most part it has retained a pragmatic approach. The lack of ideological explicitness on interracial contact does not in any way weaken or mitigate the strong white commitment to political control and racial supremacy. Since 1890 the Rhodesian government has shown determination, resolution, and skill in moving to consolidate its authority and domination wherever it was challenged.

Are there any limits to this control? The Rhodesian government can today look back over the past 80 years and see an almost unbroken string of white successes over all who have sought to induce political change in Rhodesia. Whether under the British South Africa Company, the responsible government constitution, federation, the 1961 constitution, or the post-UDI constitutions, the local settlers have sustained their own unique dominance without submitting to any meaningful external restraints. In the midst of many apparent changes, the Rhodesian white system has remained stable and in firm command of all internal matters.

The key to Rhodesia's success is that the white community is united on all important fundamentals and that the British government has been prepared to honor the commitment of internal self-government made to Rhodesia in 1923—a decision that might not have been made in the very different international atmosphere after World War II. Because of the political strength that internal self-government provided, Rhodesia has been able to try different strategies—such as expansion with federation and narrow nationalism with UDI—while the fundamentals of the society itself remained unchanged.

The unilateral declaration of independence was a most unusual step, taken partly in anger and frustration and partly in cold calculation. The move to a republic in 1970 arose from similar motives. In each case the Rhodesian Front government adequately assessed its internal position, found it solid, and proceeded on the conviction that Britain would be unable or unwilling to take the steps necessary to force change. Rhodesia's success in obtaining British acquiescence to its discriminatory laws in the pre-UDI period, and in stymieing Britain's sanctions in the post-UDI period, has revealed Britain's willingness to see Rhodesia as an independent white nation. The 1961 constitution masked British withdrawal from any serious interest in Rhodesian internal politics, and Britain's repeated subsequent efforts to confer white minority independence on Rhodesia have confirmed this predilection.

Rhodesia's success in dealing with Britain has been matched by its ability to crush the African nationalist movement. From about 1955 to 1964 African nationalism provided a comprehensive challenge to white Rhodesia. No aspect of societal relations—land policy, educational opportunities, salary differentials, urban poverty, pass laws, security legislation, access to political institutions—was ignored as the nationalist parties attempted to mobilize both the internal African population and world opinion. The nationalists used tactics that had proved successful throughout the continent. In Rhodesia, however, the nationalists failed. They failed because their leadership was indecisive and because they had no overall coherent strategy for liberating Rhodesia. And they failed for the same reason that Britain before UDI and the whole world since UDI has been unable to derail Rhodesia's white government. The reason is obvious: whites control the political system and use this power to pass whatever legislation is needed to maintain themselves in power.

The position of the African population in Rhodesia has been weak since the rebellions, and the nationalist movement was unable to pull together before the white system bore down heavily on its ability to operate. The 1959 emergency showed how the Rhodesian government intended to respond to the nationalist movement, and all subsequent challenges met with the same authority and determination. The ultimate result was the split in the nationalist movement which continues today with little prospect of reconciliation. In the meantime African leaders are either restricted or detained in Rhodesia, or else they are in exile. The fragmentation of the African nationalist movement, like the ability of the white government to ward off Britain and the world, is simply another indication of the power at the disposal of the whites and another reason for their considerable confidence.

The key to white Rhodesia's maintenance of its present authoritarian system would seem to lie in its continuing ability to maintain orderly internal control and an atmosphere of political normalcy. The long-standing pattern of white Rhodesian rule is likely to remain in the near future. Innumerable successes have given the whites great confidence, and Rhodesia's enemies are weak and disorganized. But this situation need not prevail indefinitely. The whites are inherently vulnerable for the simple but crucial reason that there are so few of them. Guerrilla actions are beginning to pose an obvious threat to internal security throughout the country despite South African assistance against the insurgents. In the long run the guerrillas have the potential to involve Rhodesia in such an extended conflict that something would have to give; an internal uprising could occur or there could be massive South African or Western intervention to restore order. But this is for the future. At the moment we would be well advised not to expect much change in Rhodesia. The Rhodesian government is resourceful and ruthless, and until its confidence erodes or internal or external threats become manifest, the present system appears strong enough to turn aside any challenges.

Appendixes

Notes

Selected Bibliography

Index

Appendix A

Rhodesia's Proclamation of Independence *

WHEREAS in the course of human affairs history has shown that it may become necessary for a people to resolve the political affiliations which have connected them with another people and to assume amongst other nations the separate and equal status to which they are entitled:

AND WHEREAS in such event a respect for the opinion of mankind requires them to declare to other nations the causes which impel them to assume full responsibility for their own affairs:

NOW, THEREFORE, WE, THE GOVERNMENT OF RHODESIA, DO HEREBY DECLARE:

THAT it is an indisputable and accepted historic fact that since 1923 the Government of Rhodesia have exercised the powers of self-government and have been responsible for the progress, development and welfare of their people;

THAT the people of Rhodesia having demonstrated their loyalty to the

---

* SOURCE: Rhodesia Government Notice No. 737N of 1965 and Rhodesia Proclamation No. 53 of 1965.

Crown and to their kith and kin in the United Kingdom and elsewhere through two world wars, and having been prepared to shed their blood and give of their substance in what they believed to be the mutual interests of freedom-loving people, now see all that they have cherished about to be shattered on the rocks of expediency;

THAT the people of Rhodesia have witnessed a process which is destructive of those very precepts upon which civilization in a primitive country has been built; they have seen the principles of Western democracy, responsible government and moral standards crumble elsewhere; nevertheless they have remained steadfast;

THAT the people of Rhodesia fully support the requests of their Government for sovereign independence but have witnessed the consistent refusal of the Government of the United Kingdom to accede to their entreaties;

THAT the Government of the United Kingdom have thus demonstrated that they are not prepared to grant sovereign independence to Rhodesia on terms acceptable to the people of Rhodesia, thereby persisting in maintaining an unwarrantable jurisdiction over Rhodesia, obstructing laws and treaties with other states and the conduct of affairs with other nations and refusing assent to laws necessary for the public good; all this to the detriment of the future peace, prosperity and good government of Rhodesia;

THAT the Government of Rhodesia have for a long period patiently and in good faith negotiated with the Government of the United Kingdom for the removal of the remaining limitations placed upon them and for the grant of sovereign independence;

THAT in the belief that procrastination and delay strike at and injure the very life of the nation, the Government of Rhodesia consider it essential that Rhodesia should attain, without delay, sovereign independence, the justice of which is beyond question;

NOW, THEREFORE, WE, THE GOVERNMENT OF RHODESIA, in humble submission to Almighty God who controls the destinies of nations, conscious that the people of Rhodesia have always shown unswerving loyalty and devotion to Her Majesty the Queen and earnestly praying that we and the people of Rhodesia will not be hindered in our determination to continue exercising our undoubted right to demonstrate the same loyalty and devotion, and seeking to promote the common good so that the dignity and freedom of all men may be assured, DO, BY THIS PROCLAMATION, adopt, enact and give to the people of Rhodesia the Constitution annexed hereto.

GOD SAVE THE QUEEN

GIVEN UNDER OUR HAND AT SALISBURY, THIS ELEVENTH DAY OF NOVEMBER IN THE YEAR OF OUR LORD ONE THOUSAND NINE HUNDRED AND SIXTY-FIVE.

Prime Minister
I. DOUGLAS SMITH

Deputy Prime Minister
CLIFFORD W. DUPONT

Ministers
WILLIAM J. HARPER

J. H. HOWMAN

D. LARDNER-BURKE

IAN F. MCLEAN

MONTROSE

B. H. MUSSETT

G. W. RUDLAND

A. P. SMITH

P. VAN HEERDEN

J. J. WRATHALL

Appendix B

The Five Principles and the 1971 Settlement *

The First Principle

The 1969 Constitution expressly precludes the Africans from ever attaining more than parity of representation with the Europeans in the House of Assembly. It also relates any increase in African representation to the amount of income tax paid by the Africans. Under the proposed terms for a settlement, these provisions will be repealed and replaced by new provisions securing unimpeded progress to majority rule. The Africans will proceed to parity of representation in the House of Assembly through the creation of a new African higher roll with the same income, property, and educational qualifications as the European roll. As the numbers registered on this roll increase, additional seats will be created on a basis that will ensure that when parity of representation is reached the number of voters on the African higher and the

* SOURCE: United Kingdom, *Rhodesia Proposals for a Settlement,* Cmd. 4835 (London, HMSO, 1971), pp. 4–7.

European rolls will be approximately equal. The first two additional African members will be elected by the voters registered on the new African higher roll and the next two by indirect election under the existing system of Electoral Colleges, of Chiefs, Headmen, and elected Councillors, and this sequence will be repeated in relation to further additional African members. By this means parity of representation will be reached with 50 European members and 50 African members in the House of Assembly. The latter will then comprise 24 indirectly elected, 18 directly elected by the new African higher roll and 8 directly elected, as at present, by the African lower roll. At this point a referendum will be held among all Africans registered on the two African rolls to decide whether or not the indirectly elected Africans should be replaced by directly elected Africans.

The Constitution will provide that, after the referendum and any elections necessary to give effect to the result, ten Common Roll seats will be created in the House of Assembly. After the result of this referendum has been implemented an independent Commission will be appointed to ascertain whether the creation of the Common Roll seats provided for in the Constitution is acceptable to the Rhodesian people at that time. But the adoption of any recommendation of this Commission to vary these arrangements will be a matter for the Rhodesian Parliament and will be subject to the normal procedure for amending specially entrenched provisions of the Constitution. Failing any such agreed amendment, the Common Roll seats will be filled by an election in a single nationwide constituency by the voters on a roll consisting of all registered voters on the African higher and the European rolls. As the number of African voters increases, they will be able to determine the result of elections to a majority of these seats, thus achieving majority rule.

The Second Principle

At all stages in the progress to majority rule it will be necessary to obtain the approval of a substantial proportion of the African representatives in the House of Assembly for any amendment to the specially entrenched provisions of the Constitution which will include all the arrangements which affect African political advance. Until the Commission appointed after parity reports, such Constitutional amendments will require, in addition to a two-thirds majority of all the members of the House of Assembly and the Senate voting separately, the affirmative votes of a majority of the total European membership and of a majority of the total African membership in the House of Assembly. This will ensure that, in the unlikely event of all the indirectly elected Africans voting in favour of a retrogressive amendment to the specially entrenched provisions of the Constitution, the blocking mechanism will still rest in the hands of the directly elected African members of the Lower House. As African representation increases the two-thirds majority will require an increasing number of African votes. Thus after parity has been reached and the referendum on the future of the indirectly elected Africans has taken place, the need for an additional safeguard over and above the requirement of a two-thirds majority will disappear and it will be dropped. At this stage the support of at least 17 African members in the House of Assembly will be required to pass any amendment of a specially entrenched provision.

The Third Principle

The creation of the new African higher roll will bring with it the prospect in the near future of increased African representation in the House of Assembly. The reduction in the franchise qualifications for the existing African lower roll will enfranchise a large number of additional Africans. These two measures amount to a substantial improvement in the political status of the Africans. In addition there is provision for the British Government to allocate substantial sums of money for an aid programme for Rhodesia over the next ten years in order to improve educational facilities for Africans and to help with the economic development of the Tribal Trust Lands, thus increasing job opportunities available for Africans. As a result of this aid the rate at which additional Africans will attain the income and educational qualifications required for the franchise will be accelerated. There will also be a new special Review of the cases of the remaining detainees by the existing Tribunal with a British observer present.

The Fourth Principle

There will be a new and strengthened Declaration of Rights, which will be enforceable in the courts . . . There will also be an independent Review Commission to examine forthwith the problem of racial discrimination in all fields, including the special problem of the allocation and use of land. The Rhodesians have undertaken to commend to Parliament legislation to give effect to the recommendations of this Commission subject to considerations that any Government would regard as overriding. Meanwhile they have made it clear that they are prepared to allocate additional land for African use as the need arises and have given an assurance that with the exception of a limited number of unauthorised occupants in certain areas, there will be no further evictions of Africans until the recommendations of the Review Commission have been considered.

The Fifth Principle

These proposals for a settlement will only be confirmed and implemented after the British Government have satisfied themselves that they are acceptable to the people of Rhodesia as a whole. Accordingly, the British Government have appointed a Commission with Lord Pearce as Chairman to canvass as thoroughly and as impartially as possible the views of all sections of Rhodesian opinion, including Rhodesians resident abroad or in detention. The Commission will start its work in the near future. Before and during this test of acceptability normal political activities will be permitted to the satisfaction of the Commission provided they are conducted in a peaceful and democratic manner. The Rhodesians will be releasing a substantial number of detainees. If the British Government are satisfied that the proposed terms are acceptable to the Rhodesian people as a whole, the Rhodesians will take the necessary steps to enact the legislative changes required to implement them. After these have been completed the British Government will recommend to Parliament that independence should be granted to Southern Rhodesia on this basis and that in these circumstances sanctions will no longer be required.

Notes

Introduction

1. Brigadier Andrew Skeen, *Prelude to Independence: Skeen's 115 Days* (Cape Town, Nasionale Boekhandel, 1966), introduction.

Chapter 1. The Foundation of White Political Control

1. On early European settlement see H. A. C. Cairns, *Prelude to Imperialism: British Reactions to Central African Society 1840–90* (London, Routledge and Kegan Paul, 1965); L. H. Gann, *A History of Southern Rhodesia: Early Days to 1934* (London, Chatto & Windus, 1965); and Philip Mason, *The Birth of a Dilemma* (London, Oxford University Press, 1958). The best study of the opening of Rhodesia from the perspective of British imperial policies is Ronald Robinson and John Gallagher with Alice Denny, *Africa and the Victorians* (London, Macmillan, 1963). Cecil John Rhodes, the "founder" of Rhodesia, has many biographers; see J. G. Lockhart and C. M. Woodhouse, *Rhodes* (London, Hodder and Stoughton, 1963) and S. G. Millin, *Rhodes* (London, Chatto & Windus, 1952).

2. In this book I have used the name Rhodesia throughout. It should be noted, however, that from 1923 to 1964 the country was commonly called Southern Rhodesia.

3. Claire Palley, *The Constitutional History and Law of Southern Rhode-*

sia 1888–1965 with Special Reference to Imperial Control (Oxford, Clarendon Press, 1966), pp. 130–132 and 187–195.

4. Milner to Asquith, November 18, 1897. Quoted in Palley, *Constitutional History*, p. 140.

5. Palley, *Constitutional History*, p. 155, has concluded, "By the end of 1898 . . . the major institutions, instruments of administration, and legislative policies, most of which were to endure until the present day, were already in existence . . . it was acknowledged that this was but a first step toward responsible government . . . [and] Britain had decided that Southern Rhodesia should follow the general pattern set by the South African colonies."

6. Colin Leys, *European Politics in Southern Rhodesia* (Oxford, Clarendon Press, 1959), p. 12. The company was unable to pay a dividend to its shareholders until 1924, the year after the charter was terminated.

7. This was a margin of 59.4 percent to 40.6 percent. The African population at this time was around 900,000. On the referendum see Gann, *History of Southern Rhodesia*, pp. 231–250, and M. A. G. Davies, *Incorporation in the Union of South Africa or Self-Government: Southern Rhodesia's Choice, 1922* (Pretoria, University of South Africa, 1965).

8. Jan Smuts, the South African prime minister, urged a unionist victory because he anticipated that the English-speaking Rhodesians would support him politically. The BSAC supported union because it believed the South African government would be more generous and expeditious than Britain in buying company assets. Britain favored union, as this had long been her expectation and she had little interest in retaining administrative ties with Rhodesia. An ironic sidelight to all of this is that Winston Churchill (then British colonial secretary) told Smuts that if Rhodesia went for union, he would throw in Northern Rhodesia as part of the bargain. On this point see Sir Roy Welensky, *Welensky's 4000 Days* (London, Collins, 1964), p. 56. What a change this would have made in the course of African politics!

9. On white Rhodesian determination to prevent the growth of a poor white class, see Giovanni Arrighi, *The Political Economy of Rhodesia* (The Hague, Mouton, 1967).

10. The classes of legislation which had to be reserved were (1) any law, except with respect to the supply of arms, ammunition, or liquor, which subjects Africans to conditions, disabilities, or restrictions that do not apply to Europeans; (2) any constitutional amendment which the legislative assembly was competent to enact; and (3) any law establishing a legislative council. Other reserve clauses were enacted to protect the financial interests of the BSAC, which continued to hold extensive mineral rights in Rhodesia and to operate the railroad.

By far the most complete study of the reserve clauses and their operation is found in Palley, *Constitutional History*, pp. 236–271. It is unfortunately the most unsatisfactory and misleading chapter in Dr. Palley's massive book. She concludes (pp. 270–271) that the reserve clauses played an important role in inhibiting the growth of discriminatory legislation. The overwhelming weight of her evidence, however, demonstrates the complete ineffectiveness with which the reserve clauses were used to prevent discriminatory legislation.

11. *Southern Rhodesia Legislative Assembly Debates* (cited hereafter as *SRLAD*), vol. 26 (July 25, 1946), 1726–1727. In 1951 Huggins described the reserve clauses as "not being worth the paper they were written on." L. H. Gann and M. Gelfand, *Huggins of Rhodesia* (London, George Allen and Unwin, 1964) is a sympathetic biography of this important Rhodesian

leader. Huggins was well aware that the British would be forced to use their army if they really wanted to override Rhodesian policy. The total weakness of the British position would only become fully apparent with the Rhodesian declaration of independence in 1965.

12. *SRLAD,* vol. 17 (October 26, 1937), 2204.

13. Leys, *European Politics,* pp. 131–144, provides the best analysis of this period. A study of white interest groups prior to 1953 is D. J. Murray, *The Governmental System in Southern Rhodesia* (Oxford, Clarendon Press, 1970).

14. For the precolonial African history of Rhodesia see the essays by D. P. Abraham and K. R. Robinson in Eric Stokes and Richard Brown, eds. *The Zambesian Past* (Manchester, Manchester University Press, 1966); Mason, *The Birth of a Dilemma,* pt. 1; D. P. Abraham, "The Early Political History of the Kingdom of Mwene Mutapa (850–1589)" (Salisbury, Leverhulme History Conference mimeo, 1960); and T. O. Ranger, "The Nineteenth Century in Southern Rhodesia," in T. O. Ranger, ed., *Aspects of Central African History* (London, Heinemann, 1968), pp. 112–153.

15. Ranger, *Aspects,* pp. 125–130, carefully reviews the extent of Ndebele raiding.

16. Ranger, *Aspects,* p. 134. The interaction between Europeans and Africans at the end of the nineteenth century is a particularly controversial subject. Students of Rhodesian history are much indebted to the pioneering work of Richard Brown, Philip Mason, and T O. Ranger, as they have endeavored to unravel African perceptions and understandings of the European occupation. See Brown's "Aspects of the Scramble for Matabeleland," in Stokes and Brown, eds., *The Zambesian Past,* pp. 63–93; Mason, *The Birth of a Dilemma,* pt. 2; and Ranger's brilliant work, *Revolt in Southern Rhodesia 1896–7: A Study in African Resistance* (London, Heinemann, 1967).

17. Ranger, *Revolt,* p. 36. Also see W. F. Rea, S. J., *The Missionary Factor in Southern Rhodesia* (Salisbury, Historical Association of Rhodesia and Nyasaland, 1962).

18. The African's understanding of the Rudd Concession is best delineated in Brown, "Aspects of the Scramble," pp. 75–83.

19. Ranger, *Revolt,* passim, and his "Connexions Between 'Primary Resistance' Movements and Modern Mass Nationalism in East and Central Africa," *Journal of African History* 9 (1968), 437–453 and 631–641.

20. A good synopsis of the vast local responsibilities passed on to the native commissioners is given in the *Report of the Commission Appointed to Inquire into and Report on Administrative and Judicial Functions in the Native Affairs and District Courts Departments* (Salisbury, Government Printing Office, 1961), esp. pars. 53–110.

21. Rhodesian land policy, far more than any other policy of the government, has been extensively examined. See Ken Brown, *Land in Southern Rhodesia* (London, Africa Bureau, 1959); Montague Yudelman, *Africans on the Land* (Cambridge, Mass., Harvard University Press, 1964), esp. pp. 57–84; *Report of the Urban African Affairs Commission* (Salisbury, Government Printing Office, 1958), esp. pp. 20–28, hereafter called the Plewman Report; *Second Report of the Select Committee on Resettlement of Natives* (Salisbury, Government Printing Office, 1960), hereafter called the Quinton Report; Barry N. Floyd, "Land Apportionment in Southern Rhodesia," *Geographical Review* (October 1962), pp. 566–582; Wolf Roder, "The Division of Land Resources in Southern Rhodesia," *Annals of the Association of American Geographers* 54 (1964), 41–58; and *Report by the Consti-*

tutional Council on the Land Apportionment Act, 1941 (Salisbury, Constitutional Council report no. 29, 1964).

22. This was particularly the attitude of the 1914 Southern Rhodesian Native Reserves Commission. See the Quinton Report, pp. 17–18.

23. Plewman Report, p. 22.

24. The Carter Commission which recommended this form of apportionment said that "until the Native has advanced much further on the paths of civilisation, it is better that the points of contact in this respect between the two races should be reduced." See the Plewman Report, p. 23.

25. T. O. Ranger, "African Politics in Twentieth-Century Southern Rhodesia," in T. O. Ranger, ed. *Aspects*, p. 227. For a favorable perspective on the LAA see L. H. Gann, "The Southern Rhodesia Land Apportionment Act 1930: An Essay in Imperial Trusteeship," *Occasional Paper No. 1* (Salisbury, National Archives, 1963), pp. 58–91.

26. This point is clearly documented in Montague Yudelman's fine study of land use in Rhodesia, *Africans on the Land,* especially the table on p. 77. The 1938 Bledisloe Commission reported that only 60 of Rhodesia's 1,350 miles of railroad were in African areas.

27. Married white Rhodesians paid *no* tax for the first 800 pounds of income.

28. Palley, *Constitutional History,* p. 177, quoting Milner.

29. Gann, *History of Southern Rhodesia,* pp. 124 and 176. The Rhodesian tax was four times higher than the Cape Colony tax upon which the Rhodesian legislation was based.

30. See F. E. Sanderson, "The Development of Labour Migration from Nyasaland, 1891–1914," *Journal of African History* 2 (1961), 259–271; M. Gelfand, "Migration of African Labourers in Rhodesia and Nyasaland (1890–1914)," *Central African Journal of Medicine* 7 (1961), 293–300; and J. R. Hooker, "The African Worker in Southern Rhodesia: Black Aspirations in a White Economy 1927–36," *Race* 6 (October 1964), 142–151.

31. *Bulawayo Chronicle,* March 31, 1938. For an earlier view of the two-pyramid policy see N. H. Wilson, *The "Two Pyramids" Policy in Diagram: A White Standard of Living for Southern Rhodesia* (Salisbury, N. H. Wilson, 1933). Also see Huggins' statement, "Native Policy in Southern Rhodesia," (November 6, 1941).

32. For African political activity before World War II see T. O. Ranger, "Traditional Authorities and the Rise of Modern Politics in Southern Rhodesia," in Stokes and Brown, *The Zambesian Past,* pp. 171–193; Richard Gray, *The Two Nations: Aspects of the Development of Race Relations in the Rhodesias and Nyasaland* (London, Oxford University Press, 1960), pp. 159–168; and J. R. Hooker, "Welfare Associations and Other Instruments of Accommodation in the Rhodesias between the World Wars," *Comparative Studies in Society and History* 9 (October 1966), 51–63.

33. Ranger, *Aspects,* p. 223, quoting the *Rhodesia Herald,* March 31, 1922.

34. On the church and African politics see T. O. Ranger, "The Early History of Independency in Southern Rhodesia," in W. Montgomery Watt, ed., *Religion in Africa* (Edinburgh, duplicated, 1964), and J. R. Hooker, "Witnesses and Watchtower in the Rhodesias and Nyasaland," *Journal of African History* 6 (1965), 91–106.

35. Gray, *The Two Nations,* pp. 167–168.

36. For a summary of early amalgamationist activity see S. H. Veats, "The Rhodesias and Amalgamation," *The Nineteenth Century and After* 124 (September 1938), 314–325, and Robert I. Rotberg, "The Federation

Movement in British East and Central Africa," *Journal of Commonwealth Political Studies* 2 (1964), 141–160.

37. This tactic had been suggested to Roy Welensky, the Northern Rhodesian white leader, at the 1948 British Africa Conference. See his *Welensky's 4000 Days*, pp. 23–26.

38. The most detailed report on these five conferences is Eugene P. Dvorin, "The Central African Federation: A Political Analysis" (Ph.D. thesis, University of California at Los Angeles, 1955). A more succinct summary can be found in Philip Mason, *Year of Decision: Rhodesia and Nyasaland 1960* (London, Oxford Univeristy Press, 1960), pp. 14–50.

The name "Central African Federation" is really a misnomer since neither Rhodesia, Northern Rhodesia, nor Nyasaland is in the central part of Africa. The name more accurately relates to the fact that all three territories are land-locked and "central" in relation to British interests in South and East Africa. The history of all three territories, both before and after federation, is better understood if we consider them as part of Southern Africa. See my paper, "The Subordinate State System of Southern Africa," *International Studies Quarterly* 12 (1968), 231–261.

39. *SRLAD*, vol. 32 (November 19, 1951), 3539.

40. *SRLAD*, vol. 33 (June 27, 1952), 2952.

41. L. H. Gann, "The Northern Rhodesian Copper Industry and the World of Copper: 1923–52," *Rhodes-Livingstone Journal* 18 (1955), 14. On Northern Rhodesian politics see Robert I. Rotberg, *The Rise of Nationalism in Central Africa* (Cambridge, Mass., Harvard University Press, 1965) and L. H. Gann, *A History of Northern Rhodesia: Early Days to 1953* (London, Chatto & Windus, 1964).

42. This theme was constantly repeated in official documents and in parliamentary debates. See United Kingdom, *Central African Territories: Report of Conference on Closer Association,* Cmd. 8233 (London, HMSO, 1951), pars. 32 and 33; and United Kingdom, *Closer Association in Central Africa,* Cmd. 8411 (London, HMSO, 1951), par. 5.

43. Arthur Hazlewood, "The Economics of Federation and Dissolution in Central Africa," in Arthur Hazlewood, ed., *African Integration and Disintegration: Case Studies in Economic and Political Union* (London, Oxford University Press, 1967), pp. 185–250.

44. *SRLAD*, vol. 32 (November 19, 1951), 3539.

45. See the debate on this issue in *SRLAD*, vol. 28 (June 23 and June 28, 1948), 1345–1378 and 1481–1500. There is no certainty that Rhodesia could have attained dominion status at this time even if Huggins had wanted it.

46. These included Ian D. Smith (first elected to the Rhodesian legislative assembly in 1948), John Wrathall, Winston Field, Fred Alexander, Harry Reedman, George Rudland, and Brigadier Andrew Skeen.

47. The *Rhodesia Herald* gave extensive coverage to both sides of the federation debate. The *Rhodesia Monthly Review, New Rhodesia,* and the various publications of the White Rhodesia Council are the best antifederation sources. See also *SRLAD*, esp. vol. 33 (June 23, 24, 26, and 27, 1952, and February 10, 12, 13, and 18–20, 1953).

48. An analogous point was made by Sir Robert Tredgold, Rhodesian chief justice, who opposed federation because he felt that assigning a common problem (race relations) to separate territorial solutions would invite disaster. In a private memo to the Rhodesia governor, Tredgold commented, "They seek to avoid an issue which is unavoidable. They endeavor to postpone a decision, which can only be made vastly more difficult by delay . . . It is impossible to have one trend of native policy in federal matters and an-

other in state matters, without a conflict arising. In the long run one trend will prevail or the federation will disintegrate." See Tredgold's *The Rhodesia That Was My Life* (London, George Allen and Unwin, 1968), pp. 193–195.

49. *Sunday Mail*, April 5, 1953.

50. *SRLAD*, vol. 33 (June 27, 1952), 2946–2947.

51. *Rhodesia Herald*, April 3, 1953.

52. These figures are taken from the *Economic and Statistical Bulletin of Southern Rhodesia* and the *Monthly Digest of Statistics*. The best analysis of Rhodesia's economic development before federation is found in C. H. Thompson and H. W. Woodruff, *Economic Development in Rhodesia and Nyasaland* (London, Dennis Dobson, 1954).

53. Yudelman, *Africans on the Land*, p. 44.

54. *SRLAD*, vol. 33 (June 27, 1952), 2957.

Chapter 2. White Rhodesian Politics, 1954–1962

1. Gann and Gelfand, *Huggins of Rhodesia*, p. 234.

2. For the election returns see the *Rhodesia Herald*, December 18, 1953, November 13, 1958, and April 28, 1962. See also E. P. Dvorin, "Central Africa's First Federal Election: Background and Issues," *Western Political Quarterly* 7 (1954), 369–390, and the *Central African Examiner*, November 22, 1958. There was little to write about the uncontested 1962 election.

3. These conclusions are supported by all major studies of the federal economy. See Arthur Hazlewood and P. D. Henderson, *Nyasaland: The Economics of Federation* (Oxford, Basil Blackwell, 1960); Shirley Williams, *Central Africa: The Economics of Inequality* (London, Africa Bureau, 1960); William J. Barber, "Federation and the Distribution of Economic Benefits," in Colin Leys and Cranford Pratt, eds., *A New Deal in Central Africa* (London, Heinemann, 1960), pp. 81–97; Michael Faber, "Southern Rhodesia Alone?: A Look at the Economic Consequences," *South African Journal of Economics* 28 (1960), 283–302; and D. S. Pearson and W. L. Taylor, *Break-up: Some Economic Consequences for the Rhodesias and Nyasaland* (Salisbury, Phoenix Group, 1963). The best single work is Arthur Hazlewood's essay in his book, *African Integration*. The major source for federal economic statistics is *National Accounts and Balance of Payments of Northern Rhodesia, Nyasaland, and Southern Rhodesia 1954–1963* (Salisbury, Central Statistical Office, 1964).

4. Hazlewood, *African Integration*, p. 205. Hazlewood's data are summarized from *National Accounts*.

5. The distribution of federal government capital formation was also skewed toward Rhodesia. Over the ten years of federation the average percentages of expenditure were Rhodesia, 57 percent; Northern Rhodesia, 32 percent; and Nyasaland, 11 percent. See *National Accounts*, Table 47.

6. Hazlewood, *African Integration*, p. 203.

7. Richard L. Sklar, "Zambia's Response to U.D.I.," *Mawazo* 1 (June 1968), 14. See Hazlewood, *African Integration*, p. 208, and Pearson and Taylor, *Break-Up*, p. 80, for similar conclusions.

8. Major books and pamphlets which emphasized these themes include Clyde Sanger, *Central African Emergency* (London, Heinemann, 1960); Guy Clutton-Brock, *Dawn in Nyasaland* (London, Hodder and Stoughton, 1959); Cyril Dunn, *Central African Witness* (London, Victor Gollancz, Ltd., 1959); Philip Mason, *Year of Decision: Rhodesia and Nyasaland 1960* (London, Oxford University Press, 1960); Faith Raven, *Central Africa:*

Background to Argument (London, Africa Bureau, 1960); and Leys and Pratt, *A New Deal in Central Africa.* About the only material that one can find in support of the federal government comes from its own public relations machinery and speeches made by federal leaders. The best single source for a variety of these viewpoints is F. S. Joelson, ed., *Rhodesia and East Africa* (London, East Africa and Rhodesia, 1958). Also consult Welensky, *Welensky's 4000 Days,* and the two official appraisals of federation: *Sir Roy Welensky's Farewell to the Federal Assembly* and *Legacy of Progress: Achievement of the Years of Federation 1953–1963*—both presented to the Federal Assembly on December 9, 1963.

9. Annual Reports of the Federal Public Service Commission and the Federal Ministry of Defence for 1959.

10. *Rhodesia Herald,* October 21, 1953.

11. Federal government press release of March 2, 1956. Italics added.

12. Ian D. Smith, who was a Federal Party member of parliament from 1954 to 1961, told the 1960 Monckton Commission that "the people of Southern Rhodesia had understood that the idea of Federation was to spread the Southern Rhodesian way of life throughout the three territories." United Kingdom, *Monckton Commission Evidence,* Cmd. 1151, vol. 4 (London, HMSO, 1960), p. 116.

13. Joint British-federal government press announcement of April 27, 1957. The text is in the *Times* (London), April 28, 1957.

14. United Kingdom, *Report of the Nyasaland Commission of Inquiry,* Cmd. 814 (London, HMSO, 1959), p. 23.

15. The federal government was particularly enraged by Prime Minister Harold Macmillan's statement on November 24, 1959, that the commission was "free in practice to hear all points of view from whatever quarter and on whatever subject." *House of Commons Debates* (H.C.D.), vol. 614, 207–218. This opened the way for the commission to consider territorial secession. Welensky, *Welensky's 4000 Days,* pp. 137–169, is mandatory for understanding federal government hostility to the commission.

16. The *Times,* January 20, 1960.

17. The *Times,* February 4, 1960.

18. The key document was United Kingdom, *Report of the Advisory Commission on the Review of the Constitution of Rhodesia and Nyasaland,* Cmd. 1148 (London, HMSO, 1960). It was supplemented by: *Survey of Development since 1953,* Cmd. 1149; *Possible Constitutional Changes,* Cmd. 1150; and *Monckton Commission Evidence,* Cmd. 1151, 5 vols. (London, HMSO, 1960). The best review of the Monckton Commission is R. Cranford Pratt, "Partnership and Consent: The Monckton Report Examined," *International Journal* 16 (winter 1960–1961), 37–49.

19. *Federal Parliamentary Debates,* vol. 19 (December 19, 1962), 2033–2057.

20. For Todd's attacks see the *Rhodesia Herald,* February 9, 1956; *Sunday Mail,* February 12, 1956; and *SRLAD,* vol. 39 (July 20, 1956), 318–341.

21. In a typical twist of white Rhodesian politics, Winston Field, when he was Rhodesian prime minister, appointed Campbell to be his high commissioner to Britain.

22. For contemporary coverage see the *Rhodesia Herald* and the *Central African Examiner.* My analysis is derived from interviews with the major participants.

23. *Principles and Policies* (Salisbury, United Rhodesia Party, 1958).

24. *Our Political Principles, Our Achievements and Our Intentions* (Salisbury, United Federal Party, 1958).

25. For contemporary analyses see Leys, *European Politics,* pp. 305–312; C. G. Rosberg, "Turning Point in Southern Rhodesia?", *Africa Special Report* (July 1958); and *Central African Examiner,* June 14, 1958.

26. *SRLAD,* vol. 39 (July 20, 1956), 337.

27. These groups included the Republican Party, the Rhodesia Republican Party, the Rhodesia Republican Army, the Rhodesia Vigilance Association, the Southern African Alliance Movement, the League of Empire Loyalists, the Southern Rhodesia Association, the United Group, and the Separate Constitutional Development Party. In addition to their (often limited) publications, see the *Rhodesia Monthly Review,* the *Citizen, Die Landgenoot,* the *Dominion Times,* and the *Rhodesia Herald* for information on their activities.

28. *Preliminary Manifesto* (Salisbury, Southern Rhodesia Association, 1959).

29. At this time, the Dominion Party was somewhat split between the DP members of the federal parliament and those in the Rhodesian parliament. The Rhodesian group opposed federation, and they represented the rank-and-file of the party. The United Group was the vehicle through which Ian Smith began his ascent to political eminence. Although he had been a backbencher in the Rhodesian parliament from 1948 to 1953 and in the federal parliament from 1953 on, he attracted little attention until 1961 when he led a minor rebellion within the United Federal Party by forming the United Group to oppose the 1961 constitution. He subsequently broke with the UFP and helped found the Rhodesian Front.

30. See *A Policy Today for Your Tomorrow* and *The Repeal of the Land Apportionment Act* (Salisbury, United Federal Party, 1962). Both are elegant examples of how the UFP could turn a liberal phrase while simultaneously guaranteeing white security. On Whitehead's favorite theme of a nonracial Rhodesian nationalism, see *SRLAD* 48 (August 24, 1961), 477–496, and 49 (December 13, 1961), 503–513.

31. Federal government press release of November 28, 1962.

32. Quoted in T. Walter Wallbank, ed., *Documents on Modern Africa* (Princeton, D. Van Nostrand Co., 1962), pp. 161–164.

33. *Principles and Policies* (Salisbury, Rhodesian Front, 1962).

34. On the election see Samuel W. Speck, Jr., "The Gap Widens in Southern Rhodesia," *Africa Report* (January 1963), and *Central African Examiner* (January 1963).

35. *Reserved Powers in the Southern Rhodesian Constitution* (London, National Democratic Party, 1960).

36. *SRLAD,* vol. 44 (March 1, 1960), 3048–3058. See also his strong statements in *SRLAD,* vol. 45 (July 6, 1960), 233–244, and vol. 46 (November 1, 1960), 2643–2663.

37. Quinton Report, par. 229.

38. *Dissent* 12 (October 22, 1959).

39. *SRLAD,* vol. 46 (October 25, 1960), 2361.

40. *SRLAD,* vol. 42 (April 1, 1959), 2911. See also Whitehead's statement in *SRLAD,* vol. 46 (October 26, 1960), 2388.

41. *SRLAD,* vol. 46 (November 18, 1960), 3443.

42. Sir Edgar Whitehead, "Southern Rhodesia," *International Affairs* 36 (1960), 186–198, is a classic white Rhodesian presentation for a British audience. *International Affairs* is the prestigious journal of the Royal Institute of International Affairs (London).

43. This pledge was similar to that given to the federal government in 1957. The relevant documents are United Kingdom, *Report of the Southern Rhodesia Constitutional Conference,* Cmd. 1291; Southern Rhodesia Consti-

tution, pt. 1, "Summary of Proposed Changes," Cmd. 1399, and pt. 2, "Detailed Provisions," Cmd. 1400 (London, HMSO, 1961). Also see M. I. Hirsch, *Focus on Southern Rhodesia* (Bulawayo, Stuart Manning, 1964). This book is an account of the conference negotiations by a UFP delegate.

44. The qualifications for each roll were based on a complex mix of income, property, and education. Translated into the realities of Rhodesian life, the A-roll was almost entirely white (and provisions were made for regularly raising the qualifications) and the B-roll potential was limited to a handful of Africans—perhaps 20,000 in an African population of 3.5 million. It was the quintessence of the middle-class strategy.

45. "Southern Rhodesia—Human Rights and the Constitution," *Bulletin of the International Commission of Jurists* (March 1964), 44.

46. *SRLAD*, vol. 47 (April 21, 1961), 5005.

47. See the *Rhodesia Herald*, June 14 and June 29, 1961, and *SRLAD*, vol. 47 (June 20, 1961), 5899–5912.

48. *The Rhodesian*, July 27, 1961.

49. Copies of the Rhodesian Vigilance Association ads and fliers are in the Rhodesian National Archives. I also have a set.

50. *Rhodesia Herald*, July 20, 21, and 25, 1961.

51. Such views were expressed to me by several of Whitehead's cabinet ministers and by others in his political circle. Whitehead subsequently stated that he had negotiated the constitution in the expectation that Rhodesia would gain independence if federation broke up. *Rhodesia Herald*, April 4, 1963.

52. *SRLAD*, vol. 49 (December 8, 1961), 322, and *Rhodesia Herald*, October 14–15 and 20–21, 1961. See also *Ukuru* (Greatness), a paper that the UFP published for Africans in 1961 and 1962. It is an excellent white statement on what the party wanted middle-class Africans to believe.

53. *Rhodesia Herald*, January 27, April 4, June 27, and August 9, 21–22, and 24, 1962.

54. *Federal Outlook* (August-September 1962).

55. Failure to make this point clear is the major problem with Leys' famous analysis of white political conflict in Rhodesia. See Leys, *European Politics*, esp. pp. 173–177.

Chapter 3. The African Nationalist Challenge

1. Ranger, *Aspects*, p. 236.

2. The National Archives in Salisbury has a fine collection of the newsletters, information sheets, programs, and miscellaneous publications of these and other liberal organizations. Of special value are *Concord* (Salisbury, Inter-racial Association, 1954–1958); the *Monthly Bulletin* of the Rhodesian Institute of African Affairs, which ceased publication with its 241st issue (August–September 1965); *Reality* (Salisbury, Central Africa Party, 1960–1961); and *Dissent* (Salisbury, 1959–1961). The *Report of the National Convention of Southern Rhodesia* (Salisbury, National Convention, 1960) should also be seen, for its ideals and goals exemplified the unreality of liberal hopes in dealing with Rhodesia's divided society.

3. The most important studies were Percy Ibbotson, *Report on a Survey of Urban African Conditions in Southern Rhodesia* (Bulawayo, Federation of Native Welfare Societies, 1943); E. G. Howman with W. A. Carnegie and H. W. Watt, "Report on Urban Conditions in Southern Rhodesia," *African Studies* 4 (March 1945), 9–22; David G. Bettison, "The Poverty Datum Line in Central Africa," *Rhodes-Livingstone Journal* 27 (June 1960), 1–40,

and "Factors in the Determination of Wage Rates in Central Africa," *Rhodes-Livingstone Journal* 28 (December 1960), 22–46; and the Plewman Report.

4. Ibbotson, *Report,* as quoted in Gray, *The Two Nations,* p. 211.

5. Plewman Report, Appendix N, pp. 186–188.

6. At constant prices the average wage growth was from 56.7 pounds per year in 1954 to 69.7 in 1963. The average non-African wage grew over the same period from 884 to 1,217 pounds. *National Accounts,* Tables 140 and 161.

7. See William J. Barber, *The Economy of British Central Africa* (London, Oxford University Press, 1961); R. W. M. Johnson, "African Agricultural Development in Southern Rhodesia: 1945–1960," *Stanford Food Research Institute Studies* 4 (1964), 165–223; Yudelman, *Africans on the Land,* esp. pp. 237–246, where he argues that output per family in rural areas has not increased for 50 years; and R. B. Sutcliffe, "Income Distribution in Rhodesia 1946–1968" (unpublished mimeo).

8. Quinton Report, par. 41.

9. Brown, *Land in Southern Rhodesia,* p. 2.

10. *What the Native Land Husbandry Act Means to the Rural African and to Southern Rhodesia: A Five Year Plan That Will Revolutionize African Agriculture* (Salisbury, Government Printer, 1955), p. 13.

11. See Brown, *Land in Southern Rhodesia,* pp. 10–22; G. Kingsley Garbett, "The Land Husbandry Act of Southern Rhodesia," in D. Biebuyck, ed., *African Agrarian Systems* (London, Oxford University Press, 1963), pp. 185–202; and Yudelman, *Africans on the Land,* pp. 115–129 and passim.

12. *SRLAD,* vol. 43 (July 2, 1959), 81, and *SRLAD,* vol. 44 (October 20, 1959), 2064.

13. Yudelman, *Africans on the Land,* pp. 76 and 85–86.

14. Ibid., p. 165.

15. *The Report of the Mangwende Reserve Commission of Inquiry* (Salisbury, Government Printing Office, 1961). This is the finest study available on the destructive impact of direct rule on Rhodesia's African society and of the political ramifications of the Native Land Husbandry Act. The report discusses implementation of the LHA on the Mangwende reserve— including the consequences following the denial of land to nearly 40 percent of the young men. Many of these youths were employed intermittently in the Salisbury area and were drawn to African nationalism because of their sense of land deprivation. Major sections of the report are reprinted in J. F. Holleman, *Chief, Council and Commissioner: Some Problems of Government in Rhodesia* (London, Oxford University Press, 1969). Holleman was chairman of the Commission of Inquiry.

16. No adequate study of Rhodesian African nationalism has been written. The major reason for this is that the political climate in Rhodesia has never been conducive to the study of African politics. It has always been difficult for whites to interact closely with Africans, and those Rhodesian Africans who might provide us with such a study generally are either in prison or restriction or engaged in the more important task of building the liberation movement. One should see, however, Nathan Shamuyarira, *Crisis in Rhodesia* (London, Andre Deutsch, 1965) and Davis M'Gabe, "Rhodesia's African Majority," *Africa Report* (February 1967), 14–20. My analysis derives largely from reading the nationalist press (which was quite important from 1957 to 1964), from interviews with nationalist leaders and supporters, and from innumerable conversations with my African students at the University College of Rhodesia and Nyasaland.

17. The Youth League and the African National Congress adopted names used by African nationalist organizations in South Africa. Many of Rhodesia's African leaders were educated in South Africa and were first active in politics there. This was because until the 1950's there were no secondary schools for Africans in Rhodesia, let alone university opportunities. Among the many Rhodesian African nationalists who studied in South Africa are Joshua Nkomo, Leopold Takawira, James Chikerema, Morton Malianga, H. Hamadziripi, Robert Mugabe, H. W. Chitepo, E. Zvogbo, George Silundika, and T. S. Parirenyatwa. It is difficult to know if any important political implications arose from this background. The tradition of South African nationalism at this time, however, was not antiwhite and opportunities were sought for cooperation with white groups. This would parallel the Rhodesian experience and perhaps account in part for the relative lack of militancy in early Rhodesian nationalism.

18. *Mukayi Africa* ran for three issues and *Chapupu* ran for eight. Both are in the Rhodesian National Archives. Their broadest attacks were reserved for those Africans who cooperated with the United Federal Party.

19. Ethnically, Rhodesia is overwhelmingly comprised of Shonas and Ndebeles, with the Shonas about twice the size of the Ndebeles. Two small groups are the Shanganis (a Zulu offshoot in eastern Rhodesia) and the Kalangas (a Shona offshoot now resident in Matabeleland). George Silundika is the most famous Kalanga politician; Edson and Ndabaningi Sithole and Morton and Washington Malianga are Shanganis. The biographical data on African nationalists used in this chapter are derived almost wholly from interviews I conducted in and out of Rhodesia. Because many nationalists were inaccessible to me because of imprisonment or detention, there may be occasional errors.

20. The full text of the ANC's principles, policy, and program is most conveniently reprinted in T. R. M. Creighton, *The Anatomy of Partnership* (London, Faber and Faber, 1960), pp. 235–247.

21. The *Central African Examiner* of August 2, 1958, p. 10, said that "Congress has, without question, the largest and broadest following of any African organization in Southern Rhodesia."

22. Plewman Report, par. 64, and Evelyn M. Bell, *Polygons,* pts. 1 and 2 (Salisbury, University College of Rhodesia and Nyasaland, 1961 and 1963).

23. Francis Nehwati, "The Social and Communal Background to 'Zhii': The African Riots in Bulawayo, Southern Rhodesia in 1960," *African Affairs* 69 (July 1970), 265.

24. Ndabaningi Sithole, *African Nationalism* (London, Oxford University Press, 1959). The first edition takes an extremely moderate position on Rhodesian questions and is very much in the multiracial tradition; a second edition, published in 1968, was revised by Sithole during his first four years of detention in Salisbury prison (1964 to 1968) and is much more critical of the Rhodesian government.

25. A fascinating source of information on this flow of intellectuals from multiracial to nationalist politics is the *Samkange Newsletter*. Published in Salisbury by Stanlake Samkange, it ran for 23 monthly issues from March 1960 to January 1962. The perspective is that of an educated African reluctantly accepting that the only hope for African political advance lies in nationalist efforts. See particularly the issue of June 27, 1960.

26. See John Day, *International Nationalism: The Extra-Territorial Relations of Southern Rhodesian African Nationalists* (London, Routledge and Kegan Paul, 1967), and William A. Payne, "Southern Rhodesia at the United Nations," *Africa Report* (November 1962).

27. The nationalists' role at the conference is clearly analyzed in John Day, "Southern Rhodesian African Nationalists and the 1961 Constitution," *Journal of Modern African Studies* 7 (1969), 221–247.

28. These speculations are presented in Day, "Southern Rhodesian African Nationalists," passim, and the *Samkange Newsletter* (February 27 and March 27, 1961).

29. Quoted in Day, "Southern Rhodesian African Nationalists," p. 230.

30. *Democratic Voice,* January 8, 1961. Compare this with the bitter tone of the September to December issues of the same year.

31. *Democratic Voice,* August 19, 1961.

32. *African Daily News,* July 6, 1963. Those named by Nkomo included the Reverend Ndabaningi Sithole, Enos Nkala, Leopold Takawira, Robert Mugabe, Nathan Shamuyarira, Washington Malianga, M. Nyagumbo, and H. Hamadziripi. All except Shamuyarira had played very important roles in the nationalist movement.

33. For information on the PCC see the *African Daily News,* the *Zimbabwe Sun,* and the *African Home News.* ZANU produced two issues of a lavish journal called *Battle Cry* as well as the *ZANU Times* and the *ZANU News.* All of these publications were banned in 1964 or 1965.

34. M'Gabe, "Rhodesia's African Majority," p. 16.

35. "The Years Behind Us," *Zimbabwe Review* (January–February 1970), 9.

36. As late as 1965 (writing from the Gonakudzingwa restriction camp with the obvious approval of the PCC executive), the *African Home News* could write, "We believe that Britain is going to do that which is right and just by us—as a matter of sheer common sense, and not as a matter of kindness or generosity." Similar views were expressed to British Prime Minister Harold Wilson when he visited Rhodesia in October 1965. See the *African Home News,* January 16, 1965, and *Memorandum to the British Prime Minister the Rt. Honourable Harold Wilson, M.P. on the Constitutional Issue of the Southern Rhodesian Colony,* October 25, 1965. This was one of several documents presented by the nationalists to Britain during 1965.

37. See, among others, James Barber, *Rhodesia: The Road to Rebellion* (London, Oxford University Press, 1967), pp. 106–108.

38. Ranger, *Aspects,* p. 243.

39. *SRLAD,* vol. 31 (June 20, 1950), 2356.

40. *Rhodesia Herald,* September 18–19, 1956. For other blunt Todd attacks on the Youth League and the African National Congress see the *Rhodesia Herald,* June 23, 1956, and June 5, 1957, and the *Sunday Mail,* December 1, 1957.

41. *Report of the Secretary for Native Affairs and the Chief Native Commissioner for the Year 1958* (Salisbury, Government Printing Office, 1959), pp. 5–6.

42. *SRLAD,* vol. 42 (February 26, 1959), 2015–2051. The government amplified its case against the African National Congress in Southern Rhodesia, *Review Tribunal: General Report: Preventive Detention (Temporary Provisions) Act, 1959.* Two Salisbury journals, *Dissent* and the *Central African Examiner,* published the best contemporary accounts of the emergency.

43. See Palley, *Constitutional History,* pp. 564–628, and Leo Baron, "Southern Rhodesia and the Rule of Law," *Journal of the International Commission of Jurists* 6 (winter 1965), 219–244.

44. African Affairs Act, chap. 92, sec. 44.

45. Unlawful Organizations Act, chap. 81.

46. Preventive Detention (Temporary Provisions) Act, chap. 74.

47. Law and Order (Maintenance) Act, chap. 39. See J. W. Horn, "Commentary on Part III of the Law and Order (Maintenance) Act [chap. 39]," *Rhodesian Law Journal* 4 (April 1964), 14–68.

48. These figures are from the annual reports of the secretary for justice and the secretary for law and order and *SRLAD,* vol. 61 (August 4, 1965), 1781–1782.

49. These figures are from *SRLAD,* vol. 61 (August 4, 1965), 1776–1778.

50. Conditions in these camps are discouraging. Gonakudzingwa, the most important camp, is in a hot and desolate part of southeastern Rhodesia near the Mozambique border. The nationalists are given little to do and they are of course separated from their families. See Amnesty International, *Prison Conditions in Rhodesia* (Gloucester, Amnesty International, 1966). The *Central African Examiner* (until it was discontinued in 1965) and *Dissent* (from 1959 to 1961) published revealing material on conditions in prisons and detention camps. I have also seen numerous unpublished letters and manuscripts from those incarcerated.

51. *Report of the Secretary for Law and Order for the Year 1964* (Salisbury, Government Printing Office, 1965).

Chapter 4. Rhodesia's Drive to Independence

1. Among the many pre-UDI voices urging Rhodesia to take this step were *Federal Outlook* (May 2 and July 10, 1958) and the Dominion Party program in 1958 and afterward. See also Palley, *Constitutional History,* p. 256.

2. *Principles and Policies* (Salisbury, Rhodesian Front, 1962).

3. *SRLAD,* vol. 52 (February 13, 1963), 35–46.

4. Southern Rhodesia, *Correspondence between Her Majesty's Government of the United Kingdom and Her Majesty's Government of Southern Rhodesia,* C.S.R. 23 (Salisbury, Government Printing Office, 1963), pp. 1–2. Because of the contentious nature of the independence negotiations and the desire of both sides to justify their stands publicly, many of the letters and reports of ministerial talks have been published. United Kingdom, *Southern Rhodesia: Correspondence between Her Majesty's Government and the Government of Southern Rhodesia, April–June 1963,* Cmd. 2073 (London, HMSO, 1963) is the corresponding British version.

5. Federal government press statement of May 11, 1963. It should not be missed that Welensky was saying that as *federal* prime minister his goal was to achieve independence for *Rhodesia.*

6. C.S.R. 23, pp. 2–4.

7. Ibid., p. 9.

8. Ibid., p. 12.

9. Ibid., p. 13.

10. Ibid., p. 15.

11. *Sunday Mail,* June 2, 1963. Field's difficulties in making concessions were exemplified by a straw poll run on the basis of these speculations. Of the 2,274 people who participated in the poll (two-thirds identifying themselves as RF supporters), only 191 considered the terms acceptable. Already, two and a half years before the event, 73 percent said they would support UDI, 98 percent wanted full independence, and 20 percent indicated a desire to join South Africa. See the full poll in the *Sunday Mail,* July 28, 1963.

12. Evan Campbell, Rhodesian high commissioner to Britain from Janu-

ary 1, 1964, to June 30, 1965, thought that although Africans might be a majority on the rolls within a decade, it would take 50 years for them to form a majority government. See his "The Political Philosophy of Rhodesia," *Commonwealth Journal* (London), 8 (June 1965), 93–96 and 116. Palley, *Constitutional History*, pp. 416–424 and Tables J–P, demonstrates how an African majority could be put off for 50 years without even altering the 50:15 A-roll/B-roll seat ratio. See also Leo Baron, "Rhodesia: Taking Stock, the 1961 Constitution and the Tiger Proposals," *World Today*, 23 (1967), 369–374.

13. C.S.R. 23, p. 17.

14. *SRLAD*, vol. 53 (June 18, 1963), 2–16. See also the full-scale debate on the independence question from June 19–21, 1963. A good local analysis of negotiations to this point is in the *Central African Examiner* (June 1963), 14–18.

15. In his statement to the Rhodesian parliament on the Victoria Falls Conference, Field said "there was goodwill at the Victoria Falls Conference" and "we did our best for Southern Rhodesia." *SRLAD*, vol. 53 (June 16, 1963), 229–231.

16. Southern Rhodesia, *Report of the Central Africa Conference, 1963* (Salisbury, Government Printer, 1963). A similar paper was published by Britain.

17. *SRLAD*, vol. 56 (February 26, 1964), 50. The speech from the throne, *SRLAD*, vol. 56 (January 25, 1964), 8, was similarly reticent about independence prospects.

18. *Rhodesia Herald*, January 3 and October 24, 1964.

19. See the *Sunday Mail*, April 12, 1964, and the *Rhodesia Herald*, April 11 and 13–16, 1964, for information on Field's removal.

20. *Rhodesia Herald*, April 16, 1964.

21. *Newsfront* (January 10, 1964). The same interview was partially reprinted in the *Rhodesia Herald* of the same day. *Newsfront* was a hard-line journal on the independence question. It published 23 issues from July 12, 1963 to May 15, 1964. It was largely financed by D. C. Lilford, a leading Rhodesian Front figure. *Newsfront* ceased publishing shortly after Smith became prime minister—in apparent certainty that its line on the independence question no longer needed a public outlet.

22. United Kingdom, *Southern Rhodesia—Documents Relating to the Negotiations between the United Kingdom and Southern Rhodesian Governments, November 1963 to November 1965*, Cmd. 2807, pp. 11–12. The Rhodesian government did not publish a document covering this period.

23. See, for instance, speeches given in Banket, Gwelo, Bulawayo, and over nationwide radio as reported in the *Rhodesia Herald* of May 13 and June 6, 16, and 26, 1964. Most of these speeches were also distributed as Rhodesian Front press releases. Sir Edgar Whitehead usefully compiled many of Smith's quotations on independence in *SRLAD*, vol. 57 (July 29, 1964), 89–115.

24. *Rhodesia Herald*, May 11, 1964. Also see Smith in *SRLAD*, vol. 53 (July 19, 1963), 419.

25. *Rhodesia Herald*, June 6, 1964.

26. On the way to London, Smith stopped to see Prime Minister Salazar in Portugal; he had visited with Dr. Verwoerd in South Africa in July.

27. Cmd. 2807, p. 39. The talks are completely summarized on pp. 21–39. The communique was reprinted in *SRLAD*, vol. 58 (September 11, 1964), 253–254.

28. During early 1964 two factions emerged within the Rhodesia Party.

They differed over independence strategies, but both factions found it hard to establish a position against the RF without appearing too pro-African for the electorate. The National Archives has issues of *Action* and *National Progress,* the newsletters put out by these RP factions. The issues of *Counterpoint* published in 1963 should also be seen.

29. *Rhodesia Herald,* September 22–23, 1964. The RP offices were also broken into and vandalized. See the *Rhodesia Herald,* September 11, 1964.

30. Southern Rhodesian Information Service press statement of September 22, 1964.

31. *Sunday Mail,* September 6, 1964.

32. *Rhodesia Herald,* September 28, 1964.

33. The Rhodesian electoral rolls were so out of date that only in relatively stable upper-income neighborhoods could the percentage poll reach even 70 percent. During the 1965 election campaign both parties estimated that 20–30 percent of the names on the rolls were incorrect. A complete reregistration took place in 1966–1967.

34. *SRLAD,* vol. 58 (September 15, 1964), 279–280.

35. Ibid.

36. Cmd. 2807, p. 41.

37. Ibid., pp. 41–42.

38. *The Domboshawa "Indaba": The Demand for Independence in Rhodesia* (Salisbury, Government Printing Office, 1964).

39. *The Domboshawa "Indaba,"* p. 30. Joshua Nkomo, the restricted African nationalist leader, addressed an appeal to the chiefs and headmen which said in part, "Dear Chiefs, your people want to be protected by the British Government. They don't want to be cut off from Britain now. They don't want Independence which will be given now while all the powers are still in the hands of the whites. If the Chiefs just say 'YES BOSS', we want Independence, the country will be sold. Sons of the soil, ask the Chiefs to say NO, we don't like Independence" (letter in the author's possession).

40. Also see G. Kingsley Garbett's important paper, "The Rhodesian Chief's Dilemma: Government Official or Tribal Leader?" *Race* 8 (October 1966), 113–128, which discusses in detail the erosion of the chiefs' authority under white rule.

41. On the Anderson dismissal see the *Rhodesia Herald,* October 24, 1964, and the *Sunday Mail,* October 25, 1964.

42. Colin Legum in *The Observer,* August 23, 1964, had predicted UDI between mid-October and the end of December 1964; *The Economist Intelligence Unit* (London) report of August 20, 1964, had predicted UDI for October 10, 1964.

43. *Rhodesia Herald,* October 28, 1964.

44. *SRLAD,* vol. 59 (October 29, 1964), 730–746.

45. *Rhodesia Herald,* November 5, 1964.

46. Unpublished letter in the author's possession.

47. The full referendum results were published in the *Rhodesia Herald,* November 7, 1964.

48. The Mutasa letter was printed in the *Rhodesia Herald,* October 19, 1964.

49. Cmd. 2807, pp. 45–46.

50. Ibid., p. 66. The five principles were publicly revealed in *The Observer,* October 10, 1965. They were to remain central to Rhodesian-British discussions even after UDI.

51. *Rhodesia Herald,* March 4, 1965.

52. Cmd. 2807, pp. 58–59.

53. *Rhodesia Herald,* April 15, 1965. Many speeches were duplicated by

the parties and distributed publicly. I was present at nearly all the election meetings.

54. For local discussion of this tactic prior to UDI see *The Citizen* (November 13, 1964); *Rhodesian Property and Finance* (July 1964); and the *Rhodesia Herald*, February 20, 1965. The original Preventive Detention Act had expired in 1964. Detentions the following year were possible only under emergency regulations.

55. *Rhodesia Herald*, April 1, 1965.

56. *The RP Policy* (Salisbury, Rhodesia Party, 1965). See also the *Rhodesia Herald*, March 24, 1965.

57. *Rhodesia Herald*, May 5, 1965.

58. *Rhodesia Herald*, April 24, 1965.

59. The *Rhodesia Herald*, April 26, 1965, published the full list of proposed constitutional changes.

60. Lardner-Burke had recently said in parliament, "I would love to have preventive detention." See *SRLAD*, vol. 60 (March 18, 1965), 1021. John Gaunt, minister of local government, said in Johannesburg the night the list was released that "we find security is sadly handicapped by the existing Declaration of Rights." *Rhodesia Herald*, April 24, 1965.

61. These reports had not been requested by the government and were virtually forced upon it by concerned business groups. Reports were submitted by the Rhodesia Tobacco Association, the Tobacco Trade Association, the Rhodesia National Farmers Union, the Rhodesian Institute of Directors, the Association of Rhodesian Industries, the Associated Chambers of Commerce of Rhodesia, the National Commercial Distribution Office Workers' Association, and the Tobacco Export Promotion Council of Rhodesia.

62. As a matter of fact, the Rhodesia Tobacco Association report was brilliantly accurate. See the *Rhodesia Herald*, January 26–28, 1965, for the controversy surrounding the publication of this memorandum.

63. Actually there was nothing that ever prevented their release except fear of government displeasure. The various interest groups hoped to educate the government about the dangers of UDI, even though many of their members (and a number of the leaders) supported the idea.

64. Rhodesia, Prime Minister's Office, *Economic Aspects of a Declaration of Independence* (Salisbury, Government Printing Office, 1965). The full text was reprinted in the *Rhodesia Herald*, April 27, 1965.

65. *Bulawayo Chronicle*, April 29, 1965.

66. *Rhodesia Herald*, May 1, 1965.

67. The full text of the Institute of Directors' report is in the *Rhodesia Herald*, April 28, 1965; the ARNI and ACCOR reports are in the *Sunday Mail*, May 2, 1965.

68. *Rhodesia Herald*, April 28, 1965.

69. *Sunday Mail*, May 2, 1965.

70. *Rhodesia Herald*, April 30 and May 5, 1965.

71. Rhodesian Front press statement of about May 1, 1965, issued from party headquarters in Salisbury.

72. *Rhodesia Herald*, May 3, 1965.

73. *Rhodesia Herald*, May 6, 1965.

74. *Rhodesia Herald*, April 30, 1965.

75. *The RP Policy*.

76. Speech given by Ian Smith on Rhodesian radio and television on election eve, May 6, 1965.

77. *Rhodesia Herald*, April 21, 1965.

78. *Rhodesia Herald*, April 2, 1965. The *African Home News* of April 3, 1965, printed the full text of the ZAPU-PCC stand on the election.

79. *The RP Policy.*

80. See Smith's opening campaign speech on the question of the B-roll in the *Rhodesia Herald* of April 15, 1965. This theory of racial representation was carried much farther in constitutional changes after UDI.

81. Information gathered from an RF memo issued April 20, in my possession. F. A. Alexander, the party chairman, inadvertently revealed at an April 27 election meeting that the RF was prepared to "advise" voters on the most desirable B-roll candidates. This was publicly denied the following day by an "RF spokesman" (*Rhodesia Herald,* April 28, 1965).

82. *Rhodesia Herald,* April 3, 1965. The chiefs' support did not go unrewarded. On July 9, 1965, the government announced pay increases for chiefs retroactive to October 1964 (the month of the independence indaba!) that more than trebled their previous salaries.

83. The percentage swing to the RF has been computed from the 28 contested constituencies.

84. *Rhodesia Herald,* May 31, 1965.

85. *The Citizen,* July 23 and July 30, 1965.

86. *Sunday Mail,* July 25, 1965.

87. Rhodesian Front press release of August 8, 1965.

88. Cmd. 2807, p. 65. It is obvious that the RF was clearly linking its plans for UDI with the exigencies of export planning, as well as reacting to considerable internal pressure from agrarian interests who dominated the RF.

89. The *Times* (London), October 13, 1965. Kenneth Young, *Rhodesia and Independence* (London, Eyre and Spottiswoode, 1967), pp. 239 and 267, sees this Wilson remark as a major error. He argues that it was in Britain's interest to spin out negotiations endlessly and never admit that there was no basis for agreement.

90. *The Observer,* October 10, 1965, summarizes the Rhodesian position. The Rhodesians also considered their dropping of a demand for the abolition of cross-voting to be a major concession.

91. Skeen, *Prelude to Independence,* p. 51.

92. Cmd. 2807, p. 90.

93. *The Observer,* October 10, 1965.

94. Cmd. 2807, p. 98. This statement was issued publicly.

95. Skeen, *Prelude to Independence,* pp. 103 and 108, and D. Lardner-Burke, *Rhodesia: The Story of the Crisis* (London, Oldbourne, 1966), p. 48.

96. Cmd. 2807, pp. 102–135. The talks were held between October 26 and 29, 1965—just two weeks before UDI.

97. Ibid., p. 125.

98. About the only thing the nationalists could agree on was that they were hungry and about the only satisfaction Wilson got from the white Rhodesians all week was to get the African nationalist leaders he met with a good meal. This pathetic incident pretty much reveals the limit of British power within Rhodesia. See Harold Wilson, *A Personal Record: The Labour Government 1964–1970* (Boston, Little, Brown, 1971), pp. 159–160.

99. *Sunday Mail,* October 31, 1965. It should be remembered that constitutional rule equaled white rule.

100. See the *Rhodesia Herald* and the *Times* during September 1965.

101. Brigadier Skeen's perspective, given at the beginning of this book, is suggestive of how involved with the excitement of taking UDI some RF leaders were.

102. R. B. Sutcliffe, "Was Smith Not Told?," *Venture* (March 1966), 4–5, argues that this was the *worst* time of year for UDI since it gave importers four months to find alternative sources for tobacco.

103. This summation is distilled from numerous RF speeches, the Rhodesian case as presented in Cmd. 2807, and *Rhodesia's Case for Independence* (Salisbury, Rhodesia Ministry of Information, 1965).

104. I have constructed this breakdown from personal interview information.

105. Lardner-Burke, *Rhodesia*, p. 47.

106. Palley, *Constitutional History*, p. 749.

107. The full text of the independence proclamation is given in Appendix A.

Chapter 5. The Rhodesian Front: Political Power in Contemporary Rhodesia

1. My evidence for this analysis comes from printed and unpublished Rhodesian Front documents and from interviews with RF activists at all levels of the party organization. An earlier draft of much of this chapter (which now has been revised and updated) was published under the title, "Organisation, Power, and Decision-Making within the Rhodesian Front," *Journal of Commonwealth Political Studies* 7 (1969), 145–165.

2. In comparison, Leys in *European Politics*, p. 145, notes that in 1957 the governing United Rhodesia Party claimed only 42 active branches in Rhodesia and the Federal Party 69, many of which were inactive.

3. This argument has carried less weight since Rhodesia became a republic in 1970. See, for instance, *Rhodesian Property and Finance* (October 1970), where it was vigorously asserted that the RF government was selling out its white constituency by refusing to implement immediately new restrictive racial laws. Dissident former members of the RF carried this argument to the electorate in the 1970 election with a notable lack of success.

4. Until 1967 there were only 46 divisional representatives with a slightly weighted advantage given to rural areas. This structure was unwieldy, however, and disliked by the constituencies who did not get an executive representative. It was changed by the 1967 congress.

5. *Rhodesia Herald*, September 21, 1963. This kind of statement would have been unthinkable during the Huggins-Welensky era.

6. See the *Rhodesia Herald*, January 14, 1967, and *Rhodesian Property and Finance* (February and April 1967).

7. *Rhodesia Herald*, October 24, 1970.

8. Cyril A. Rogers and C. Frantz, *Racial Themes in Southern Rhodesia: The Attitudes and Behavior of the White Population* (New Haven: Yale University Press, 1962), p. 338.

9. Failure to handle this problem seems to me to be a critical weakness in Rogers and Frantz, *Racial Themes*.

10. This perspective on Rhodesian white politics has dominated British thinking on Rhodesia, even after UDI. Within Rhodesia *The Citizen* and *Rhodesian Property and Finance* (a weekly newspaper and a monthly journal, respectively) often make this argument.

11. Palley, *Constitutional History*, p. 457.

Chapter 6. Isolation and Survival: White Rhodesia under International Sanctions

1. A great deal has been written about the use of sanctions against Rhodesia, but the literature must be used with care. Within Rhodesia the government has censored economic data in order to conceal both successes and

failures; yet these are the only statistics we have on the overall effect of sanctions. With regard to internal Rhodesian data, see the annual budget address of the minister of finance and the annual economic survey. Good articles have occasionally appeared in the *Rhodesian Journal of Economics* and *Rhodesian Property and Finance*.

Magazines and newspapers published outside Rhodesia have carefully followed the impact of sanctions. Of particular importance are the *Times*, the *Sunday Times*, the *Observer*, the *Financial Times*, and the *Economist* (all from London), and the *Financial Mail* and the *South African Financial Gazette* (from Johannesburg).

See also T. R. C. Curtin, "Rhodesian Economic Development under Sanctions and 'the Long Haul'," *African Affairs* 67 (April 1968), 100–110; Curtin, "Total Sanctions and the Economic Development in Rhodesia," *Journal of Commonwealth Political Studies* 7 (1969), 126–131; Curtin and David Murray, *Economic Sanctions and Rhodesia* (London, Institute of Economic Affairs, 1967); Johan Galtung, "On the Effects of International Economic Sanctions with Examples from the Case of Rhodesia," *World Politics* 19 (April 1967), 378–416; R. T. McKinnell, "Sanctions and the Rhodesian Economy," *Journal of Modern African Studies* 7 (1969), 559–581; R. B. Sutcliffe, "The Political Economy of Rhodesian Sanctions," *Journal of Commonwealth Political Studies,* 7 (1969), 113–125; Sutcliffe, *Sanctions against Rhodesia: The Economic Background* (London, Africa Bureau, 1966); and Sutcliffe, "Rhodesian Trade since UDI," *World Today* 23 (1967), 418–422.

2. There is considerable literature on UN involvement with Rhodesia. See Charles Burton Marshall, *Crisis over Rhodesia: A Skeptical View* (Baltimore, Johns Hopkins Press, 1967); Catherine Hoskyns, "The African States and the United Nations," *International Affairs* 40 (1964), 466–480; Republic of Ghana, *A Memorandum in Regard to Southern Rhodesia Submitted to the Security Council on the 2nd August 1963* (Accra, Government Printer, 1963); A. G. Mezerik, ed., *Rhodesia and the United Nations* (New York, International Review Service, 1966); Rosalyn Higgins, "International Law, Rhodesia, and the U.N.," *World Today* 23 (1967), 97–106; J. Leo Cefkin, "The Rhodesian Question at the United Nations," *International Organization* 22 (summer 1968), 649–669; Ralph Zacklin, "Challenge of Rhodesia: Toward an International Public Policy," *International Conciliation,* no. 575 (November 1969), 1–72; George Alfred Mudge, "Domestic Policies and UN Activities: The Case of Rhodesia and the Republic of South Africa," *International Organization* 21 (winter 1967), 55–78; C. G. Fenwick, "When is There a Threat to Peace?—Rhodesia," *American Journal of International Law* 61 (1967), 753–755; and C. A. Crause, *Rhodesia Independence and the Security Council of the United Nations* (Cape Province, Fort Hare Univeristy Press, 1966).

3. The June resolution 1747 (XVI) passed by 73 for, 1 opposed, and 27 abstaining; the October resolution 1760 (XVII) passed by 81 for, 2 opposed, and 19 abstaining. Britain did not participate in either vote.

4. Hugh Foot, *A Start in Freedom* (London, Hodder and Stoughton, 1964), pp. 215–226.

5. *SRLAD,* vol. 59 (October 27, 1964), 420.

6. The October resolution 2012 (XX) passed by 107 to 2 with one abstention. The November resolution 2022 (XX) passed 82-9-18. Britain again did not participate in the voting.

7. Security Council resolution 217 (1965). The other resolutions were General Assembly 2024 (XX), November 11, 1965, and Security Council resolution 216 (1965).

8. Security Council resolution 221 (1966).

9. Security Council resolution 232 (1966).

10. The *Times* (London), January 1, 1966. R. B. Sutcliffe has pointed out that the issue now is whether sanctions will work in "years rather than decades." See his "Political Economy of Rhodesian Sanctions," p. 114.

11. *New York Times,* March 18–19, 1970, and February 5, 1972. The U.S. veto was the first ever cast by the United States at the United Nations. The vetoed resolution also called for the rupture of all telegraphic, radio, postal, and telephone ties with Rhodesia and urged the UN to give both moral and material support to the liberation forces.

12. See R. L. Cole and D. S. Pearson, "The Tobacco Industry of Central Africa," *East African Economic Review* 1 (December 1965), 46–77.

13. *Financial Mail,* July 10, 1970.

14. *SRLAD,* vol. 77 (July 16, 1970), 693.

15. For Zambia's dilemmas at the time of UDI see Richard L. Sklar, "Zambia's Response to U.D.I.," *Mawazo* 1 (June 1968), 11–32; F. Taylor Ostrander, "Zambia in the Aftermath of Rhodesian UDI: Logistical and Economic Problems," *African Forum* 2 (winter 1967), 50–65; R. B. Sutcliffe, "Zambia in the Strains of UDI," *World Today* 23 (1967), 506–511; and the work of Richard Hall, "Zambia and Rhodesia: Links and Fetters," *Africa Report* (January 1966), 8–12, and *The High Price of Principles: Kaunda and the White South* (London, Hodder and Stoughton, 1969).

16. See McKinnell, "Sanctions and the Rhodesian Economy," 578; Sanctions Committee of the Security Council, *U.N. document S/9252 plus Add. 1* (June 12–13, 1969); Committee of 24, *Economic Conditions in Southern Rhodesia with Particular Reference to Foreign Interests,* SCI/71/7 (26 July 1971) and the *New York Times,* September 24, 1971, and June 1, 1972.

17. Zacklin, "Challenge of Rhodesia," 43–63, provides the best analysis of the problems of enforcement.

18. H.C.D. 720 (November 11, 1965), 353. See the full British debate on UDI in H.C.D. 720 (November 12, 1965), 523–637.

19. H.C.D. 722 (December 10, 1965), 769. On December 1, 1965, Wilson had said that it is "better that the measures be quick and sharp rather than a long and drawn out agony on Rhodesia." H.C.D. 721 (December 1, 1965), 1432.

20. Press release from British High Commission (Salisbury), November 11, 1965.

21. H.C.D. 720 (November 11, 1965), 362.

22. Richard L. Sklar, "On Returning 'to the Road of Legality' in Rhodesia," (unpublished, 1968) makes this point very well. Ali A. Mazrui, a distinguished African political scientist, has commented that it was racial fellowship between white Rhodesia and white Britain that prevented stronger British actions. He has written, "When all is said and done, only a fellow Briton in the colonies could threaten rebellion against Great Britain and still entertain a British Prime Minister to dinner pending the final break." See his "The Rhodesian Problem and the Kenya Precedent," in *The Anglo-African Commonwealth* (Oxford, Pergamon, 1967), pp. 45–46.

23. H.C.D. 738 (December 20, 1966), 1177.

24. H.C.D. 720 (November 11, 1965), 352.

25. *Judgement . . . between Stella Madzimbamuto, Leo Solomon Baron and Desmond Lardner-Burke, et al.* (Salisbury, Government Printing Office, 1966).

26. J. Leo Cefkin, "Zimbabwe Nationalists Hanged," *Africa Today*

(April–May 1968), 4–5. See also Wilson's angry statement in H.C.D. 760 (March 7, 1968), 652–659, and the full-scale debate on Rhodesia at H.C.D. 761 (March 27, 1968), 1543–1678. The hangings led directly to the United Nations vote for compulsory mandatory sanctions.

27. See the *Rhodesia Herald* of January, February, and September 1968, passim, and the *Times* (London), August 10 and September 14, 1968.

28. H.C.D. 722 (December 10, 1965), 771. Wilson also charged the RF with running a "very, very competent brain-washing police state." H.C.D. 723 (January 25, 1966), 51.

29. H.C.D. 723 (January 25, 1966), 40.

30. The major documents on British-Rhodesian relations since UDI are Rhodesia, *Rhodesia Independence Constitution* (Salisbury, Government Printing Office, 1967); Rhodesia, *Relations between the Rhodesian Government and the United Kingdom Government, November 1965–December 1966* (Salisbury, Government Printing Office, 1966); Rhodesia, *Statement on Anglo-Rhodesian Relations, December 1966 to May 1969* (Salisbury, Government Printing Office, 1969); United Kingdom, *Rhodesia: Documents Relating to Proposals for a Settlement 1966*, Cmd. 3171 (London, HMSO, 1966); United Kingdom, *Rhodesia: Proposals for a Settlement 1966*, Cmd. 3159 (London, HMSO, 1966); United Kingdom, *Rhodesia: Report on Exchanges with the Regime since the Talks Held in Salisbury in November 1968*, Cmd. 4065 (London, HMSO, 1969); United Kingdom, *Rhodesia Proposals for a Settlement*, Cmd. 4835 (London, HMSO, 1971); and United Kingdom, *Rhodesia: Report of the Commission on Rhodesian Opinion under the Chairmanship of the Right Honourable the Lord Pearce*, Cmd. 4964 (London, HMSO, 1972). See also Leo Baron, "Rhodesia: Taking Stock, the 1961 Constitution and the Tiger Proposals," *World Today* 23 (1967), 369–374; M. J. Christie, *Rhodesia: The "Fearless" Proposals and the Six Principles* (London, Africa Bureau, 1968) and the *Sunday Times* and the *Observer* (London), esp. the issues of November 28, 1971.

31. The working document is reprinted in Cmd. 3171, pp. 87–90.

32. Rhodesia, *Relations between . . .* , p. 135.

33. Rhodesia, *Rhodesia Independence Constitution*, is the fullest statement of Rhodesian reasons for rejecting the *Tiger* working document. For the British side see Wilson's statements in H.C.D. 737 (December 5, 1966), 1053–1080, and H.C.D. 737 (December 8, 1966), 1598–1631.

34. H.C.D. 738 (December 20, 1966), 1175–1183.

35. Richard L. Sklar, "The End of NIBMAR on the Fearless," *Africa Today* (October–November 1968), 4.

36. The nations closing their missions in Salisbury were Denmark, Norway, Italy, the Netherlands, West Germany, France, Belgium, Austria, Switzerland, Greece, and the United States.

37. *Rhodesia Herald*, July 13, 1971.

38. See Cmd. 4835. The portion of the document showing how the five principles are met is given in Appendix B.

39. The most complete analysis of the potential time frame for majority rule was made by Dr. Claire Palley for the *Sunday Times*, November 28, 1971. Assuming the most favorable circumstances including absolute good faith by all white governments, no manipulation of the law or constitution, acceleration in African educational opportunities, low rates of white immigration, no rise in the level of financial qualifications, and the registration and voting of every eligible African, Dr. Palley computed that the year 2035 would be the earliest possible African "majority." Less favorable assumptions would put it off until late in the twenty-first century, if even then.

40. *Rhodesia: Proposals for a Sell-Out* (London, Southern African Research Office, 1972) is the best of many analyses explaining and interpreting the terms of the agreement.

41. H.C.D. 826 (November 25, 1971), 1548.

42. H.C.D. 826 (November 25, 1971), 1550. See also the *Times* of December 2, 1971, where Home specifically defends the agreement because all alternatives are worse.

43. *House of Lords,* vol. 326 (December 1, 1971), 325–338, and "My Case for Settling with Ian Smith," *The Observer,* December 3, 1971.

44. *The Observer,* December 3, 1971.

45. *Rhodesia Herald,* November 26, 1971.

46. Cmd. 4964, p. 2.

47. Ibid., pp. 57–58 and 75–78.

48. Ibid., p. 76.

49. Ibid., p. 112.

50. Ibid., pp. 44–51, 53, and 72–73.

51. *Rhodesia Herald,* January 22, 1972.

52. Desmond Frost, Rhodesian Front chairman, made a similar point when he presented the RF's views to the Pearce Commission on February 4, 1972. He noted that "the Africans' reaction is tantamount to a slap in the face for the European . . . unless the Africans show some willingness to reciprocal cooperation with the European I cannot in all honesty guarantee that the RF party will continue to support wholeheartedly the proposals as a package deal." *Rhodesia Herald,* February 5, 1972.

53. Cmd. 4964, p. 112.

54. Ibid., p. 80.

55. Ibid., pp. 58–59.

56. Ibid., p. 26.

57. Ibid., p. 49.

58. Ibid., pp. 109–111.

59. Ibid., pp. 88–96.

60. The *Times* (London), May 24, 1972.

61. Ibid.

62. *New York Times,* June 7, 1972.

63. The *Times* (London), May 24, 1972.

64. See James Barber, "The Impact of the Rhodesian Crisis on the Commonwealth," *Journal of Commonwealth Political Studies* (1969), 83–95; D. Rothchild, "Rhodesian Rebellion and African Response," *Africa Quarterly* 6 (1966), 184–196; A. Gupta, "The Rhodesian Crisis and the Organization of African Unity," *International Studies* 9 (July 1967), 55–64; R. Cranford Pratt, "African Reaction to the Rhodesian Crisis," *International Journal* 21 (spring 1966), 186–198; J. Nyerere, "Rhodesia in the Context of Southern Africa," *Foreign Affairs* 44 (April 1966), 373–386; and George W. Shepherd, Jr., "The Failure of Sanctions against Rhodesia and the Effect on African States: A Growing Racial Crisis," *Africa Today* (February–March 1968), 8–12.

65. Nyerere, "Rhodesia in Context," p. 373.

66. Pratt, "African Reaction," p. 186.

67. Nyerere, "Rhodesia in Context," p. 378.

68. J. Nyerere, "Independence Means Power," *Africa Report* (December 1968), 22–23.

69. My own analysis of evolving relations throughout Southern Africa may be found in "The Subordinate State System of Southern Africa," *International Studies Quarterly* 12 (1968), 231–261. See also Ernest A. Gross,

"The Coalescing Problem of Southern Africa," *Foreign Affairs* 44 (July 1968), 743–757, and Christopher R. Hill, "UDI and South African Foreign Policy," *Journal of Commonwealth Political Studies* 7 (1969), 96–103.

Chapter 7. Internal Politics and Control since the Unilateral Declaration of Independence

1. Skeen, *Prelude to Independence.* Other books of this genre include D. Lardner-Burke, *Rhodesia: The Story of the Crisis* (London, Oldbourne, 1966); Douglas Reed, *The Battle for Rhodesia* (Cape Town, HAUM, 1966); B. G. Spurling, *Reluctant Rebel* (Johannesburg, Voortrekkerpers, 1966); A. J. Peck, *Rhodesia Condemns* (Salisbury, Three Sisters, 1967); Phillippa Berlyn, *Rhodesia: Beleaguered Country* (London, Mitre, 1967); and A. Harrigan, *One against the Mob* (Arlington, Va., Crestwood Books, 1966). The opposite view is expressed in Judith Todd, *Rhodesia* (London, Macgibbon, 1966) and B. V. Mtshali, *Rhodesia: Background to Conflict* (New York, Hawthorn Books, 1967).

2. Rhodesia, *Report of the Constitutional Commission, 1968* (Salisbury, Government Printing Office, 1968), p. 1. The full report was 180 pages.

3. Ibid., p. 11.

4. Ibid., p. 12.

5. See the local Rhodesian press and *Rhodesian Property and Finance* from May through July 1968.

6. *Rhodesia Herald,* September 6, 1968.

7. The Yellow Paper was dropped on February 11, 1969. The new constitutional proposals were published in May. See Rhodesia, *Proposals for a New Constitution for Rhodesia* (Salisbury, Government Printing Office, 1969).

8. *SRLAD,* vol. 75 (October 8, 1969), 1196.

9. Qualifications for the African voter roll are as follows: income of not less than 300 pounds, or ownership of immovable property in Rhodesia valued at not less than 600 pounds; or income of not less than 200 pounds, or ownership of immovable property in Rhodesia valued at not less than 400 pounds, and in addition completion of a course of not less than two years' secondary education. See *SRLAD,* vol. 76 (October 29, 1969), 349.

10. The most current estimate of Rhodesia's indigenous African population is Shona 3,341,000 and Ndebele 1,589,000 for a total of 4,930,000. See *SRLAD,* vol. 76 (January 30, 1970), 1687–1688.

11. Subpar. 10 of the Declaration of Rights in the 1969 constitution.

12. *Rhodesia Herald,* May 8, 1969.

13. *Rhodesia Herald,* May 31 and June 11, 1969.

14. See *Rhodesia Needs the Centre Party* and *Ten Vital Questions: Centre Party Answers* (Salisbury, Centre Party, 1969).

15. *Sunday Mail,* June 1, 1969, and *Rhodesia Herald,* June 18, 1969.

16. *Rhodesia Herald,* June 6, 1969.

17. *Rhodesia Herald,* June 23, 1969, and *SRLAD,* vol. 74 (July 2, 1969), 232–236.

18. *Sunday Mail,* June 22, 1969.

19. *SRLAD,* vol. 75 (October 2, 1969), 1046.

20. Ibid., p. 1076.

21. *Rhodesia Herald,* June 23, 1969, and *SRLAD,* vol. 74 (July 2, 1969), 232–236.

22. During the campaign for the republic, RF speakers had commonly

suggested that only by declaring a republic could Rhodesia fully demonstrate its independence to the world and therefore be recognized. This argument, used previously to support UDI, brought the sour comment from the *Sunday Mail* of June 1, 1969, that "there is no guarantee whatever that Rhodesia will gain recognition under a republican constitution. The only recognition likely is from international smugglers."

23. *Rhodesia and You in the Super 70's* (Salisbury, Rhodesian Front, 1970).

24. *Sunday Mail*, March 3, 1970.

25. *SRLAD*, vol. 64 (July 21, 1966), 707–718, and vol. 66 (February 16, 1967), 1714–1721.

26. Statement by Minister of Justice D. Lardner-Burke in *SRLAD*, vol. 75 (October 2, 1969), 1054.

27. *SRLAD*, vol. 75 (October 15, 1969), 1478.

28. *SRLAD*, vol. 76 (February 13, 1970), 2246. This would be the long-promised Residential (Property Owners) Protection Bill sought by Salisbury residents. A draft of this bill was released on November 26, 1970. Because of the small size of the Asian and Coloured populations, they are theoretically considered as part of the European population under the terms of the LTA and the new constitution.

29. The Municipal Amendment Act passed virtually without debate. See *SRLAD*, vol. 69 (September 6, 1967), 86–126.

30. *SRLAD*, vol. 76 (February 11, 1970), 2090–2127.

31. *SRLAD*, vol. 63 (April 20, 1966), 1847–1860, and vol. 76 (February 4, 1970), 1843–1890. See also Lester K. Weiner, "African Education in Rhodesia since UDI," *Africa Today* (March–April 1967), 14–15.

32. *SRLAD*, vol. 74 (July 25, 1969), 737.

33. *SRLAD*, vol. 76 (February 4, 1970), 1845–1847.

34. African (Registration and Identification) Act prosecutions were as follows: 1965—14,786; 1966—11,569; 1967—11,006; 1968—17,680; and 1969 (through November 11)—14,904. African (Urban Areas) Accommodation and Registration Act prosecutions were as follows: 1965—3,931; 1966—7,041; 1967—7,908; 1968—8,443; and 1969 (through November 11)—6,028. See *SRLAD*, vol. 76 (January 28, 1970), 1575–1576.

35. *Rhodesia Herald*, February 13, 1969.

36. Cmd. 4964, p. 92. Before the commission left Rhodesia, 923 of those arrested had been acquitted or released without trial, 689 had been convicted of some charge, and the remaining 124 still had their cases pending. The most notable detainees were former prime minister Garfield Todd and his daughter Judy, two of the few whites who opposed the settlement, and Josiah and Ruth Chinamano, two African leaders closely associated with ZAPU and Nkomo.

37. *Rhodesia Herald* and the *Times* (London), March 11, 1972.

38. Evidence on guerrilla activities in Rhodesia comes from a variety of sources. The British press carries occasional articles, and the African nationalist exile press (*Zimbabwe Review* for ZAPU and *Zimbabwe News* for ZANU—both printed in Lusaka) gives its version. The following articles should also be seen: Davis M'Gabe, "The Beginnings of Guerrilla Warfare," *Monthly Review* (March 1969), 39–47; Alan Rake, "Black Guerrillas in Rhodesia," *Africa Report* (December 1968), 23–25; John Day, "The Rhodesian African Nationalists and the Commonwealth African States," *Journal of Commonwealth Political Studies*, 7 (1969), 132–144; Russell Warren Howe, "War in Southern Africa," *Foreign Affairs* 48 (October 1969), 150–165; Colin Legum, "Guerrilla Warfare and Africa Liberation Move-

ments," *Africa Today* (August 1967), 5–10; and Martin Legassick, "The Consequences of African Guerrilla Activity for South Africa's Relations with her Neighbours" (unpublished, 1967).

39. *Zimbabwe News* (July 1970), 7.

40. Rake, "Black Guerrillas," 23–25.

41. Howe, "War in Southern Africa," 150. This is the most optimistic report on the Rhodesian insurgency yet published in a nonnationalist journal.

42. The *Standard* (Dar es Salaam), December 11, 1970; *The Times of Zambia* (Lusaka), December 10, 1970; and the *Nationalist* (Dar es Salaam), December 14, 1970. The ZANU paper, the *Zimbabwe News*, of January 5, 1971, blasted members of ZAPU, whom they called "cool professional tricksters who, because they personally thrive on the ZANU-ZAPU split, have not hesitated to denounce as treacherous any effort aimed at reconciling our differences." This is about the level of dialogue at which the two parties have approached each other since 1963.

43. See the *Zimbabwe Review* (August–October 1967) and *Sechaba,* the African National Congress paper from London, during the same months, for information on the merger. ZANU called the merger "irresponsible clowning at its best. James Chikerema and Oliver Tambo are unwittingly granting South Africa a perfect diplomatic excuse for military intervention in Rhodesia." *Zimbabwe News,* September 30, 1967, p. 3.

44. *Rhodesia Herald,* September 7, 16, and 18, 1971.

45. It is estimated that there are between two and three thousand South African police in Rhodesia. See Howe, "War in Southern Africa," 155; Martin Legassick, "The Southern African Bloc: Integration for Defense or Expansion?", *Africa Today* (October–November 1968), 9–12; Martin Legassick, "Racism and Guerrilla Struggle in Southern Africa," *Africa Today* (February–March 1968), 3–5, and Bowman, "The Subordinate State System," passim.

46. *No Hide-Out* (Salisbury, Government Printing Office, 1966). Also see *Murder by Radio* (Salisbury, Government Printing Office, 1966), which attacked the African nationalist broadcasts over Zambian radio beamed to Rhodesia.

47. See *SRLAD*, vol. 70 (February 2, 1968), 623–657, and vol. 76 (February 6, 1970), 1967–1971. The *Report of the Select Committee on Political Boycott* (Salisbury, Government Printing Office, 1966) had recommended various tough new measures to deal with all types of dissent.

48. Richard Booth, *The Armed Forces of African States* (London, Institute for Strategic Studies, Adelphi Paper No. 67, 1970), pp. 19–20.

49. See J. Bowyer Bell, "The Frustration of Insurgency: The Rhodesian Example in the Sixties," *Military Affairs* 35 (February 1971), 1–5.

50. Sutcliffe, "The Political Economy of Sanctions," 113.

Selected Bibliography

I. Government Documents

THE FEDERATION OF RHODESIA AND NYASALAND

The Constitution of the Federation of Rhodesia and Nyasaland.
Federal Parliamentary Debates, 1954–1963.
The Federation of Rhodesia and Nyasaland Newsletter, Washington, D.C.
Report to the Federal Minister of Agriculture by the Federal Standing Committee on Agriculture Production (the Engledow Report), 1958.
The Development of Manufacturing Industry within the Federation and Nyasaland, 1961.
The Constitutional Convention: Britain's Power to Legislate for the Secession of a Territory from the Federation of Rhodesia and Nyasaland, 1962.
Federal Government Economic Policy: Principles, 1962.
The Issue of Nyasaland's Secession, 1962.
The Break-Up: Effects and Consequences on the Two Rhodesias, 1963.
Legacy of Progress: Achievements of the Years of Federation 1953–1963, 1963.
Sir Roy Welensky's Farewell to the Federal Assembly, 1963.
Balance of Payments of the Federation of Rhodesia and Nyasaland, 1954–1963, 1964.
National Accounts of the Federation of Rhodesia and Nyasaland, 1954–1963, 1964.

RHODESIA

Annual Reports

Bank of Rhodesia and Nyasaland.
City of Bulawayo: Director of Housing and Amenities.
City of Salisbury: Director of African Administration.
Commissioner, British South Africa Police.
Comptroller and Auditor General.
Constitutional Council.
Director, Information Service.
Director of Mines.
Economic Survey of Rhodesia.
Estimates of Expenditures.
External Trade.
Financial Statements.
National Accounts and Balance of Payments.
Natural Resources Board.
Public Sector Investment.
Rhodesia National Labour Supply Commission.
Secretary for African Education.
Secretary for Agriculture.
Secretary for Commerce and Industry.
Secretary for Defence.
Secretary for External Affairs.
Secretary for Education.
Secretary for Housing.
Secretary for Justice.
Secretary for Law and Order.
Secretary for Local Government.
Secretary for Native Affairs and the Chief Native Commissioner (subsequently *Internal Affairs*).
Tobacco Export Council of Rhodesia.

Other Publications and Reports

The Constitution of Southern Rhodesia, 1923 and 1961.
The Constitution of Rhodesia, 1965 and 1969.
Economic and Statistical Bulletin.
Export Opportunities Bulletin.
Monthly Digest of Statistics.
Quarterly Bulletin of Financial Statistics.
Rhodesian Commentary.
Southern Rhodesia Legislative Assembly Debates (subsequently *Parliamentary Debates*).
Southern Rhodesia Legislative Assembly Votes and Proceedings.
This is Rhodesia.
Statement of Native Policy in Southern Rhodesia, 1941.
Secretary for Native Affairs: Report on the Question of Native Housing and Implementation of the Land Apportionment Act in the Urban Areas of the Colony, 1944.
Report of the Commission . . . to Investigate the Grievances Which Gave Rise to the Strike amongst the African Employees of the Rhodesia Railways and Certain Other Matters Affecting Africans Employed in Industry, 1946.

Report of the Commission Appointed . . . to Inquire into and Report upon All Matters Concerning Recent Native Disturbances in the Colony (the Hudson Report), 1948.

Select Committee on the Amendment of the Constitution, *Some Aspects of Dominion Status*, 1950.

Survey of Native Policy, confidential, 1950.

Report of the Native Education Inquiry Commission, 1951.

What the Native Land Husbandry Act Means to the Rural African and to Southern Rhodesia: A Five Year Plan That Will Revolutionize African Agriculture, 1955.

Report of the Franchise Commission, 1957.

African Resettlement and the Native Purchase Areas (by S. M. Makings), 1958.

Preliminary Report on the Salisbury African Demographic Survey, August/ September, 1958, 1958.

Report of the Urban African Affairs Commission (the Plewman Report), 1958.

First Report of the Select Committee on Resettlement of Natives, 1959.

The 1953–55 Demographic Sample Survey of the Indigenous African Population of Southern Rhodesia, 1959.

Review Tribunal [Prevention Detention (Temporary Provisions) Act 1959], General Report, 1959.

Second Report on the Salisbury African Demographic Survey August/ September 1958, 1959.

A Note on the Economics of African Development in Southern Rhodesia with Special Reference to Agriculture (by S. M. Makings and M. Yudelman), 1960.

Second Report of the Select Committee on Resettlement of Natives (the Quinton Report), 1960.

The African of Southern Rhodesia: A Brief Research Paper for Visitors, Lecturers, Students, Immigrants, and Others (by K. D. Leaver and W. T. Nesham), 1961.

Minority Report of Rev. J. A. C. Shaw, a Member of the Commission of Inquiry into Alleged Discontent in the Mangwende Reserve, 1961.

Report of the Commission Appointed to Inquire into and Report on Administrative and Judicial Functions in the Native Affairs and District Courts Departments (the Robinson Commission), 1961.

Report of the Commission of Inquiry into Allegations of Interference with the Courts, 1961.

Report of the Commission of Inquiry into Alleged Discontent in the Mangwende Reserve, 1961.

First (and Second) Reports of the Commission of Inquiry into the Organization and Development of the Southern Rhodesia Public Services (the Paterson Commission), 1962.

Report of the Advisory Committee: The Development of the Economic Resources of Southern Rhodesia with Particular Reference to the Role of African Agriculture (the Phillips Report), 1962.

Report of the Survey of the British South African Police, 1962.

Report on the Zimbabwe African Peoples Union, 1962.

Southern Rhodesian Africans Speak: "Our Fight against Hooliganism and Thuggery," 1962.

Correspondence between Her Majesty's Government of the United Kingdom and Her Majesty's Government of Southern Rhodesia, 1963.

Report of the Central Africa Conference, 1963, 1963.
Report of the Southern Rhodesia Education Commission 1962 (the Judges Commission), 1963.
The Domboshawa "Indaba": The Demand for Independence in Rhodesia (consultation with the African tribesmen through their chiefs and headmen), 1964.
Final Report of the April/May 1962 Census of Africans in Southern Rhodesia, 1964.
1961 Census of the European, Asian and Coloured Population, 1965(?).
Economic Aspects of a Declaration of Independence, 1965.
Final Report on the September, 1961 Census of Employees, 1965.
Local Government and Community Development: The Roll of Ministries and Co-ordination, 1965.
Report on Urban African Budget Survey in Salisbury, 1963/64, 1965.
Judgement . . . between Stella Madzimbamuto, Leo Solomon Baron and Desmond Lardner-Burke, et al., 1966.
Murder by Radio, 1966.
No Hide-Out, 1966.
Relations between the Rhodesian Government and the United Kingdom Government, November 1965–December 1966, 1966.
Report of the Select Committee on Political Boycott, 1966.
Rhodesia in the Context of Africa, 1966.
The General Report of the Review Tribunal, 1967.
Report by J. L. Sadie on Planning for the Economic Development of Rhodesia, 1967.
Report of the Beit Bridge Rail Link Commission, 1967.
Rhodesia Independence Constitution, 1967.
Terrorist Incursions from Zambia, 1967.
Report of the Constitutional Commission (the Whaley Commission), 1968.
Proposals for a New Constitution for Rhodesia, 1969.
Statement on Anglo-Rhodesian Relations, December 1966 to May 1969, 1969.

UNITED KINGDOM

House of Commons Debates.
Report of the Commission on Closer Union of the Dependencies in Eastern and Central Africa, Cmd. 3234 (the Hilton-Young Commission), 1929.
Rhodesia-Nyasaland Royal Commission Report, Cmd. 5949 (the Bledisloe Commission), 1939.
The British Territories in East and Central Africa 1945–50, Cmd. 7987, 1950.
Central African Territories: Comparative Survey of Native Policy, Cmd. 8235, 1951.
Central African Territories: Geographical, Historical and Economic Survey, Cmd. 8234, 1951.
Central African Territories: Report of Conference on Closer Association, Cmd. 8233, 1951.
Closer Association in Central Africa, Cmd. 8411, 1951.
Draft Federal Scheme, Cmd. 8573, 1952.
*Report of the Fiscal Commission,*Cmd. 8673, 1952.
Report of the Judicial Commission, Cmd. 8672, 1952.
The Federal Scheme for Southern Rhodesia, Northern Rhodesia and Nyasaland Prepared by a Conference Held in London, January 1953, Cmd. 8754, 1953.

Report by the Conference on Federation Held in London in January 1953, Cmd. 8753, 1953.

The Federation of Rhodesia and Nyasaland: Economic and Commercial Conditions in the Federation of Rhodesia and Nyasaland (by H.W. Woodruff), 1955.

Nyasaland Despatch by the Governor Relating to the Report of the Nyasaland Commission of Inquiry, Cmd. 815, 1959.

Report of the Nyasaland Commission of Inquiry, Cmd. 814 (the Devlin Report), 1959.

Advisory Commission on the Review of the Constitution of the Federation of Rhodesia and Nyasaland, Cmd. 1151, 5 vols. (evidence presented to the Monckton Commission), 1960.

Possible Constitutional Changes, Cmd. 1150 (the Monckton Commission), 1960.

Report of the Advisory Commission on the Review of the Constitution of Rhodesia and Nyasaland, Cmd. 1148 (the Monckton Commission), 1960.

Survey of Developments since 1953, Cmd. 1149 (the Monckton Commission), 1960.

Report of the Southern Rhodesia Constitutional Conference, Cmd. 1291, 1961.

Southern Rhodesian Constitution, Part I. Summary of Proposed Changes, Cmd. 1399, 1961.

Southern Rhodesian Constitution, Part II. Detailed Provisions Cmd. 1400, 1961.

Southern Rhodesia: Correspondence between Her Majesty's Government and the Government of Southern Rhodesia, Cmd. 2000, 1963.

Southern Rhodesia: Correspondence between Her Majesty's Government and the Government of Southern Rhodesia April–June 1963, Cmd. 2073, 1963.

Southern Rhodesia: Documents Relating to the Negotiations between the United Kingdom and Southern Rhodesian Governments, November 1963 to November 1965, Cmd. 2807, 1965.

Rhodesia: Proposals for a Settlement 1966, Cmd. 3159, 1966.

Rhodesia: Documents Relating to Proposals for a Settlement 1966, Cmd. 3171, 1966.

Rhodesia: Report on the Discussions Held aboard H.M.S. Fearless October 1968, Cmd. 3793, 1968.

Rhodesia: Report on Exchanges with the Regime since the Talks Held in Salisbury in November 1968, Cmd. 4065, 1969.

Rhodesia: Proposals for a Settlement, Cmd. 4835, 1971.

Rhodesia: Report of the Commission on Rhodesian Opinion under the Chairmanship of the Right Honourable the Lord Pearce, Cmd. 4964, 1972.

OTHER

Ghana. *A Memorandum in Regard to Southern Rhodesia Submitted to the Security Council on the 2nd August 1963*, 1963.

Portugal. *Some Portuguese Documents on the Question of Rhodesia*, 1966.

UNESCO. *Educational Planning Mission: Southern Rhodesia*, 1965.

United Nations, Committee of 24. *Economic Conditions in Southern Rhodesia with Particular Reference to Foreign Economic Interests*, restricted, 1968.

United Nations, Office of Public Information. *A Principle in Torment: The United Nations and Southern Rhodesia*, 1969.

United States, House of Representatives Subcommittee on Africa. *Rhodesia and United States Foreign Policy,* 1969.

II. Newspapers, Periodicals, and Political Party Publications *

Action, Que Que Group, Que Que, 1964.
Africa Institute Bulletin, Pretoria.
African Daily News, also called the *Bantu Mirror,* Salisbury, 1934–1964.
African Home News, Bulawayo and Gonakudzingwa, 1953–1965.
African Labour News, Salisbury, 1963.
African Mail, Lusaka, 1960–1961.
African Pilot, Salisbury, 1965.
African Times, Fort Victoria, 1963.
African Times, Salisbury, 1965–1966.
Assegai, magazine of the Rhodesian army, Salisbury.
Barclays Trade Review, London and Salisbury.
Battle Cry, Zimbabwe African National Union, Salisbury, 1963–1964.
Black and White, Salisbury, 1966–1967.
Candid Opinion, Salisbury, 1930–1931, 1949–1953.
Capricorn Africa Society, Salisbury: *The Zebra* (1956–1957); *The Capricorn Chronicle* (1955–1956); and *Equinox* (1958).
Central Africa Intelligence Report, Salisbury, 1962–1963.
Central African Examiner, Salisbury, 1957–1965.
Chapupu, Youth League and African National Congress, Salisbury, 1957.
Christian Action, Salisbury, 1958–1960, 1962–1963.
Citizen, Salisbury.
Community Development and Local Government Bulletin, Salisbury.
Concord, Interracial Association, Salisbury, 1954–1958.
Confidential News Report, Salisbury, 1961–1965.
Counterpoint, 1963 Group, Bulawayo, 1963.
Democratic Voice, National Democratic Party, Salisbury, 1960–1961.
Die Landgenoot, Salisbury, 1958–1960.
Dissent, Salisbury, 1959–1961.
Dominion Party Newsletter, Salisbury, 1956–1958.
Dominion Times, Salisbury, 1961.
East Africa and Rhodesia, also called *Rhodesia and Eastern Africa,* London, terminated 1967.
Evening Standard, Salisbury, 1958–1962.
Fact, Salisbury, 1960–1963.
Federal Outlook, Federal Party, Salisbury, 1956–1962.
Federal Tribune, Bulawayo, 1957.
Financial Mail, Johannesburg.
The Liberal, Liberal Party, Bulawayo, 1947–1948.
Monthly Bulletin, Rhodesian Institute of African Affairs, terminated 1965.
Mukayi Africa, Salisbury, 1955–1956, 1958.

* Political party miscellany such as constitutions, minutes of meetings, convention agendas, policy statements, internal party communications, press releases, election materials, and biographical data have not been individually listed here. They have, however, been referenced in the text where specifically utilized.

Inclusive dates are given for those newspapers, periodicals, and party papers that have ceased publication; undated entries are still being published.

Murimi, journal of the Rhodesian African Farmers' Union, Salisbury.
NADA, Native Affairs Department Annual, Salisbury.
National Progress, Rhodesia National Party, Salisbury, 1964.
The Nationalist, Salisbury, 1962.
The New Rhodesia, Salisbury, 1933–1954.
Newsfront, Salisbury, 1963–1964.
Nhume, Salisbury, 1958–1963.
The Observer, London.
Optima, Anglo-American Corporation, Johannesburg.
Outpost, also called *Mapolisa,* journal of the African members of the British South Africa Police, Salisbury.
The People's Voice, Zimbabwe African People's Union, Salisbury, 1962.
Prospect, London, 1962–1964.
Reality, Central Africa Party, Salisbury, 1960–1961.
Rhodesia and World Report, Candour League, Salisbury.
Rhodesia Herald, Salisbury.
The Rhodesian, Dominion Party, Salisbury, 1958–1961.
The Rhodesian Farmer, Rhodesia National Farmers Union, Salisbury.
Rhodesian Journal of Economics, Salisbury.
Rhodesian Law Journal, Salisbury.
Rhodesian Monthly Review, Salisbury, 1939–1964.
The Rhodesian Newsletter, Rhodesia Party, Salisbury, 1951–1953.
Rhodesian Property and Finance, Salisbury.
Rhodesian Tobacco Journal, Salisbury.
Round Table, London.
Samkange Newsletter, Salisbury, 1960–1962.
The Shield, journal of the Catholic church, Salisbury.
Sitima, African Affairs Department of the Rhodesia railways, Bulawayo.
Standard Bank Review, London and Salisbury.
Sunday Mail, Salisbury.
The Sunday Times, London.
The Times, London.
Ukuru, United Federal Party, Salisbury, 1961–1962.
Venture, Fabian Society, London.
Voice of the Unions, later *Voice of the Workers,* Reformed Industrial and Commercial Union, Bulawayo and Salisbury, 1949–1951, 1957–1960.
Weekly Express, Salisbury, 1965–1966.
Workers Voice, African Trade Union Congress, Salisbury, 1962–1963.
ZANU News, Zimbabwe African National Union, Salisbury, 1964.
ZANU Times, Zimbabwe African National Union, Bulawayo, 1963.
Zimbabwe News, Zimbabwe African National Union, Dar es Salaam and Lusaka.
Zimbabwe Review, Zimbabwe African People's Union, London, Lusaka, and Cairo.
Zimbabwe Sun, Zimbabwe African People's Union, People's Caretaker Council, Salisbury, 1964.
Zimbabwe Times, Salisbury, 1964.

III. Secondary Sources

Arrighi, Giovanni. *The Political Economy of Rhodesia.* The Hague, Mouton, 1967.
Austin, Reg. *The Character and Legislation of the Rhodesian Front since UDI.* London, Africa Bureau, 1968.

Barber, James. *Rhodesia: The Road to Rebellion.* London, Oxford University Press, 1967.

Baron, Leo. "Southern Rhodesia and the Rule of Law," *Journal of the International Commission of Jurists* 6 (winter 1965), 219–244.

Bettison, David G. "The Poverty Datum Line in Central Africa," *Rhodes-Livingstone Journal* 27 (June 1960), 1–40.

Bowman, Larry W. "The Subordinate State System of Southern Africa," *International Studies Quarterly* 12 (1968), 231–261.

Brown, Ken. *Land in Southern Rhodesia.* London, Africa Bureau, 1959.

Build a Nation Campaign. "Field Organizer's Training Course" (Salisbury, cyclostyled, 1961).

Cairns, H. A. C. *Prelude to Imperialism: British Reactions to Central African Society 1840–90.* London, Routledge and Kegan Paul, 1965.

Cefkin, J. Leo. "The Rhodesian Question at the United Nations," *International Organization* 22 (summer 1968), 649–669.

Christie, M. J. *Rhodesia: The "Fearless" Proposals and the Six Principles.* London, Africa Bureau, 1968.

Davies, M. A. G. *Incorporation in the Union of South Africa or Self-Government: Southern Rhodesia's Choice, 1922.* Pretoria, University of South Africa, 1965.

Day, John. *International Nationalism: The Extra-Territorial Relations of Southern Rhodesian Nationalists.* London, Routledge and Kegan Paul, 1967.

——— "Southern Rhodesian African Nationalists and the 1961 Constitution," *Journal of Modern African Studies* 7 (1969), 221–247.

Drew, J. D. C. "The Four Southern Rhodesian Referendums: Their Organization and Social and Political Background," *Occasional Paper No. 1 of the National Archives of Rhodesia and Nyasaland* (1963), 42–57.

Dvorin, Eugene P. "The Central African Federation: A Political Analysis" (Ph.D. thesis, University of California at Los Angeles, 1955).

Faber, Michael. "The Distribution of Income between Racial Groups in Southern Rhodesia," *Race* 2 (1961), 41–52.

Floyd, Barry N. "Land Apportionment in Southern Rhodesia," *Geographical Review* (October 1962), 566–582.

Gann, L. H. "The Southern Rhodesia Land Apportionment Act 1930: An Essay in Imperial Trusteeship," *Occasional Paper No. 1 of the National Archives of Rhodesia and Nyasaland* (1963), 58–91.

——— *A History of Southern Rhodesia: Early Days to 1934.* London, Chatto & Windus, 1965.

——— and M. Gelfand. *Huggins of Rhodesia.* London, George Allen and Unwin, 1964.

Garbett, G. Kingsley. "The Land Husbandry Act of Southern Rhodesia," in D. Biebuyck, ed., *African Agrarian Systems.* London, Oxford University Press, 1963, pp. 185–202.

——— "The Rhodesian Chief's Dilemma: Government Official or Tribal Leader?" *Race* 8 (October 1966), 113–128.

Gray, Richard. *The Two Nations: Aspects of the Development of Race Relations in the Rhodesias and Nyasaland.* London, Oxford University Press, 1960.

Hall, Richard. *The High Price of Principles: Kaunda and the White South.* London, Hodder and Stoughton, 1969.

Hartley, George. "The Development of an African Urban Community," *NADA* 35 (1958), 87–98.

Hazlewood, Arthur. "The Economics of Federation and Dissolution in Central Africa," in Arthur Hazlewood, ed., *African Integration and Disintegration: Case Studies in Economic and Political Union.* London, Oxford University Press, 1967, pp. 185–250.

Hirsch, M. I. *Focus on Southern Rhodesia.* Bulawayo, Stuart Manning, 1964.

Holleman, J. F. *Chief, Council and Commissioner: Some Problems of Government in Rhodesia.* London, Oxford University Press, 1969.

Horn, J. W. "Commentary on Part III of the Law and Order (Maintenance) Act [Chap. 39]," *Rhodesian Law Journal* 4 (April 1964), 14–68.

Howman, E. G., with W. A. Carnegie and H. W. Watt. "Report on Urban Conditions in Southern Rhodesia," *African Studies* 4 (March 1945), 9–22.

Howman, Roger. "The Native Affairs Department and the African," *NADA* 31 (1954), 42–49.

———— "African Leadership in Transition," *NADA* 33 (1956), 13–25.

———— "Chieftainship," *NADA* 43 (1966), 10–14.

Ibbotson, Percy. *Report on a Survey of Urban African Conditions in Southern Rhodesia.* Bulawayo, Federation of Native Welfare Societies, 1943.

———— "Report on Effect on Africans of the Implementation of the Native (Urban Areas) Accommodation and Registration Act of 1946" (Salisbury, cyclostyled, 1949).

Kaplan, Marion. "Their Rhodesia," *Transition* 23 (1965), 33–43.

Lardner-Burke, Desmond. *Rhodesia: The Story of the Crisis.* London, Oldbourne, 1966.

Lawrence, W. G. "Report on the Detentions, Restrictions and Loss of Freedom in Rhodesia" (Salisbury, typescript, 1965).

Legassick, Martin. "The Consequences of African Guerrilla Activity for South Africa's Relations with her Neighbors" (New York, African Studies Association mimeo, 1967).

Leys, Colin. *European Politics in Southern Rhodesia.* Oxford, Clarendon Press, 1959.

———— and Cranford Pratt, eds. *A New Deal in Central Africa.* London, Heinemann, 1960.

Lukhero, M. B. "Social Characteristics of an Emergent Elite in Harare," in P. C. Lloyd, ed., *The New Elites of Tropical Africa.* London, Oxford University Press, 1966, pp. 126–137.

McEwan, P. J. M. "The Urban African Population of Southern Rhodesia," *Civilisations* 13 (1963), 267–290.

———— "The European Population of Southern Rhodesia," *Civilisations* 13 (1963), 429–441.

M'Gabe, Davis. "Rhodesia's African Majority," *Africa Report* (February 1967), 14–20.

Mason, Philip. *The Birth of a Dilemma.* London, Oxford University Press, 1958.

Mazrui, A. A. "The Rhodesian Problem and the Kenya Precedent," in A. A. Mazrui, ed., *The Anglo-African Commonwealth.* Oxford, Pergamon, 1967, pp. 42–59.

Mezerik, A. G., ed. *Rhodesia and the United Nations.* New York, International Review Service, 1966.

Nehwati, Francis. "The Social and Communal Background to 'Zhii': The African Riots in Bulawayo, Southern Rhodesia in 1960," *African Affairs* 69 (July 1970), 250–266.

Nyerere, Julius K. "Rhodesia in the Context of Southern Africa," *Foreign Affairs* 44 (1966), 373–386.

Palley, Claire. *The Constitutional History and Law of Southern Rhodesia 1888–1965 with Special Reference to Imperial Control.* Oxford, Clarendon Press, 1966.

Prison Conditions in Rhodesia. London, Amnesty International, 1966.

Ranger, T. O. *Crisis in Southern Rhodesia.* London, Fabian Commonwealth Bureau, 1960.

———— *Revolt in Southern Rhodesia 1896–7: A Study in African Resistance.* London, Heinemann, 1967.

———— "The Nineteenth Century in Southern Rhodesia," and "African Politics in Twentieth-Century Southern Rhodesia," in T. O. Ranger, ed., *Aspects of Central African History.* London, Heinemann, 1968, pp. 112–153 and 210–245.

Report of the National Convention of Southern Rhodesia. Salisbury, National Convention, 1960.

Reserved Powers in the Southern Rhodesian Constitution. London, National Democratic Party, 1961?

Rhodesia: Proposals for a Sell-Out. London, Southern African Research Office, 1972.

Roder, Wolf. "The Division of Land Resources in Southern Rhodesia," *Annals of the Association of American Geographers* 54 (1964), 41–58.

Rotberg, Robert I. "The Federation Movement in British East and Central Africa, 1889–1953," *Journal of Commonwealth Political Studies* 2 (1964), 141–160.

Shamuyarira, Nathan. *Crisis in Rhodesia.* London, Andre Deutsch, 1965.

Sithole, Ndabaningi. *African Nationalism.* 2nd ed. London, Oxford University Press, 1968.

Skeen, Brigadier Andrew. *Prelude to Independence: Skeen's 115 Days.* Cape Town, Nasionale Boekhandel, 1966.

Sklar, Richard L. "On Returning 'to the Road of Legality' in Rhodesia" (Los Angeles, African Studies Association mimeo, 1968).

Stokes, Eric, and Richard Brown, eds. *The Zambesian Past.* Manchester, Manchester University Press, 1966.

Sutcliffe, R. B. "The Political Economy of Rhodesian Sanctions," *Journal of Commonwealth Political Studies* 7 (1969), 113–125.

Todd, R. S. Garfield. "The Meaning of Racial Partnership in the Rhodesian Federation," *Optima* (December 1967), 174–180.

Trillin, Calvin. "Letter from Salisbury," *The New Yorker* (November 12, 1966), 139–193.

Welensky, Sir Roy. "Development of Central Africa through Federation," *Optima* (December 1952), 5–10.

———— *Welensky's 4000 Days.* London, Collins, 1964.

Whitehead, Sir Edgar. "Southern Rhodesia," *International Affairs* 36 (1960), 188–196.

Willson, F. M. G., ed. *Source Book of Parliamentary Elections and Referenda in Southern Rhodesia, 1898–1962.* Salisbury, Department of Government, University College of Rhodesia and Nyasaland, 1963.

Wilson, Harold. *A Personal Record: The Labour Government 1964–1970.* Boston, Little, Brown, 1971.

Yudelman, Montague. *Africans on the Land.* Cambridge, Mass., Harvard University Press, 1964.

Zacklin, Ralph. "Challenge of Rhodesia: Toward an International Public Policy," *International Conciliation* (November 1969), 1–72.

Index

Administration, African: under British South Africa Company, 10–16; under responsible government, 10–16; under United Federal Party, 38–39; under Rhodesian Front, 104–105, 142–144

Africa, southern, 21, 114, and passim; and economic sanctions, 113, 116; and guerrilla warfare, 147–150

African National Congress, 16, 45, 49; formation, 50–51; rural focus, 51–52, 57; program, 51; banning, 51–52, 58

African National Congress (of South Africa), 148

African National Council, 50, 125, 127–128, 146–147

African (Registration and Identification) Act, 39, 60, 145

African (Urban Areas) Accommodation and Registration Act, 11, 145–146

Alexander, Fred, 100–102

All-African Convention, 46

Anderson, Maj. Gen. John, 67, 73

Associated Chamber of Commerce of Rhodesia (ACCOR), 79, 80

Association of Rhodesian Industries (ARNI), 79

Banana, Rev. Canaan, 127, 146

Banda, Dr. H. Kamuzu, 28, 131

Bledisloe Commission, 17

Bottomley, Arthur, 72, 75, 85

Bradburn, Lt. Cmdr. F. W., 97

British South Africa Company (BSAC): relations with United Kingdom, 6–8; relations with white settlers, 6–7; invasion of Ndebele kingdom, 10; and African administration, 10–16

Build-a-Nation Campaign, 42–43

Butler, David, 77

Butler, R. A., 63–66

Campbell, Evan, 29, 67

Capricorn Africa Society, 46

Cary, W., 101

Central Africa Party, 46, 52

Central African Federation: white demand for, 17–20; constitution, 17–18, 26; African opposition, 17, 27; white opposition, 19–20; refer-

Central African Federation (*contd.*)
endum on, 19–20; and Federal
Review Conference, 19, 26, 27;
allocation of functions under, 21, 23,
25, 29, 32; economic development
during, 22–25; white Rhodesian
domination, 22–28; conflicts with
Rhodesian territorial government,
29; erosion of white support for, 29–
30, 33, 37; breakup, 63–68
Centre Party, 127, 139, 141
Chiefs, 38, 123, 127, 138, 153;
Rhodesian Front support for, 38, 70,
74, 81, 83, 86, 142; threatened by
Native Land Husbandry Act, 49–50;
and African National Congress, 57–
58; and 1964 indaba, 71, 72–73;
and 1965 election, 82
Chikerema, James, 50, 51, 52, 148
Chitepo, Herbert, 52, 53, 148
Church of the White Bird, 16
Coleman, H., 101
Commonwealth of Nations, 69, 74, 88,
111, 120–121, 129–130
Commonwealth preferences, 69, 78, 79
Conflict: nature in Rhodesia, 4–5,
151–152; among whites, 7, 19–20,
29–35, 41–44, 62–90 passim, 134–
142; between whites and Africans,
10, 46–61, 124–129, 145–150,
151–155
Constitution Amendment Act (federal),
26
Constitutional Council, 138; under 1961
constitution, 40, 53
Constitutions: of 1923, nature, 7–8, 37;
African administration under, 10–16;
1953 federal, 17–18, 26; of 1961,
terms, 34, 40–41; negotiation,
37–41; Declaration of Rights under,
40–41; as basis for independence,
41, 43, 65, 70, 86–87; as cover for
United Kingdom withdrawal, 43,
154; African rejection of, 54, 83;
and 1965 election, 76; status after
UDI, 119–121; of 1965, 119;
of 1969, 128; debate over, 134–142;
terms, 137–139; as basis for
1971 proposed settlement, 137

Danziger, Max, 19
Declaration of Rights, 123, 126, 138;
under 1961 constitution, 40, 41, 53
Devlin report, 27
Dominion Party, 29–31, 33, 37, 106,
108; and 1961 referendum, 41
Douglas-Home, Sir Alec, *see* Home,
Sir Alec Douglas-
Dumbetshena, Enoch, 52
Dupont, Clifford, 33, 34, 68, 69, 89;

and 1964 by-election, 71–72; as
Officer Administering the Government, 100; as Rhodesian Front
chairman, 100–102

Eastwood, S. N., 101
Economic development, 20, 24, 47;
as rationalization for federation, 18;
during federation, 22–25; since UDI,
114, and passim
Economic sanctions: threat by United
Kingdom, 69, 73–74, 86; anticipated
effects, 78–80, 89; actual effects,
111–117; limited goal, 118; effect
of proposed settlement, 129
Elections, 29; of 1924–1948, 8; federal,
22, 34, 77; of 1958, 31–32; of 1962,
33–37, 42; 1964 by-elections, 71–72;
of 1965, 75–84; of 1970, 109, 134,
141
Electoral Act, 31
Emergency, states of, 51, 58–60, 70,
73, 89–90, 148–149
Emergency Powers Act, 58, 59, 145,
146, 149
Employment: of Africans, 14–16, 25,
47–48, 144; of Europeans, 104

Fearless talks, 120–122, 134, 137, 140,
141
Federal Party, 22, 29. *See also* United
Federal Party
Field, Winston, 29, 33–34, 63, 88, 99;
independence negotiations under, 63–
69; ouster, 67–69, 91–92, 96, 103,
107; as prime minister, 91, 106–107
Fletcher, Patrick, 31
Foot, Sir Hugh (Lord Caradon), 111
France, 115
Frantz, Charles, 103
Frelimo, 148
Frost, Desmond, 101, 102
Future prospects, 132, 148–150, 151–
155

Gardiner, Lord, 75
Gaunt, J., 101
Gibbs, Sir Humphrey, 120, 141
Goodman, Lord, 122, 124
Graham, Lord, 78, 89, 100, 101, 108;
constitutional proposals, 137, 141,
142
Grant, S. M., 39
Greenfield, Julian, 30
Guerrillas, 139, 155; beginning of war-
fare, 147–150
Guest, Sir Ernest, 19

Harper, William J., 33, 69, 85, 101, 106,
108, 109; constitutional proposals,
137, 141, 142

Heath, Edward, 117
Home, Sir Alec Douglas-, 67, 70, 138;
efforts to reach settlement with
Rhodesia, 122–124; response to
Pearce Commission report, 128–129
Howe, Russell Warren, 147
Howman, John, 68, 89
Huggins, Sir Godfrey, 8, 15, 17, 31, 63,
68, 88; and move to federation, 17–
20, 51; as prime minister, 22, 25–26,
29, 91, 106, 107
Hughes, Cledwyn, 84, 85

Idensohn, Len, 108
Indabas, 71, 72–73
Independence: and 1961 constitution,
41, 43, 65, 70, 86–87; prospects
under United Federal Party, 42;
white desire for, 62, 68, and passim;
negotiations under Rhodesian Front,
62–90 passim. See also UDI
Industrial and Commercial Union, 16
Industrial Conciliation Act, 14–15,
38–39, 152
Interracial Association, 46

Japan, 115

Kafue Dam, 24, 115
Kariba Dam, 22, 24, 115
Kaunda, Kenneth, 28, 148
Knox, Lt. Col. W. M., 84, 101, 102
Kock, Steve, 42
de Kock, W., 101

Labor migration, 14, 49; impact on
African politics, 52
Land Apportionment Act, 12, 14, 34,
35, 38, 142, 152; African protest,
12–13; enforcement, 49; and Na-
tive Land Husbandry Act, 49–50;
and Rhodesian independence, 65, 86
Land policy, 11–14, 38, 49, 123; and
Native Land Husbandry Act, 49–50
Land Tenure Act, 12, 142–143, 144
Lardner-Burke, Desmond, 33, 77, 85,
89, 101, 136; and 1969 constitution,
139–140; and guerrillas, 148
Law and Order (Maintenance) Act, 58,
59, 60, 145, 149, 153
Liberal Party, 19
Lilford, D. C. ("Boss"), 97, 100, 101
Lobengula, 5, 9, 10

McAllister, D., 101
M'Gabe, Davis, 56
McLean, I., 101
Macmillan, Harold, 28
Malawi, and Rhodesia after UDI, 130–
131. See also Nyasaland

Master and Servants Act, 14, 60
Mawema, Matthew, 52
Monckton Commission, 27–28, 39, 52
Morris, Stan, 135
Moyo, J. Z., 50
Mozambique, 14, 148; and economic
sanctions, 112, 115. See also Portugal
Msika, J., 50
Mugabe, R., 148
Multiracial organizations, 46–47, 52;
United Federal Party, 36–37, 42–
43; Rhodesia Party, 77, 81, 82, 84
Municipal Amendment Act, 143, 144
Mushonga, Paul, 50, 52
Mutasa, Dr. E. C., 74
Muzorewa, Bishop Abel, 127, 146

National Commercial Distribution and
Office Workers' Association, 79
National Democratic Party, 50; formation and optimism, 52–53; errors
at 1961 constitutional conference, 53;
banning, 54
Nationalists, African, 45–61; support
for reserve clauses, 37, 53; and Build-
a-Nation Campaign, 42; white commitment to crush, 44, 58–61; and
1961 constitution, 53, 56–57; split
in movement, 54–56; Smith's
opposition, 70, 126, and passim; and
1965 election, 83; and talks with
Wilson, 87–88; hangings after UDI,
119; response to Pearce Commission,
125–128; activities since UDI, 145–
150
Native Affairs Act, 11, 152
Native Affairs Amendment Act, 58
Native Affairs Department, 11, 51
Native Land Husbandry Act, 49–50,
51
Native Registration Act, 11
Native (Urban Areas) Accommoda-
tion and Registration Act, see African
(Urban Areas) Accommodation and
Registration Act
Ndebele, 138, 143, 147; relations with
Shona, 9; invasion of kingdom, 10
Nehwati, Francis, 52
Nilson, Ralph, 101, 102
Nkala, Enos, 52
Nkomo, Joshua: as nationalist leader,
50–54 passim, 67, 69; and African
nationalist split, 54–56
Northern Rhodesia, 5, 8, 16, 28, 63,
152; and movement to federation,
17–20; and African opposition to
federation, 17, 27, 46; exploited by
Rhodesia, 23–25. See also Zambia
Nyandoro, George, 49, 50, 51, 52

Nyasaland, 14; and federation, 17, 19, 23, 28, 63; and African opposition to federation, 17, 27, 46. *See also* Malawi

Nyerere, Julius, 54, 129–130, 148

Officer Administering the Government, 100, 141

Olley, Charles, 19

Organization of African Unity (OAU), 54, 55, 113, 129–130, 148

Palley, Ahrn, 81, 138

Partnership, 18, 20, 46; absence during federation, 25–26, 28

Pass laws, 11, 39

Pearce Commission, 113, 125–128, 146

People's Caretaker Council (PCC), *see* ZAPU

Phillips, Chris, 101, 108, 109

Political parties, *see* names of individual parties

Portugal, 88, 122, 149; and economic sanctions, 113, 115, 116; and relations with Rhodesia after UDI, 129–132. *See also* Mozambique

Pratt, R. Cranford, 130

Preventive Detention (Temporary Provisions) Act, 58–59, 153

Protests, African: rebellions (1896–1897), 10, 147; before 1945, 12–13, 16, 46; 1945 and 1948 strikes, 46, 57; conditions spawning, 47–51, 144. *See also* Nationalists, African

Public Order Act, 57

Public Services Act, 16, 39

Putterhill, Maj. Gen. Sam, 139

Quinton, H. J., 38

Rebellions (1896–1897), 10, 147

Reedman, Harry, 80

Referenda: of 1922, 7–8; of 1953, 19–20; of 1961, 41–43, 54; of 1964, 71, 73–74; on 1971 settlement, 124; of 1969, on constitution, 137, 139; of 1969, on republic, 140

Republic, 122, 135; movement to, 140–142

Republican Alliance, 141

Reserve clauses, 8, 12, 19, 39–41, 43; African nationalist position, 37, 53

Rhodes, Cecil, 5, 10

Rhodesia Party, 71, 72; and 1965 election, 76–84; as multiracial party, 77, 81, 82, 84; and UDI, 80

Rhodesian Bantu Voters Association, 16

Rhodesian Front, 19, 29, 30, 42, 43, 44; formation, 33–34; in 1962 election, 35–36; support for chiefs, 38, 70, 74, 81, 83, 86, 142; and UDI, 62, 78–81, 84–90, 95, 107–109; desire for independence, 62–90 passim; party principles, 63, 84, 85, 95, 141; and 1961 constitution, 65; ouster of Field, 67–69; power structure within, 68–69, 85, 88–89, 91, 97–109; attempts to defeat Welensky, 71; and 1965 election, 75–84; congresses, 85, 94–96, 100, 102, 137; basis of support, 91, 92, 109; organization, 92–97, 109; members of parliament, 94, 99, 102–105; and 1966 proposed settlement (*Tiger* talks), 102, 107–108, 121; constitutional dispute (1968–1969), 102, 108–109; nature of conflict within, 105–109; and 1968 proposed settlement (*Fearless* talks), 108, 122; actions after UDI, 110–150 passim; and proposed 1971 settlement, 123–125, 128; 1970 election, 134, 141; conflict over 1969 constitution, 134–142; and apartheid, 134, 135, 143–144, 153–154; and 1969 constitutional referendum, 139; and demand for republic, 140–142; and legislation since UDI, 142–144

Rhodesian government: defense of segregation, 15–16, 153; desire for federation, 17–20; domination of federation, 22–28; relations with United Kingdom, 27–28, 62–90 passim, 117–129, 154–155. *See also* Field, Winston; Huggins, Sir Godfrey; Rhodesian Front; Smith, Ian D.; Todd, Garfield; United Federal Party; Welensky, Sir Roy; Whitehead, Sir Edgar

Rhodesian Institute of Directors, 79, 80

Rhodesian Tobacco Association, 78, 79, 80

Rhodesian Vigilance Association, 41

Robertson, Olive, 101, 103

Rogers, Cyril, 103

Rudd Concession, 5, 6, 10

Rudland, G., 101

Salisbury, 6, 24, 25, 55, 67, 98; state of emergency, 70, 73

Sandys, Duncan, 53, 66, 67

Sawyer, Sidney, 72

Security legislation, 51, 52, 57–61, 89–90, 123, 139, 145, 148–149. *See also* names of specific laws

Shona, 138, 143, 147; relations with Ndebele, 9; leadership during rebellions, 10

Silundika, George, 52, 53

Sithole, Rev. Ndabaningi, 52, 53, 54, 146; and African nationalist split, 55–56

Skeen, Brigadier Andrew, 1, 86, 134

Smit, J. H., 19

Smith, D., 101

Smith, Ian D., 1, 33, 34, 41, 63, 78, 117, 146; and drive to independence, 67, 69–90 passim; as prime minister, 68, 71, 99–102, 107–108, 119, 137; and UDI, 69, 71, 74, 79, 80, 81, 84–90, 107, 111, 118; on African politics, 70, 126, and passim; in British view, 118–119; negotiations with United Kingdom after UDI, 120–124; analysis of 1971 proposed settlement, 124; and 1969 constitution, 135–142 passim

South Africa, 7, 10, 16, 43, 109, 122, 140, 144; and federation, 18, 28; and economic sanctions, 112–116; relations with Rhodesia after UDI, 129–132, 134; military forces in Rhodesia, 148–150

Southern Rhodesia Association, 33, 41

Stockil, R. O., 19

Subversive Activities Act, 57

Sutcliffe, R. B., 150

Takawira, Leopold, 52, 53

Tanner, D., 101

Tan-Zam railroad, 130

Tanzania, 130

Taxation: African, 14; as basis for African vote, 137–138

Tiger talks, 120–121, 134, 135, 141

Tobacco industry, 78, 79, 113–114, 116

Todd, Garfield, 42, 43, 91; as prime minister, 29, 32; ouster, 30–32, 68; restriction, 89

Tredgold, Sir Robert, 42

Twala, Abraham, 16

UDI (unilateral declaration of independence): justification, 1–2, 134, 154–155; Field's opposition, 67–68; Smith's perspective, 69, 71, 74, 79, 81; anticipated economic consequences, 77–80; movement to, 84–90; and Rhodesian Front, 107–109; aftermath, 110–150. *See also* Economic sanctions; Independence; Rhodesian Front

United Federal Party (UFP), 29–31, 68–69, 106, 143; political structure, 30; and 1962 election, 34–37; independence strategy, 34–44; as multiracial organization, 36–37, 42–43; and 1961 referendum, 41–43; and African nationalists, 58–61; and UDI, 62; membership, 92, 93. *See also* Constitution (1961); Federal Party; Rhodesia Party; Welensky, Sir Roy; Whitehead, Sir Edgar

United Group, 33, 41

United Kingdom: relations with British South Africa Company, 6–8, 10; reserve clauses, 8; land policy, 12; African taxation, 14; and federation, 17–20; relations with federal government, 26–28; relations with Rhodesian government, 27–28, 62–90 passim, 117–129, 154–155; negotiation of 1961 constitution, 37, 39–40, 43; and African nationalists, 56–57, 87–88; and UDI, 62, 69, 73–75, 84–90; independence negotiations, 63–67, 70–72, 74–90; and proposed agreement following UDI, 102, 120–129, 137–138, 141; application of economic sanctions, 111–117, 118; and United Nations re Rhodesia, 111–113; and Portugal re Rhodesia, 112, 115, 120; and South Africa re Rhodesia, 115, 120, 131–132, 149; expectations following UDI, 117–120; and question of republic, 140–142

United Nations, 35, 69, 109, 129, 130, 140; and actions opposing Rhodesia before UDI, 111–112; and actions opposing Rhodesia after UDI, 112–113

United Party, 8, 19, 29

United Rhodesia Party, 31–32

United States of America, 113, 115, 129

Unlawful Organizations Act, 58, 60, 145, 153

Vagrancy Act, 60

Van der Byl, P. K. F. V., 80

Van Heerden, Philip, 143

Victoria Falls Conference, 65–67, 68, 106

Voters, African, 20, 36, 76

Wages, African, 14–15, 25, 46–48

Watchtower movement, 16

Welensky, Sir Roy, 18, 19, 33, 68, 91, 136; as federal prime minister, 22, 25–26, 28, 29, 37, 63, 106, 107; support for United Federal Party, 35, 41; and Land Apportionment Act, 38; and Rhodesian independence, 63, 88; opposition to UDI, 71; comeback attempt, 71–72, 74, 93

West Germany, 115

Whaley, William R., 135

Whaley Commission, 135–137

White Rhodesia Council, 19
Whitehead, Sir Edgar, 29, 31, 68, 91, 136; as prime minister, 33–44; conception of African "majority," 35; changing commitment to federation, 37; negotiation of 1961 constitution, 37–41, 43, 53; African administration under, 38–39; and 1961 referendum, 41; and African nationalists, 54, 58; and Rhodesian independence, 63. *See also* United Federal Party
Wilson, Harold, 73, 78, 113, 137, 141; views on Rhodesian independence, 74–75, 85–90; reaction to UDI, 117, 118, 120; negotiations following UDI, 120–122
Wrathall, John J., 85, 89, 101, 114

Yellow Paper, 136–137, 141
Youth League, 50, 51, 57

Zambia, 5, 133; and effects of UDI, 114–115, 130; as base for guerrillas, 147–150. *See also* Northern Rhodesia
ZANU (Zimbabwe African National Union), 50, 54, 70, 133; goals, 55; and split in nationalist movement, 55–56; and beginning of guerrilla warfare, 146–148
ZAPU (Zimbabwe African Peoples Union), 50, 70, 133; urban orientation, 52; banning, 54; goals, 55; and split in nationalist movement, 55–56; and beginning of guerrilla warfare, 147–148
Zwimba, Matthew, 16